Managing Creativity

Managing Creativity

JOHN J. KAO
Harvard Business School

Prentice Hall, Englewood Cliffs, New Jersey 07632

Library of Congress Cataloging-in-Publication Data

KAO, JOHN J.
   Managing creativity: text, cases & readings/John J. Kao.
      p.   cm.
   ISBN 0-13-556705-X
   1. Creative ability in business—Management.   I. Title.
HD53.K36   1991
658.4—dc20
                                          90-34673
                                             CIP

Editorial/production supervision and
   interior design: *Carol Burgett*
Cover design: *Mike Fender*
Manufacturing buyer: *Peter Havens*

Printed in the United States of America

10 9 8 7 6 5 4 3 2 1

ISBN 0-13-556705-X

Prentice-Hall International (UK) Limited, *London*
Prentice-Hall of Australia Pty. Limited, *Sydney*
Prentice-Hall Canada Inc., *Toronto*
Prentice-Hall Hispanoamericana, S.A., *Mexico*
Prentice-Hall of India Private Limited, *New Delhi*
Prentice-Hall of Japan, Inc., *Tokyo*
Simon & Schuster Asia Pte. Ltd., *Singapore*
Editora Prentice-Hall do Brasil, Ltda., *Rio de Janeiro*

For my mother, Edith Ling Kao

Contents

CASES

READINGS

INDEX

Preface

The present volume focuses on the topic of managing creativity. In the author's view, creativity and entrepreneurship are intimately linked—part of an overall flow of events. All entrepreneurial processes begin with the idea. The lightbulb which goes off may not necessarily conform to the commonplace notion of a breakthrough theory or a radically new product. It may equally well be an idea about a process, a different way of doing things, a perception of the market-place, or an approach to building the organization. Creative ideas are generated by people working alone or together, and thus it is worth knowing how creativity operates at both the individual level and in the setting of working groups. In addition, the management of creativity involves virtually every organizational design and human resource tool which has been identified for mainstream business organizations, including structure, work design, recruiting, reward system design, and corporate culture development. It may seem counterintuitive to talk about "managing" creativity, and yet, managing the process by which ideas are generated, whether by people working alone or together, is critical for the entrepreneurial process.

Conceptually, I view creativity as one part of a three-legged stool, a three-stage process. After the idea is generated, a person must step forward to champion the idea—to run with and implement it—and in so doing to achieve some tangible result. This is the figure of the entrepreneur, who is the subject of the second volume in this series, *The Entrepreneur*. If innovation is creativity implemented, then the entrepreneur may be seen as the agency for innovation.

Finally, the entrepreneur, if he or she is not to work alone as a sole proprietor, is faced with the challenge of designing, starting, and building an organization which will provide the appropriate leverage for translating the idea into reality. These issues are taken up in the third volume of this series. *The Entrepreneurial Organization*. Entrepreneurial organizations, with their volatility and flux, have long interested me. There is much to observe and learn in entrepreneurial environments, where standard operating procedures are lacking and organizational structure, culture, and leadership style are created anew each day. Like the art of Japanese ink-brush painting, developing entrepreneurial firms requires a sure and steady hand. They grow and evolve rapidly. A movement made too fast, and the ink will be too thin; too slow, and the ink will make an unsightly blot. The trick, simply stated but difficult to practice, lies in following the motion's natural course.

From a historical perspective, it is worth noting that this present volume, *Managing Creativity,* is the long-awaited offspring of a body of work begun in 1983 when I developed a course called "Entrepreneurship, Creativity, and Organization" at Harvard Business School. At that time, entrepreneurship had burst into bloom as a topic of concern among both academics and practitioners. Many central management issues of the day—competitiveness, innovation, managing change, and human resources theory—were all refracted through the new lens of entrepreneurial studies. As knowledge grew, it became clear that entrepreneurship contained broad intellectual and practical lessons for the mainstream of business. Greater perspective has since grown around the topic. Kanter and others have even begun to refer to a "post-entrepreneurial" revolution in which the dynamism of the entrepreneurial process would be coupled with the resources and organizational disciplines of the larger, more established organization.

My primary objective in developing my course was to capture some essential skills, attitudes, and experiences which I felt were not adequately included in traditional entrepreneurship courses. Through research on hundreds of entrepreneurs and their ventures, the voice of experience spoke clearly. Familiarity with human and organizational dilemmas of the entrepreneurial process was seen as critical to the success of a wide range of ventures. In many instances it was the "make or break" ingredient in a venture's progress to a desired level of organizational maturity and business success. In addition, entrepreneurs frequently reported that it was these types of responsibilities which, to their surprise, occupied the greater portion of their time. This motivated me to write the textbook *Entrepreneurship, Creativity, and Organization.* The response to this effort has been gratifying. More than one thousand MBA students at HBS have elected this course as part of their second-year program. And the course has been adopted by educational institutions around the world.

As these materials came into wider use, it became increasingly important to me that they be made available to a wider audience. In consultation with my ever-supportive editor at Prentice Hall, Alison Reeves, I conceived the idea of publishing three follow-on daughter textbooks based on the three broad topic areas of the parent course: Managing Creativity, The Entrepreneur, and the Entrepreneurial Organization.

We had several motives. First, we wanted to publish some of the newer material that had been developed, including such cases as Windham Hill, The Los Angeles Olympic Organizing Committee, Activision, and Managing Entrepreneurship at the CML Group. We also felt that creating three modular textbooks would allow for expanded and more flexible "menus of use" within more traditional courses in general management, organizational behavior, and entrepreneurial studies. We hoped that courses treating such topics as leadership, innovation, managing change, managerial behavior, and managing technology could benefit from using the material contained in these three volumes. At the same time, we decided to retain the original overview chapter in each volume because of its importance in presenting the overall conceptual scheme of the "Entrepreneurship, Creativity, and Organization" course, within which the material in each volume plays a role.

Preparing and compiling these books has been a labor of love. I hope that they find the audiences they so earnestly seek. Entrepreneurship contains important lessons for the mainstream of business practice and research. The experiences of those living on the cutting edge of organizational and product/service innovation deserve to be presented to a wider audience. In this effort, I hope to have been deemed at least partly successful.

*　　*　　*　　*　　*

Harvard Business School proved to be a fertile and nurturing environment within which to incubate this venture in pedagogy. Many people contributed to the start-up. John McArthur, Dean of the Faculty at Harvard Business School, provided warm support and encouragement for the project. In many ways, he is the real champion of this corporate venture. Howard Stevenson, Sarofim-Rock Professor of Entrepreneurship, and Associate Professor Bill Sahlman, have been immensely valued colleagues and friends. Professors John Kotter, Michael Beer, John Gabarro, and Chris Argris, and Associate Professor Jeffrey Sonnenfeld from the area of organizational behavior have also given valuable feedback and encouragement. Other colleagues who provided valued help include Professors Chris Christensen and Abraham Zaleznik, Lecturer Pierre Wack, and Tony Athos. Professors Shervert Frazier, Fritz Redlich, and Thomas Detre of Harvard, UCLA, and Yale Medical Schools nurtured the development of my interest in psychiatric practice and research. The Harvard Business School Division of Research has also been supportive. Professor Jay Lorsch, my current research director, has encouraged the research agenda based on my course's concern.

Entrepreneurs and entrepreneurial managers in a variety of settings also helped immeasurably in creating *Entrepreneurship, Creativity, and Organization.* They include Lou Gerstner, Jerry Welsh, Kathi Kuhn, Fred Wilkinson, Jamie Dimond, and many others at American Express Travel Related Services Company; Jim Ferry of Creative Realities; Charlie Atkinson from The Whole Brain Corporation; Mitch Kapor, Janet Axelrod, and Cathy Faulkner of Lotus Development Corporation; Wendell Butler of the Young Astronaut Program; Bob Norton and Bob Greber of Lucasfilm Ltd; Peter Ueberroth, Commissioner of Major League Baseball; Robert Saunders and Michael Cornfeld of Robert Michael Companies; Linda Linsalata of Orange Nassau; Jim Morgan of Morgan Holland; Steve Ricci of The Palmer Organization; Art Snyder of U.S. Trust; Diana Frazier of BancBoston Ventures; Leo Castelli; Ron Shaich, Len Schlesinger, and Louis Kane of Au Bon Pain; Nolan Bushnell, Larry Calof, and John Anderson of Catalyst Technologies; Ann Piestrup and Marcia Klein of The Learning Company; Peter Schwartz of Royal Dutch Shell Group; Jan Carlzon and John Herbert at Scandinavian Airline Systems; Al Vezza of Infocom; Bob Carpenter, David Housman, and others at Integrated Genetics; Burt Morrison of the Ladd Company; Anne Robinson and Will Ackerman of Windham Hill; Charles Leighton of the CML Group; Akira Kimishima of Dainana Securities Company; Jerry DeLa Vega of Hot Rock; Jim Levy, Ken Coleman, Linda Parker, Brad Fegger, David Crane, Ralph Guiffre, Larry Hicks, Alison Elwers, and others at Activision.

The opportunity to form intellectual partnerships with these outstanding people cannot be overvalued.

John Kao
Cambridge, Massachusetts

Managing Creativity

Overview to *Entrepreneurship, Creativity, & Organization*

Entrepreneurship emerged in the 1980s as an important focus of attention for business students, practitioners, and academics across the United States, indeed around the world. Much is happening on today's campus. Would-be entrepreneurs look for appropriate courses of study to prepare for their envisioned career. Groups of student entrepreneurs practice the ancient art of networking, enhanced by the advent of the personal computer. Entrepreneurial alumni return to campus to tell their stories before packed lecture halls. Established companies position themselves on campus as "entrepreneurial," "intrapreneurial," and "creative."

Such activity mirrors the world at large. The business press is replete with accounts of the most recent public offering, the newest mousetrap. New ventures are lionized as the source of new opportunities and new jobs. Major corporations experiment with ways of introducing the "entrepreneurial spirit" into the established environment. Their tools are new approaches to organizational structure, people management, and leadership. The flow of money continues to fuel the flames of initiative, with the formation of vast, multi-billion-dollar pools of venture capital in the United States and world wide. New streams of opportunity are evident everywhere. They come from new rules of the game such as deregulation and tax policy; they depend on new technology, exemplified by the microprocessor and recombinant genetic material. These opportunities are inspired by a significant shift in social values and career expectations. They are also fueled by a new willingness to experiment with public/private partnerships.

This current interest in entrepreneurship is appropriate. We need what entrepreneurs can give us: new products; new jobs; creative work environments; new ways of doing business. And yet, we should consider critically some of the ways entrepreneurship is being discussed today. Far from being easy, entrepreneurship is hard work, involving an unpredictable blend of calculation and luck; it is a tonic laced with the ever-present possibility of failure. Thus, it is important to put the current enthusiasm for entrepreneurship into perspective. As a nation we have spent a number of years questioning our basic business competence. Whether it be the Japanese challenge or our overvaluation of analytical management at the expense of common sense, we have had plenty of opportunity to doubt ourselves. In our search for answers, we must beware that entrepreneurship does not become a magic portion or a panacea. We do not yet know how to turn frogs into princes.

Keeping in mind, then, both the renewed attention to entrepreneurial and creative behavior and that it is not a cure-all, we can ask two questions: How do you "do" entrepreneurship well? What do you really have to know?

This textbook, and the course on which it was based, were developed to address these questions and fulfill a need. Existing entrepreneurship courses have tended to focus on technical skills: writing business plans; analyzing financial data; exploring legal issues. Yet entrepreneurship is fundamentally less about technical skills than about people and their passions. An old dictum of real estate holds that its three principles are "location, location, location." It could be said that the three principles of entrepreneurship are "people, people, people." Clearly, the entrepreneur must be skilled at identifying and pursuing opportunity. Yet, human issues are also predominant. Equally, the entrepreneur's task involves finding leverage through the efforts of others to amplify his or her own vision. Crusades are usually not entered into alone. Instead, the entrepreneur may find it necessary to enter into a partnership or start a new company. In creating the organizational means appropriate to pursuing a particular opportunity, the entrepreneur must work with and through people. By generating and communicating a vision of what is possible, the entrepreneur gathers together, leads, and inspires human beings.

The human issues of entrepreneurship also wear another, individual face. The entrepreneur must also manage him or herself effectively in dealing with the ambiguity and uncertainty that surround the creation of an idea and the organizational vehicle developed around it. The ability to take on such human challenges, indeed, to seek them out, is fundamental to entrepreneurial success and is emphasized constantly by those who have been through the process. Such knowledge is essential and complementary to entrepreneurial skills involving a mastery of technical subjects like finance, strategy, and marketing.

ENTREPRENEURSHIP, CREATIVITY, AND ORGANIZATION: GOALS AND PRINCIPLES

"Entrepreneurship, Creativity, and Organization" was originally an MBA elective developed for second-year students at Harvard Business School. Taught for the first time in 1984, it is directed to the needs of several groups of students:

- would-be entrepreneurs;
- would-be managers of entrepreneurial processes in established firms;
- would-be managers in creativity-driven businesses.

The material that makes up the course derives from field research questions, and the case study serves as the primary vehicle for the educational process. Students are introduced to a range of people, companies, and industries—some well known, others obscure. Because of the importance of these human stories, interview material appears from time to time. The use of video material, specifically developed for this course, is recommended as a means of making these human dramas more vivid and sharpening diagnostic and analytical skills.

Not all the course material chronicles success by any means, nor is there an underlying assumption that any one approach is "correct." Rather, the course presents students with a variety of people and situations from which they can extract general principles regarding the recurring issues and problems of entrepreneurs and entrepreneurial organizations.

Entrepreneurship, Creativity, and Organization's aim is *to contribute to the success of the entrepreneurial and/or creative venture* by helping students recognize—and anticipate—these recurring issues; to improve their sensitivity to human and organizational factors in the entrepreneurial environment; and to enhance their ability to make effective decisions and to find resolution of these issues. As a concentrated dose of preventive medicine, the course encourages a pattern recognition approach to learning, whose objective is an internalized sense of how things should be done. This does not derive from intellectualizing or theory but is lived; it is not free of charge but comes primarily from extensive and often painful personal experience.

The course is predicated on three underlying beliefs. First, entrepreneurship and creativity are seen as intimately related, timeless human qualities. Creativity implies generating new ideas and approaches. Entrepreneurial behavior involves the ability to identify opportunities based on these new ideas and approaches, and to turn them into something tangible. Outstanding organizations have always sought to mobilize both these qualities. Entrepreneurship and creativity are not topics of the moment but valuable corporate resources that can be managed for competitive advantage.

Second, the would-be entrepreneur needs facility in an array of human and organizational skills: self-understanding; interpersonal understanding; leadership; conflict resolution; stress management; tolerance for ambiguity; team and project management; creating appropriate rewards and incentives; and organization design.

Third, rigorous examination of entrepreneurial and creativity-dependent companies provides fresh insights into the relationships between organizations, strategies, and environments. Such companies operate in highly uncertain environments and exhibit great fluidity in their internal structure. Thus, they are continually challenged to generate mechanisms for fostering organizational integration and coherence. In addition, these firms evolve rapidly. Studying them reveals a panorama of the stages and dilemmas of leadership and organizational development. Put another way, they provide a significant laboratory for examining issues of generic importance to all managers.

Building on themes of basic organizational behavior and human resource management courses, *Entrepreneurship, Creativity, and Organization* poses some recurrent questions:

- What are the issues and concerns SPECIFIC to entrepreneurial companies?
- What is the impact on entrepreneurial organizations of:
  rapid growth;
  lack of established structure;
  balancing short-term and long-term decision making;
  shortages of resources such as managerial skills, time, and money;
  value conflicts between founders and newcomers;
  interaction patterns among functional groups in embryonic and rapidly changing organizations;
  the ongoing need to deal with stress and ambiguity
- What are the differences and similarities between entrepreneurial and managerial behavior at individual, group, and organizational levels?
- How do the human and organizational challenges of fostering entrepreneurship and creativity in large established firms and small entrepreneurial ones compare?

This course is organized around a process flow model. Four modules, each adopting a different point of view, and a group of related questions comprise the "golden thread" of this course. They are:

Managing creativity.   This module adopts the perspective of the manager of creative processes. It poses such basic questions as: Where do ideas come from? Which processes—individual and organizational—facilitate creativity?

The entrepreneur.   This module includes cases written from the entrepreneur's perspective. It allows students to clarify for themselves such issues as: What characterizes the person who recognizes the opportunity in an idea and translates it into reality? Is there a prototypical entrepreneurial personality?

The evolving organization.   This module also takes the entrepreneur's perspective. Once the idea and the people have been found, how can an appropriate company organization be developed and nurtured? How can the external environment influence the progress of an evolving firm? What are the predictable crises of organizational life that affect the viability of the enterprise?

The established organization.   This module adopts two related perspectives, that of the entrepreneurial leader/CEO and of the entrepreneurial middle manager.

When an organization is established in size, complexity, history, and corporate culture, how can the creative and entrepreneurial spirit be preserved and stimulated? What are the advantages and disadvantages of an established organization in pursuing these objectives? How do they influence the corporate or "internal" entrepreneur? What are important contrasts between bureaucratic and entrepreneurial organizations?

The four course modules suggest a number of additional questions specific to business students as they develop their career objectives and strive to achieve the highest possible level of professional effectiveness. These issues provide a subtext to the flow of course topics and include:

Managing creativity.   How can I understand the creative process better in terms of my own experience? What facilitates or blocks it for me? How effective am I in managing creative people? How do I evaluate the quality of a creative environment? How can I enhance creative results in a given organization?

The entrepreneur.   Where do I fall on a spectrum of entrepreneurial and managerial behavior? What aspects of my interpersonal and problem-solving style affect my potential as an entrepreneur or a productive member of an entrepreneurial and creativity-dependent organization?

The evolving organization.   How do I assess the fit between myself and an evolving and dynamic organization? Am I comfortable with the ambiguity inherent in such an environment? What must I do to enter successfully such a company and manage my career within it?

The established organization.   How can I create greater discretion for myself within the boundaries of an established organization? How do I gain the right to pursue entrepreneurial objectives? How do I make new things happen within the traditions and rules of an established company?

THE ENTREPRENEURSHIP, CREATIVITY, AND ORGANIZATION (ECO) ANALYTICAL FRAMEWORK

A basic assumption of this course is that entrepreneurship and creativity cannot be studied exclusively from one frame of reference such as the person or the organization, but must be dealt with more holistically. Entrepreneurship and creativity result from the interrelationship of three elements as shown in Figure 1:

- the person
- the task
- the organizational context

The first element, the "person," is obvious. New ideas are not generated or implemented by organizations or technology but come into being through the efforts of dedicated people. Thus, it is important to understand people's personalities, motivations, skills, levels of experience, and psychological preferences. It

FIGURE 1 THE ECO ANALYTICAL FRAMEWORK

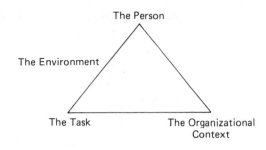

may be useful to know, for example, that someone has problems with authority stemming from previous relationships (personality issues); or is highly driven by a need for achievement (motivation); or has a particular facility with interpersonal relationships (skills); or has had work experience only in large bureaucratic organizations (level of experience); or finally, that someone prefers unstructured environments where intuition can be extensively used (psychological preferences).

The "task" is what a given group of people or an organization does. Tasks may be determined by an individual's personality or private vision. They are shaped by organizational strategy, as well as influenced by the external environment. For the entrepreneur, relevant tasks include generating new ideas or insights about new opportunities (creative tasks) and making those ideas come into some tangible form (operational/managerial tasks). As the entrepreneur develops an organization to serve as an appropriate lever for his or her vision, the nature and variety of tasks must inevitably change as the organization evolves and becomes more complex.

The "organizational context" is the immediate setting in which creative and entrepreneurial work takes place. Such issues as organizational structure and systems, the definition of work roles, and group culture affect significantly the nature of the creative or entrepreneurial environment. Such factors may limit or facilitate creativity and entrepreneurship, and become an increasing factor to contend with as the organization evolves.

Finally, these elements exist in an "environment," which refers to the outside world surrounding the organization. It is obviously significant as a source of external resources such as capital, people, information, and expertise, as well as various forms of professional services. It, too, can facilitate or impede creative and entrepreneurial endeavor to the extent that an appropriate infrastructure, for example, is either absent or present. The environment also defines the competitive situation, which may be composed of such factors as competitors, regulatory forces, and the development state of technology. Figure 2 summarizes the ECO analytical framework.

In general, the form an organization assumes and the tasks it undertakes are defined by and depend on both its strategy and environment.[1] Strategy gives

---

[1] John P. Kotter, "Organizational Design," *Organizational Behavior and Administration*, Paul Lawrence, Louis Barnes, and Jay Lorsch, eds. (Homewood, Ill.: Richard D. Irwin, 1976).

FIGURE 2 THE ECO ANALYTICAL FRAMEWORK

THE PERSON	THE TASK	THE ORGANIZATIONAL CONTEXT
Motives	What the person does	Structure
Personality	Inner/outer influences	Culture
Skills		Roles
Experience	Creative tasks	Policies
Psychological preferences	Operation/managerial tasks	Human resource systems
		Communication systems
		May limit or facilitate creativity and entrepreneurship

KEY ISSUE		
Modes of influence may change as the organization evolves	Nature and variety of tasks change as the organization evolves	Becomes more significant as the organization evolves
		Need for coordination, integration, and leadership increase

THE ENVIRONMENT

External resources
    capital
    people
    expertise
Infrastructure
Competitive pressures
Social values/mores
Regulation
State of technology

shape to tasks by defining the overall goals and purpose of the organization. The environment's influence on tasks comes from the relative availability of resources and influences on the operating environment. An organization's viability depends significantly on how it fits with its strategy and environment.

Regardless of their strategy or environment, all organizations must address several basic challenges. First, they must handle information effectively. For some organizational theorists, such as Galbraith, organizations are information processing mechanisms whose central tasks include getting information, disseminating it within the organization, and using it to make decisions.[2] Information

---

[2] Jay Galbraith, *Designing Complex Organizations* (Reading, Mass.: Addison-Wesley Publishing Company, 1973).

processes define an organization's relative ability to interact efficiently with its environment and to pursue its specific goals.

Second, they must balance the need for what Lawrence and Lorsch[3] label differentiation and integration. Differentiation refers to diversity in cognitive and emotional point of view that characterizes people with different functional orientations. For example, software designers and marketing managers may see problems and priorities in a significantly different light. Integration means an organization's ability to effect needed collaboration between functional specialists and organizational units to meet the challenges of the environment. Achieving integration is a guiding objective of the entrepreneurial firm, where tasks are highly diverse, interdependent, and important. The more diversity and interdependence, the more potential for information and work overload and for organizational conflict, requiring different organizational strategies. Differentiation also affects the ability of an organization to respond to change. Specialization may lead to a decrease in flexibility at both individual and operating unit levels. Changes in the environment, strategy, and available resources can also cause difficulty in achieving a required level of integration.

Third, organizations must achieve a degree of structural formality appropriate to the degree of uncertainty and ambiguity that characterizes their key tasks. For example, a high degree of task certainty encourages the development of formal structures to attain operational efficiency. On the other hand, a high degree of task uncertainty suggests a need for flexibility and greater informality. Obviously, entrepreneurial organizations are those with the highest degree of uncertainty and ambiguity, as Figure 3 indicates.

THE CRITICAL ROLE OF A HUMAN RESOURCE MANAGEMENT (HRM) PERSPECTIVE IN ENTREPRENEURIAL FIRMS

It is a basic orientation of this course that the concepts and skills represented by a human resource perspective are critical for the pursuit of creative and entrepreneurial objectives. The traditional entrepreneur's job description includes responsibilities like product development, business planning, and finance. But unless the company is a sole proprietorship, the entrepreneur quickly discovers that a substantial amount of time in the early phases of a company's life is taken up with human resource issues. The right people must be found, hired, and integrated into the organization; they must share the entrepreneur's vision of the future, be given appropriate direction, goals, and measures. The entrepreneur also must define agendas, make compensation deals and reward standards, clarify responsibilities, allocate status, resolve conflict, and manage interpersonal trade-offs, as well as evaluate and develop key people.

[3] Paul Lawrence and Jay Lorsch, *Organization and Environment* (Homewood, Ill.: Richard D. Irwin, 1967).

FIGURE 3 SOURCES OF UNCERTAINTY IN ENTREPRENEURIAL ORGANIZATIONS

THE OPPORTUNITY

Market size
Pricing
Viability of original business idea
Customer response
Value of proprietary position/patents/know-how
Product/service life-cycle

EXTERNAL: THE EMERGING INDUSTRY AS ENVIRONMENT

Competitors
Regulation
Technology
Word-of-mouth information

INTERNAL: "THE ENTREPRENEURIAL SCRAMBLE"

The Organization

Fit between key people and organization
Access to key resources: capital, people

The Person

Management/leadership ability of founder(s)

Tasks

Identifying
Prioritizing
Executing
Ability to create product/service
Length of time to develop product/service

What might be considered hard assets in a more established firm are to the embryonic firm often quite intangible. Technology may be in the process of development, finances contingent on performance, brand name unknown, comparative advantage and anticipated market position unproven. People are, on the other hand, among the most tangible and most expensive assets of the entrepreneurial company. One might think carefully about an investment decision involving a costly piece of equipment, yet in their haste to "get the job done," entrepreneurs are often less attentive to the managerial and financial implications of choosing and investing in people than they should be.

Difficulties in pursuing the human resource agenda may spring from an apparent tension between the "entrepreneurial spirit" and human resource management systems. The early-stage organization may be notable for its informality; people decisions like allocating responsibilities and rewards are made face to face. For some, creating human resource management systems may suggest the onset of bureaucracy. Such steps as hiring a human resource specialist, defining a human resources function, and embarking on human resource programs are often perceived, particularly by old-timers, as the imposition of unwanted structure on the company's free-wheeling entrepreneurial environment.

Yet, developing a human resource perspective is indispensable for the entrepreneur because it provides crucial leverage for influencing the development of the organization as well as the people in it. Human resource issues are important because entrepreneurs typically face an imbalance between the people resources at their disposal and the work that needs to be done. Hence, making the most of available human resources is clearly a central entrepreneurial challenge.

Growth provides another reason for valuing the leverage from effective human resource management. Growth rates of 50 percent to 100 percent per year are not uncommon as companies "ramp up" and attempt to win market acceptance. Early success, while ardently desired, can also lead to unique organizational risks and burdens for the entrepreneurial firm, which must maintain the flexibility and capacity to adapt to a changing and dynamic environment. To deal with emerging needs the firm must modify its organizational structure, find new methods of internal communication, develop new human skills, and assimilate new people into the organization.

Managing expectations is another human issue important to the entrepreneurial firm. First are the expectations of key people. A firm may be very dependent on the creative and/or technical talents of one or more "stars" who, in such high-tech areas as computer software and biotechnology, may be responsible for a product's successful development. If retaining such people and maintaining their productivity are important, then they must be kept happy and their role continually developed in relation to the company's evolution. Second, there are the expectations of people who have been drawn to the entrepreneurial firm because of their perceptions of it: as a successful company; a vehicle for personal financial gain; an opportunity for advancement; an attractive company environment in which employees are treated well. Continually balancing expectations with reality is critical to maintaining a company atmosphere of excitement and productivity.

What specifically can a human resource management function do for an entrepreneurial company? Properly conceived, human resource management can be an important source of leverage for the entrepreneur in addressing the following key issues:

- Selecting the right person for the right job.
- Planning for change in a dynamic environment as both people and jobs evolve.

- Maximizing productivity through job design, clear expectations and performance appraisal, encouraging shared values, skill development and training, managing morale, managing nonfinancial incentives, encouraging communications within the company.

Human resources can influence each element in the ECO analytical framework. Clearly, the human resource function is critical in identifying and bringing the right people into the organization. It has a significant effect on people's progression in the organization through training, promotion systems, and career planning. HRM affects the task through job design and the creation of rewards appropriate to the behavior desired. It affects the organizational setting through such interactions as communication systems, counseling senior managers, managing company culture, and handling company climate. Figure 4 summarizes the role of human resource management as a source of managerial leverage and influence. Human resource management deals with each element by providing an answer to a key question:

- *The person:* Do we have the people we need today? Are we looking for the people we will need tomorrow?
- *The task:* Are tasks being defined to best satisfy individual and organizational needs?
- *The organizational context:* Is the organization developing so as to best support its strategy?

Human resource management acts on each element, but it is in the area of assuring fit that it realizes its greatest value: as a transmission system for linking the person, the task, and the organizational context. In this role human re-

FIGURE 4 HRM AS A SOURCE OF LEVERAGE AND INFLUENCE

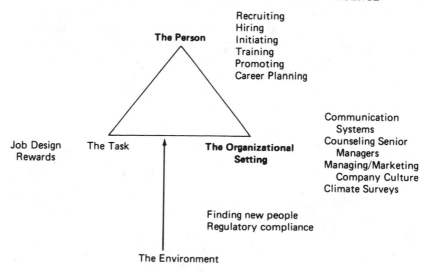

sources can buffer the effects of rapid or discontinuous change by operating in three critical dimensions:

- person-organization fit;
- person-task fit;
- task-organization fit.

Assuring fit between person and organization is critical to entrepreneurial and creative success. Variables such as personal style, needs, and ability to tolerate uncertainty may critically influence a person's ability to be successful in a given company environment. It is imperative that an organization understand itself in terms of culture and environment, and that it maintain a clear image of the type of person likely to be successful in it. Such an image increases the likelihood that the right people will be found through highly focused recruiting practices. It also determines the manner in which new people will be introduced to the norms and expectations of the organization. Finally, the fit between person and organization is dynamic, and influenced by change on both sides of the equation. Providing ways for both careers and organizational capabilities to develop will assure the continuous and mutual adaptation of person and organization.

Assuring person-task fit is also a critical responsibility of the human resources function. As an organization evolves, the nature and complexity of tasks to be accomplished will change. Developing people's skills through training and development allows them to keep pace with an organization's changing needs. Varying their opportunities to gain experience through job rotation and redeployment can lead to the development of critically needed skills.

Finally, achieving an ongoing fit between an organization's needs and the tasks to be accomplished is of fundamental importance. An organization must constantly ask itself whether the right things are being done relative to an organization's strategy and resources. Modifying the definition and design of jobs is an important way to redefine tasks as an organization's needs evolve.

Further issues of human resource management are explored in the companion volumes to this book as they relate to specific issues of the entrepreneur, the evolving organization, and the established organization.

Introduction to
Managing Creativity

Understanding creativity provides a foundation for the understanding of entrepreneurship. Central to the entrepreneur's role is the constant desire to create something: a new organization, new insights into the market, new corporate values, new manufacturing processes, new products or services, new ways of managing. All entrepreneurial activity unfolds around the birth of new ideas. Understanding how the creative process begins and evolves is therefore critical for entrepreneurial success.

Creativity is a topic relevant not only to the entrepreneurial start-up but to business in general. It is an important source of competitive strength for all organizations concerned with growth and change. For, to be responsive to change *is* to be creative: in such terms as perceiving the environment; developing new products and services; establishing new business procedures.

Creativity presents a variety of management challenges and it may require significant tangible investment. As an example, Hallmark Cards has spent substantial resources on an Innovation Center that houses several hundred employees involved with generating new product ideas. Creativity may be an integral part of a corporate culture that management wishes to instill. It may also determine organizational structure and human resource practices.

The management of creativity may proceed intentionally or by default. This book's purpose is to examine how to manage creativity *better* and to dispel the notion that it is simply brainstorming on a pink cloud.

Creativity is a large and complex topic. In this book, it is considered from a managerial perspective, with the cases revolving around what the manager must do to manage creativity effectively. Three major issues are addressed: first, a working definition of creativity useful in business terms is established; second,

FIGURE 1-1

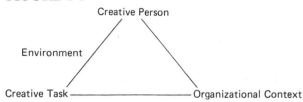

the importance of managing creativity is demonstrated in terms of nurturing the competitive strength of a given organization; and third, a set of tools is presented for managers to influence the creative process. These tools reflect the importance of understanding creativity in both individual and organizational terms. Stated differently, the following sections are entitled:

1. Creativity—What is it?
2. Managing Creativity—Why is it important?
3. Managing Creativity—How do you do it?

In seeking to foster creativity, the manager must differentiate among interventions which influence person, task, and organizational context. Figure 1-1 illustrates the model.

Appreciating the challenges facing creative individuals and their needs is an essential task for the would-be manager of creative process. Different interpersonal approaches to managing creative people are explored using such examples as Leo Castelli and George Lucas. Managers may influence the creative task through job design and the manner in which expectations and goals are communicated. At the organizational level, it will be shown that creativity, far from being unmanageable, is a resource deeply influenced by basic decisions about such organizational issues as structure, culture, and style of leadership. Such issues are taken up in the George Lucas, Ladd, Windham Hill, Catalyst, and Activision cases in this book. Finally, managers must also be aware of the environment to the extent that it facilitates or hinders creative work through the availability of resources, supportive social values, and infrastructure.

CREATIVITY—WHAT IS IT?

Webster[1] defines creativity as "the ability to bring something new into existence." To others, it is a human process leading to a result which is novel (new), useful (solves an existing problem or satisfies an existing need), and understandable (can be reproduced). But this tells us little about the process. A quote on creativ-

---

[1] *Webster's Third New International Dictionary* (Springfield: G&C Merriam and Company, 1976).

ity from Jasper Johns, a noted modern painter, captures this dilemma: "It's simple. Take something and do something to it and then do something else. Do it for a while and pretty soon you've got something." Pablo Picasso makes a wry distinction between technique and inspiration: "Some painters transform the sun into a yellow spot, others transform a yellow spot into the sun." The difficulty in defining creativity for the creative individual is highlighted in the article "On My Painting" by Max Beckmann which accompanies the Leo Castelli case in this book.

Creativity has a flavor of something revolutionary or subversive. For example, Degas once said that a painter paints a picture with the same feeling as that with which a criminal commits a crime. Creativity is intimately linked to the idea of change. "Every act of creation is first of all an act of destruction," says Picasso. Interestingly, the economist Shumpeter also referred to entrepreneurship as "creative destruction."

A most useful definition of creativity comes from a recent literature on social psychology. According to Amabile,[2] a product or response will be judged creative to the extent that it is a novel and appropriate, useful, correct, or valuable response to the task at hand, and the task is *heuristic* rather than *algorithmic*.

Algorithmic tasks are those governed by fixed rules. The path to a solution is clear and straightforward. Broiling a steak and repairing a carburetor are governed by specific rules. Painting a picture and designing a new computer chip, on the other hand, are heuristic tasks. They have not been done before; the task is not specifically defined, there is no established path to a solution. The algorithm must be developed from scratch, which involves a new interplay among a person, a task, and a social environment.

What are the characteristics of creative people? Can everyone be creative? While most would agree that the creativity of Mozart or Einstein operated at a high level sometimes described as "genius," others would argue that creativity is at least latent in everyone. The psychologist Maslow[3] writes that there is a type of creativity which "is the universal heritage of every human being" and strongly associated with psychological health. He distinguishes between "special talent creativeness" such as the musical talent of a Mozart, and "self-actualizing creativeness" which he believed originated in the personality and was visible in the ordinary affairs of life.

Many attempts have been made to list the attributes of the creative person. In reviewing the literature, Roe[4] offers the following:

- openness to experience
- observance—seeing things in unusual ways

---

[2] Teresa Amabile, *The Social Psychology of Creativity* (New York: Springer Verlag, 1983).

[3] Abraham Maslow, *Creativity in Self-Actualizing People, Toward a Psychology of Being* (New York: Van Nostrand Reinhold Company, 1968).

[4] A. Roe, "Psychological Approaches to Creativity in Science," *Essays on Creativity in the Sciences*, ed. M. A. Coler and H. K. Hughes (New York: New York University, 1963).

- curiosity
- accepting and reconciling apparent opposites
- tolerance of ambiguity
- independence in judgment, thought, and action
- needing and assuming autonomy
- self-reliance
- not being subject to group standards and control
- willingness to take calculated risks
- persistence

Raudsepp[5] adds further attributes:

- sensitivity to problems
- fluency—the ability to generate a large number of ideas
- flexibility
- originality
- responsiveness to feelings
- openness to unconscious phenomena
- motivation
- freedom from fear of failure
- the ability to concentrate
- thinking in images
- selectivity

Other definitions of creativity come from an eclectic tradition of research. For instance, it is associated with neuropsychological theories which show specialization in the two cerebral hemispheres of the brain.[6] The left side of the brain is said to stress logical, rational, and analytical modes of thinking, while the right side governs emotional and intuitive experience. It is not a major leap to conceive in metaphorical terms of our left hemispheres as "managerial" and our right as "entrepreneurial."

Integrating these predispositions appropriately then becomes the central challenge. Logic without passion is sterile, while inspiration without analysis is often arbitrary or misguided. The bureaucrat without the taste for change and innovation is as stuck as the entrepreneur with brilliant ideas but limited management skills. Rothenberg has coined the term "Janusian thinking"[7] to refer to the capacity for "conceiving and utilizing two or more opposite or contradictory ideas, concepts, or images simultaneously." Janusian is derived from Janus, the two-headed god looking simultaneously into the future and the past, the god of beginnings. The idea of integrating apparent opposites is also contained in the

---

[5] E. Raudsepp, "Profile of the Creative Individual," *Creative Computing,* August 1983.

[6] H. Mintzberg, "Planning on the Left Side and Managing on the Right," *Harvard Business Review,* July–August, 1976.

[7] A. Rothenberg, *Janusian Thinking in the Creativity Questions,* A. Rothenberg and eds. (Chapel Hill: Duke University Press, 1976).

FIGURE 1-2 THE PROCESS APPROACH TO CREATIVITY

CREATIVITY STAGE	ACTIVITY	PSYCHOLOGICAL STYLE
Interest	environmental scanning	intuition/emotion
Preparation	preparing the expedition	details/planning
Incubation	"mulling things over"	intuition
Illumination	the "eureka" experience	intuition
Verification	market research	details/rationality
Exploitation	captain of industry	details/rationality

notion referred to by Peters and Waterman as "simultaneous loose-tight proper-ties."[8] This involves a process of controlling and not controlling, for example managing certain organizational agendas tightly while creating slack around others so that new initiatives can emerge.

Other disciplines have also explored creativity. Because it involves an inter-play between a person, a task, and an organizational context, creativity has been the subject of extensive psychological research. Wallas,[9] an early American psy-chologist, described several stages of the creative process. For him, creativity begins with *interest:* There has to be something inherently compelling about the problem. This is followed by the stage of *preparation,* when the ensuing intellec-tual journey is planned, much as one would pack supplies for a voyage. *Incuba-tion* then follows as an intuitive, "back burner," nonintentional style of working on the problem. *Illumination*—the intuitive, synthetic "ah-ha" experience—fol-lows.

Finally, the results must be *verified.* Are they arbitrary or capable of replica-tion and understanding? Subsequently the stage of *exploitation* or capturing value from the creative act has been added to Wallas' model. Figure 1-2 illustrates this process approach to creativity.

A central theme of this book is demonstrating the strong linkages between creativity and entrepreneurship. An entrepreneur can be defined as someone who is responsive to opportunity and has a sense of freedom both in personal and in organizational terms to act on that opportunity. Entrepreneurship con-notes implementation, *doing.* While creativity implies a vision of what is possible, the entrepreneur translates that creative vision into action, into a human vision which guides the work of a group of people. If the term "innovation" suggests the implementation process by which creative inspiration leads to practical results, then entrepreneurship is the human and organizational process by which innovation takes place. Figure 1-3 illustrates the link between creativity and entrepreneurship.

[8] Thomas Peters and Robert H. Waterman, Jr., *In Search of Excellence* (New York: Harper and Row, 1981).

[9] Graham Wallas, "Stages of Control," *The Art of Thought* (New York: Harcourt Brace Jovanovich, 1926).

FIGURE 1-3 ENTREPRENEURIAL CAPACITY

	High	Low
High	③ Lotus Lucasfilm	① Think Tank Artists Coop
Low	② Fast Food Franchiser	④ Mature Bureaucracy

Creative Capacity

Thus, while the concepts of creativity and entrepreneurship are highly related and overlap, they are not identical. The capacity to develop new ideas, concepts, and processes is not the same as the capacity to make things happen, to implement in practical terms. In Figure 1-3, we have four categories of companies differentiated by creative and entrepreneurial capacity. Capacity in this sense refers to all investment in people, infrastructure, or intellectual assets. Category 1 companies are high in creative resources but low in entrepreneurial resources. These might be think tanks or artists' cooperatives which are in the business of generating creative ideas without the responsibility of having necessarily to *do* anything with them. Category 2 firms are low in creativity, but high in entrepreneurship. These are companies involved in existing businesses, for example franchising fast-food businesses in a relentless and opportunity-driven manner. Category 3 involves firms well endowed with both creative and entrepreneurial resources, for example Lucasfilm Ltd. Finally, Category 4 refers to companies high in neither creativity nor entrepreneurship, for example, mature bureaucracies like the postal service.

This matrix also relates to the predispositions of individuals. Some people may be good conceptualizers or artists, adept at generating new ideas but weak in the areas of implementation. Others are entrepreneurial but not particularly creative. Like the owner of 20 McDonald's franchises, they may be able to spot opportunity and act on it with zeal but not be concerned about generating new kinds of businesses. It is important to keep in mind that the entrepreneur is not necessarily creative, but is able to recognize and take advantage of the creativity of others. Some people may be capable of both creative and entrepreneurial work, while others may have talent for neither and are content instead to work in a well-defined environment according to rules established by others.

There is a final distinction which should be made between creativity and entrepreneurship. Creativity may or may not be externally focused on the environment. Most painters will do whatever is required to pursue a personal vision. The creative process is inner-directed. The notion of doing market research to validate a creative vision is often anathema to people on the creative side of a business. This issue emerges strongly in the cases on the videogame industry in this book. On the other hand, the entrepreneur must keep at least one eye sharply focused on the environment if business success is to be assured. Ultimately what the entrepreneur accomplishes must be validated by a response from the "real world."

Again, managing creativity is a process, combining issues of the creative person, task, and organizational context. One could make a comparison between creative efforts in the organization and the biological process of conception, gestation, and birth. The act of inspiration, the "ah-hah" experience, is only the beginning: the combining of disparate elements in an act of fertilization. Gestation then requires a healthy environment, necessary resources, support without undue interference, patience with a natural evolutionary process, tolerance of anxiety, and other feelings that result from the uncertainty of the process, change, and adaptation in the host to accommodate development. When the creative product/organism is "born," the parallels continue. Does it fit with expectations when it sees the light of day? Birth raises a number of "parenting" issues. Who is to be responsible? What models and values of parenting seem most appropriate? Birth has an important impact on the environment. The experience of successful birth can validate a system in important ways. Conversely, birth can also bring with it the prospect of complications. How does one deal with something which doesn't turn out as expected? How does one deal with the attendant guilt, anger, or denial? How does one deal with grief over a "business death" from such causes as bankruptcy or premature project termination? Psychology gives us some important guidelines for dealing with such losses in ways that can contribute to growth. While not fully applicable, biological images can be a useful descriptive model for the task of managing creativity.

Creativity comes with a price. The costs within a competitive industry of maintaining a creative atmosphere and of retaining key personnel can be high. Top managers are increasingly aware of the extent to which "climate" and "corporate culture" can translate into expensive, tangible investment. Yet, the costs of failing to foster creativity can be significantly higher. Well-positioned indeed is the organization that facilitates the progress of its creative members toward the next "1-2-3," the next biotechnology breakthrough, the next Pac Man videogame, the next Macintosh computer, the next "Star Wars" movie. Thus, managing creativity can be seen as an important strategic dimension for long-term planning and decision making.

MANAGING CREATIVITY— WHY IS IT IMPORTANT?

To speak of "managing creativity" may sound paradoxical or even frivolous; the search for creativity has often been linked to magic, the demonic, or the divine. How could such a process be *managed*? But creativity is a central preoccupation of many managers every day in many types of firms: a biotechnology company where 50 percent of the employees are scientists; a financial services company that is constantly innovating in service and marketing strategies; a consulting firm continuously striving to develop new analytical tools; a real estate developer who designs original financings for unique opportunities. For companies in these situations, managing creativity is of critical competitive importance. Lucasfilm Ltd. and the firms described in the videogame industry cases are only as secure as their most recent successes. Their business strategy requires them to maintain a constant flow of creative output. "Create or die" might be their motto.

Yet what does *managing* creativity mean? According to popular definitions of these words, "creativity" springs from the most inner recesses of human vision, the most intimate reaches of human experience. Creativity is thought by many to be "inspired," its comings and goings unpredictable and highly idiosyncratic. "Management" seems opposed to creativity, suggesting a valuation of collective attitudes above personal vision. The pragmatic, rational, and judgmental style frequently associated with business management seems at the outset inhospitable to creative efforts and threatens to dilute them.

Furthermore, creativity is commonly attributed primarily to artistic endeavor and the expression of cultural talent. Artists are by definition creative, it is believed. Something about their talent is innate; they are born and not made. But it is a guiding assumption of this book that far from being germane only to the arts, creativity is a resource important for the basic institutions of society: industrial and business organizations; educational institutions; social and community agencies.

In fact, there is no such thing as creativity divorced from a particular human group, from a particular set of political constraints. Creativity for *whom* is as important as the value-laden issues raised by the question of creativity for *what*. Indeed, creativity is latent in most collective situations, and the extent to which it is fully expressed determines whether a group reaches the fulfillment of its goals. Creativity and organizational processes then must engage, must mesh, if social institutions are to be fully productive. Seen in this way, creativity is not something for special people in special situations, but belonging to everyone.

Why is attention to the management of creativity important? As mentioned earlier, creativity is a competitive issue, not just something nice. It is a valuable resource that must be nurtured, not wasted, given the significant costs associated with creative talent and infrastructure supportive of creative work. Finally, managing creativity may require an experimental attitude towards developing new types of organizations. Many entrepreneurial organizations, in a sense, are laboratories in which the organizational structures appropriate to future business challenges are currently under development. How such organizations treat the question of managing creativity will be of considerable importance for their continued survival. New challenges will be faced by such organizations: managing explosive growth; dealing with greater work force diversity; establishing a culture supportive of creative activity; maintaining fairness.

This concern with managing creativity also tells a demographic story. New entrants to the workplace come with an expectation of more creative and fulfilling work. This "corporate new wave"[10] is concerned with self-actualization, and

---

[10] John Kao, "The Corporate New Wave" in "Entrepreneurship: What It Is and How to Teach It," John Kao and Howard Stevenson, eds., Division of Research, Harvard Business School, 1984.

the demands for creative work are higher. The pace of technological change is also relevant. Creativity is an important plane of competition, particularly in what Porter calls emerging industries.[11] The explosion of creativity which surrounds emerging industries involves not only new technology, but business practices and strategy. It frequently gives rise to a variety of organizational experiments in how to maximize creativity. The cases describing the range of companies placing bets on creativity in the videogame industry provide a dramatic illustration of this point.

Creativity, however, preoccupies more than start-up organizations. It is at the heart of much work on industrial policy at state and regional levels; it is also a challenge to established business organizations. Many significant experiments managing creativity are being carried out at considerable expense of resources, for example, the approaches of 3M, Hewlett-Packard, and IBM towards fostering innovation in established organizations. Other examples include such innovative organizations as MCC (Microelectronics and Computer Consortium), a joint venture of leading semiconductor and computer companies aimed at pooling knowledge and resources in a new fashion.

Meanwhile, managing creativity has become a highly visible topic of public debate in other parts of the world. Nowhere is this more apparent than in Japan. As the president of Fujitsu Computers, Tuma Yamamoto, said: "The creativity of the Japanese people will be called into question . . . through the 1990s. The whole nation must work like one possessed to meet this great challenge."[12] Japan's MITI (Ministry of International Trade and Industry) has urged Japanese industry to make the transition from imitation to creativity. As part of addressing this challenge, Japan has embarked on an ambitious national effort called the Technopolis Strategy,[13] a program of developing high technology zones or miniature Silicon Valleys all over Japan. This involves a massive investment in constructing environments conducive to industrial creativity. Will creativity become an explicit plan of global industrial competition in the future? Will "creativity gaps" emerge in the industrial societies of the future?

MANAGING CREATIVITY—HOW DO YOU DO IT?

The very management of creativity is heuristic and hard to reduce to a fixed set of rules. Yet, the goal of this book will be to provide tools for managers to apply in dealing with creativity.

We may learn more about creativity in a particular organization by understanding what facilitates or blocks its expression. Common sense tells us that to hinder creative expression we should:

- emphasize bureaucratic structures and attitudes
- pile on tradition and established culture

[11]   Michael Porter, *Competitive Strategy* (New York: Free Press, 1980).
[12]   Sheridan Tatsuno, *The Technopolis Challenge* (New York: Prentice Hall Press, 1986).
[13]   Ibid.

- stress the importance of standard operating procedures
- suppress suitable role models for creative expression
- minimize the availability of needed resources
- ensure poor communication which blocks the flow of ideas
- have tight control systems which eliminate slack required for unofficial initiatives
- enforce strict penalties for failure
- omit rewards for success
- emphasize values which inhibit risk taking and questioning
- reinforce the expectation of external evaluation
- carry out surveillance of creative activity
- emphasize tight deadlines
- prefer specialization; emphasize authority over responsibility

On the other hand, a number of organizational actions can enhance creativity:

- create an open, decentralized organizational structure
- support a culture which provides leverage for creative experimentation
- encourage experimental attitudes
- circulate success stories
- emphasize the role of the champion
- provide the freedom to fail
- stress effective communication at all levels
- make resources available for new initiatives
- ensure that new ideas cannot be easily killed
- remove bureaucracy from the resource allocation process
- provide appropriate financial and nonfinancial rewards for success
- ensure a corporate culture which supports risk taking and questioning
- minimize administrative interference
- provide freedom from surveillance and evaluation
- loosen deadlines
- delegate responsibility for initiating new activity

As mentioned earlier the manager must consider several elements to gain perspective on the challenge of fostering creativity, including those outlined in Figure 1-4. Each of these elements provides an entry point for managerial intervention.

The manager influences creative people by selecting them, initiating them into the organization, and providing for their development. Through the medium of personal relationships, creative people can be motivated, their agendas clarified and adjusted, their connections to the organization fostered. The manager must be an astute psychologist, attentive to communication at all levels, sensitive to needs.

In managing creative people, managers need to be aware of their sources of leverage. Are they dealing with a uniquely talented individual or is the person replaceable? If replaceable, how easily? To what extent does the creative individual perceive you, the manager, as credible in your personal style, track record, or

FIGURE 1-4 FOSTERING CREATIVITY

Person	Appreciating the creative person's process and the manager–creative person relationship
Task	Defining the creative task without stifling creativity
Organizational Context	Creating/influencing the organization in terms of structure and culture to maximize the creative atmosphere
Environment	Recognizing creativity as a resource influenced by competitive factors

technical expertise? To what extent do you, as manager, control resources which the creative individual needs, whether in terms of technology, money, management expertise, marketing clout, company reputation, or brand name? How much cooperation from creative individuals can be garnered through such sources of leverage?

The manager influences the creative task by defining it, setting expectations, and by providing goals and objectives. *He or she frames the problem.* Despite the heuristic nature of the task, he or she is nevertheless able to provide a map of what needs to be done. Hence, managerial style is important. The manager must be willing to practice "loose-tight" management. An excessive amount of evaluation or surveillance of creative work will place an inhibiting burden on it. Yet, the manager must work within the world of budgets, resource allocation procedures, deadlines, market demands, and competitive pressures. Thus, the manager of creativity must become an integrator[14] between the creative and business priorities of the organization. He or she must know when to melt into the background, and when to push; when to leave expectations ambiguous, and when to clarify them. These skills involve the development of sensibilities rather than the memorization of rules. This is why studying the examples of such masters of creativity management as Leo Castelli can be so instructive.

Finally, the manager influences the organizational context by a range of organizational tools and "design factors." These include organizational structure and culture, human resource practices, and leadership style.

How an organization is designed is important: Relevant issues include organizable structure and the attendant communications network; physical layout; and resulting patterns of human interaction. Organizational systems for functions, such as resource allocation and formal communication between organization levels, can either support or inhibit creativity. It is important to foster the development of a corporate culture supportive of creativity, the freedom to question, and the freedom to fail. Many experiments in organization design have attempted to maintain the flavor of a creative "hot shop" within an established

---

[14] Paul Lawrence and Jay Lorsch, *Organization and Environment* (Boston, Mass.: Harvard Business School Press, 1986).

organization. In a sense, this means creating an officially sanctioned counterculture or a company within a company. Examples include the creation of the Convergent Technologies' laptop computer, and the design of the personal computer by IBM's entry systems group. At other times, creativity is maintained by delegating design tasks to outside firms. Apple, for example, delegated the design of the "mouse" for its Macintosh computer.[15]

Much managers' leverage in fostering creative efforts rests with the human resource management agenda. Seen in managerial terms, creative people are an important company asset: the "process" by which a creative "product" is developed or a creative "service" rendered. Managing this human process for maximum effect is vital. Reward systems are critical both in monetary and nonmonetary terms. "Signing the painting" is an important source of reward. For example, the Macintosh design team was permitted to sign their names inside the injection molded case of the computer.[16] Recognition programs are also important as with the IBM Fellows Program. Other areas for HRM intervention include evaluation and career development, perception of employee influence, participation in decision making, human resource planning, and job design.

Another set of people-related issues involves dealing with creative talent. How should "mavericks" and "stars" be treated? How can creative success and failure be dealt with? The role of the "special person" must be clarified. While creativity may not be an outcome of democratic consensus, it is important that perceived fairness be maintained or that trade-offs around special treatment for some members of the organization be explicitly recognized.

In looking at creative people themselves, whether they be scientists, artists, engineers, or computer programmers, the manager is faced with a series of basic questions. What do they need to be most creative? How many of such people are needed, and how much will they cost the organization? How do you design jobs which will take best advantage of people's creative talents? What kind of leadership styles and role models best support an organization's creative needs? How much managerial latitude is provided in terms of the freedom to fail and/or to question? There are questions of what style seems appropriate to a given situation and set of needs. Many potential sources of conflict between managers and creative people exist stemming from the need for evaluation, resource allocation, planning, rewards, and standards of comparison. Classic situations include account executives and creative designers in advertising, scientists and marketing managers in biotechnology. Assumptions, perceptions, and feelings can easily become polarized. Which managerial interventions seem to work best? How far should management go to accommodate creative people? In this regard, Michael Eisner, chairman and CEO of Walt Disney, has remarked that "the only people I let roll around the floor having a tantrum are my three-year-olds."

[15] Michael Rogers, "Silicon Valley's Newest Wizards," *Newsweek,* January 5, 1987, p. 36.
[16] *In Search of Excellence: The Video,* produced by Nathan Tyler Productions, Waltham, Mass., 1985.

Managerial responsibilities are diverse in a creative organization. They include:

- creating and sharing a vision
- communicating clearly and flexibly
- providing interpersonal support
- cheerleading and coaching
- praising accomplishments—providing applause
- honoring failures
- using conflict resolution skills
- knowing when to open the process up and when to close it down
- balancing originality with resource constraints
- balancing vision with attention to detail

The manager orchestrates the creative process by organizing the flow of communication and human interaction around it. For example, the manager may wish to make use of creativity techniques which enhance creativity and allow it to emerge. Osborne[17] pioneered the technique of brainstorming, letting ideas emerge without substantial editing. Synectics[18] is a process of creative problem solving through attention to group process. De Bono[19] has developed the notion of lateral thinking as an anchor for training systems designed to foster creative thinking.

The manager must also be alert to questions of how the climate for creativity changes as an organization matures. How can it maintain creative excitement and productivity at later stages in its "life cycle"? What differences exist in managing creativity in the embryonic as opposed to the mature organization? What types of people are needed at what organizational stage? Can creativity be institutionalized? This issue of managing change is addressed through such cases as the Videogame Industry, Windham Hill, and Activision.

Managing creativity in organizations brings a number of classic dilemmas and trade-offs. Can you have creativity on demand? How do you balance the need for freedom in an organization with the need for structure? How can you balance the creative person's desire for unlimited development time with the manager's desire for deadlines? How can you reconcile the creative need for participation and informal communication with the management need for hierarchy and structured authority in more complex kinds of organizations? What kinds of systems for planning, resource allocation, and information flow are useful? If predictable conflicts arise between the managerial and creative sides of an organization, how can they best be managed? To what extent is there value for the organization in such conflicts?

[17] Alex F. Osborne, *Applied Imagination: Principles and Procedures of Creative Problem Solving* (New York: Scribner's Sons, 1979).
[18] George Prince, *The Practiced Creativity* (New York: Macmillan, 1970).
[19] Edward De Bono, *Lateral Thinking* (New York: Harper and Row, 1970).

THE CASES

Leo Castelli

This case permits a deeper exploration of creativity in terms of the relationship between creator and manager. Leo Castelli is the preeminent New York art dealer who has nurtured the careers of such modern artists as Jasper Johns, Roy Lichtenstein, Robert Rauschenberg, and Frank Stella. The case explores Castelli's development as an entrepreneur and catalyst, examines his personal style, and suggests a framework for looking at the creative process from the managerial perspective. The accompanying reading, "On My Painting" by Max Beckmann, introduces and allows an assessment of the world of the creative artist.

The Videogame Industry and The Videogame Design Process

These cases look at the specific issue of managing videogame designers within the broader contours of an emerging industry. They have general applicability since the explosive growth of the entertainment software industry shared characteristics with the development of the television and automobile industries. The case on the videogame design process presents various approaches to managing creativity, some often contradictory. It allows for discussion of how a particular approach is shaped by specific organizational culture and strategy. Students consider such questions as: How does a firm establish and defend a guiding emphasis on creative quality? What are the appropriate incentives to sustain this focus? What happens to creativity in a volatile industry which suddenly experiences rapid decline?

George Lucas and Skywalking

This case presents an individual who has experienced exceptional success in turning his creative vision into a successful organization, Lucasfilm Ltd., to implement this vision. The company possesses both entrepreneurial and creative features, and appears skilled at dealing with ambiguity and human behavior. Analysis provides an opportunity to look at one person's concept of creativity and how this definition is translated into a company culture and operating system. In addition, individual and organizational issues are related to the question: What does this type of company have to do to manage the creative process successfully?

Jerry Welsh

In the mid-1980s, the American Express Travel Related Services company was a highly visible, successful, and mature business organization. Yet its management was constantly on the lookout for ways of enhancing its creative and entrepreneurial results. One method employed by TRS's CEO, Lou Gerstner, involved making unusual hires who would serve as internal entrepreneurs to shake things up within the organization. One of the most well-known examples of this approach is Jerry Welsh, executive vice president of Worldwide Marketing, whose unusual attitudes towards managing people and balancing creativity and management made him an important emblem of the officially sanctioned TRS "counterculture." The Jerry Welsh case may also be used in conjunction with the American Express TRS Company cases which are published in *The Entrepreneurial Organization*.[20]

The Ladd Company

Riding high on the wings of success as president of Twentieth Century Fox Film Corporation, Alan Ladd undertook to create a model environment for encouraging the diverse forms of creativity required to make successful motion pictures. Called The Ladd Company, this new venture was designed to enhance the ability of a select group of professionals to generate results unhampered by bureaucratic interference. Integral to The Ladd Company's approach was the leadership style of Alan Ladd himself, a creator, head of The Ladd Company, and an entrepreneur.

Windham Hill Productions

This well-known firm in the recorded entertainment business started as a highly informal "labor of love" by Will Ackerman and Anne Robinson. Pioneering the genre of "new age music," the company quickly became a runaway success—balancing the need for special relationships with special people (the firm's stable of creative artists) with the need for management efficiencies in the marketing and distribution of the company's products. Furthermore, the company had to deal with the challenges of being more professional within a culture strongly influenced by the entrepreneurial and non-mainstream attitudes of the company's founders.

Catalyst Technologies

Catalyst Technologies was founded by high-technology mogul Nolan Bushnell, whose previous enterprises had included Atari and Pizza Time theater. Established as a "venture incubator," the purpose of Catalyst lay in providing a nur-

---

[20]   John J. Kao, *The Entrepreneurial Organization* (Englewood Cliffs, NJ: Prentice Hall, 1991).

turing environment for the establishment of new ventures that at the same time enjoyed economies of scale from providing a variety of shared services within the incubator environment. In a sense, Catalyst was set up to be a venture in the business of creating new ventures—a venture factory. This case provides an opportunity to assess the concept of venture incubation in general, and Catalyst's approach in particular.

Activision

Activision was one of the earliest and most successful companies in the videogame cartridge business. Deciding to leave the videogame hardware business to other manufacturers, the company based its strategy on attracting an elite group of outstanding game designers who were freed from the usual interference in the creative process originating from such functions as management and marketing. Instead, game designers were treated like stars, sheltered from outside influence, and taken care of in a variety of tangible and intangible ways. The company represented a conscious attempt to design a company whose culture, organizational structure, human resource strategy, and leadership style were all congruent with one another and dedicated to the strategic goal of maximizing creative results.

Activision was severely affected by an unexpected downturn in the videogame industry. The Activision (B) case describes the company's response to unforeseen and adverse shifts in its operating environment that forced tough decisions in terms of what it should or could keep from its innovative corporate culture.

FOR FURTHER READING

ADAMS, JAMES, *Conceptual Blockbusting*. New York: W. W. Norton and Company, 1974.

AMABILE, TERESA, *The Social Psychology of Creativity*. New York: Springer-Verlag, 1983.

DE BONO, EDWARD, *Lateral Thinking*. New York: Harper and Row, 1970.

HERBERT, ROBERT, ed., *Modern Artists on Art*. Englewood Cliffs, N.J.: Prentice-Hall, Inc., 1964.

JOHN-STEINER, VERA, *Notebooks of the Mind*. Albuquerque: University of Mexico Press, 1985.

KAO, JOHN, *Taking Stock of Creative Resources*. Working Paper 83-80, Division of Research, Harvard Business School, 1983.

KAO, JOHN, The Corporate New Wave, in *Entrepreneurship: What It Is and How to Teach It*, John Kao and Howard Stevenson, eds., Division of Research, Harvard Business School, 1984.

KIDDER, TRACY, *The Soul of a New Machine*. Boston: Little, Brown, 1981.

MAY, ROLLO, *The Courage to Create*. New York: W. W. Norton and Company, 1975.

PERKINS, DAVID, *The Mind's Best Work*. Cambridge: Harvard University Press, 1981.

POLLACK, DALE, *Skywalking*. New York: Harmony Books, 1983.

PRINCE, GEORGE, "Synectics," from Shirley Olsen, ed., *Group Planning and Problem-Solving Methods in Engineering*. New York: John Wiley & Sons, Inc., 1982.

RAUDSEPP, EUGENE, *How to Create New Ideas*. Englewood Cliffs, N.J.: Prentice-Hall, Inc., 1982.

RAY, MICHAEL, *Creativity in Business*. New York: Doubleday, 1986.

ROTHENBERG, ALBERT, and CARL HAUSMAN, *The Creativity Question*. Chapel Hill: Duke University Press, 1976.

Leo Castelli

Ask the international art community to name the single most important figure in the world of contemporary art and the overwhelming favorite would not be a painter, sculptor, critic, or collector. The likely choice would be New York art dealer Leo Castelli. His Castelli Gallery, founded in 1957, represented artists such as Jasper Johns, Robert Rauschenberg, Frank Stella, Roy Lichtenstein, Claes Oldenburg, James Rosenquist, Robert Norris, Ellsworth Kelly, Kenneth Noland, Cy Twombly, Donald Judd, Dan Flavin, Bruce Nauman, Richard Serra, and Andy Warhol, many of whom were not only successful proponents of their period, but also creators of an entirely new art movement (see *Exhibit 1*). Their contributions helped make New York the center of the art world. Leading them was the European-born Castelli, 50 years old at the gallery's inception.

Equally impressive was the longevity of Castelli's success and partnership with his artists. He remarked:

> Some other dealers have had a better eye or sense of discovery; yet they have failed while I have succeeded. I do attribute this in part to my background. To me, a business has to be treated with a certain seriousness. You can't live in a cloud and think that things will take care of themselves. The new, successful dealers understand this. They also seem to have an incredible talent for public relations.

Many of his artists no longer need an agent to sell their work; they are famous and in great demand. Yet they continue to sell work through Castelli Gallery, giving up some of their profit. What has Castelli done to inspire this uncommon loyalty? What must be done to manage successfully this creative process?

THE ART BUSINESS

While art may be plentiful, good art is rare; while beauty may be in the eye of the beholder, many mistrust their own eyes. Hence, for hundreds of years art

This case was prepared by Associate Professor John Kao, Research Associate Lee Field, and Terence Eagleton.

buyers have relied on experts to judge what was "good." Traditionally, these experts have been dealers and critics. With the increasing number and power of museums in the twentieth century, museum curators have been added to that list.

Once an expert labeled an artist or a group of artists and their works gifted, the market of supply and demand took over. The number of works an artist could produce in a lifetime was finite; the number of collectors who might desire one of those works was potentially much greater.

In the 1960s and 1970s, as wealth and inflation both increased, prices of old masters paintings skyrocketed, which created interest from a new segment of buyers—those seeking a good investment. This buyer relied to an even greater extent on experts. Further, rising prices of old masters spilled over to contemporary (living) artists. Would one of them someday be labeled a master? And who would first discover and aid the new talents and make them known to critics, curators, and collectors? Dealers.

The Dealers' Role

Art dealers have bridged the gap between artists and buyers. Ideally they make it easier for artists to produce their work by separating the business aspects of making a living from making art, thus freeing the artist to do more creative work. The association from the artist's viewpoint, however, has often been unpleasant. Marcel Duchamp, the French Surrealist, referred to dealers as "lice on the backs of artists—useful, but lice all the same." This characterization echoed the sentiments of many generations of artists who felt used or even abused by dealers. In fact, with some noteworthy exceptions such as Rembrandt, only recently (in this century) have artists actually made substantial amounts of money. Recently, the notion of "artists contracts" has been addressed as a mechanism whereby artists would share in profits from resale of their work as well as maintaining certain rights to it.

The basic strategy a dealer follows is to find an unknown artist or group of artists and make a market for him, her, or them. With success, the dealer then can attract new artists of increasingly high quality. At the same time, buyers will become interested in the other artists the dealer represents because the ability to judge good works has been proven.

Dealers provide several services. First, they set up shows for individual artists, averaging perhaps one show a month. Second, dealers obtain exclusive agreements with their artists or with a "stable" of artists. Commissions are usually 50-50, 60-40 (artist/dealer), or on occasion some other arrangement. A monthly allowance for the artist in the range of $1,000–$5,000 (or by negotiation) is not uncommon and is drawn against proceeds from sales. Third, the dealer publicizes the artist by finding buyers, soliciting museum acquisitions, and by ensuring reviews from appropriate critics and media. Finally, the dealer adds value to the buyer by providing him or her with art that appreciates in value and has investment qualities.

From the dealer's perspective, the relationship with the artist is important as well: Referrals to new artists often come through the artists whom he or she represents. The number of artists who have either shown in a gallery and/or were represented by a dealer grew from a few hundred in 1960 to almost 24,000 in 1985. The number of art galleries in New York City alone rose from a handful in the 1950s, to 450 by 1970, to over 650 in 1985.

The Price of Art

Overall, the price of art has risen dramatically in recent years. Alfred Taubman, chairman of the auction house of Sotheby, Parke Bernet, estimated that the total 1985 worldwide market sales of art and collectibles approached $25 billion. Resale prices of individual pieces indicate the trend. One early collector, for example, purchased a Jasper Johns' painting for $900; less than a decade later he had resold it at auction for $90,000. Records are constantly broken, a vivid example being the May 30, 1987, auction at Christie's in London, during which Van Gogh's "Sunflowers" fetched an astonishing $39.9 million, *triple* the price ever paid for a work of art at auction.

Prices vary for a new work, but a 20″ × 24″ painting by an unknown artist might sell in the $500–$1,800 range. If the artist has a successful first show, the price will rise by 20% and fluctuate with demand. If the demand exists, the artist's 2′ × 3′ canvas will rise to $10,000 in a few years, and after five or six shows to $20,000. The time needed to achieve a $20,000 price is a reflection of the dealer's judgment about how much exposure the artist can bear and how quickly, without saturating the market.

But as the prices of art have risen, the pool of interested buyers has also broadened. According to *The Wall Street Journal:*

> Art collecting has become a respectable, even trendy activity for rich American businessmen. Many have found that, apart from the investment value, buying a famous painting at auction can bring them a good deal of publicity. In addition, cheap dollars have made art increasingly attractive among European and, more prominently, Japanese collectors.[1]

Nonetheless, skyrocketing prices have brought concern that this burgeoning market will bottom out. Opinion is divided, as Klaus Perls, a New York dealer, notes:

> Anybody who says it [the art market] can't collapse wasn't there in 1930 to 1933. You couldn't sell anything. [Today] is a fantasy world like 1929, when people didn't want to believe that another group of suckers wasn't going to bail them out tomorrow. I think it can crash completely from here, or go sky high. It's anybody's guess.[2]

[1] *The Wall Street Journal,* May 19, 1987.
[2] Ibid.

CASTELLI BEFORE THE GALLERY

Born in 1907 in Trieste (part of the Austro-Hungarian Empire until ceded to Italy in 1919), Leo Castelli was from a privileged and cosmopolitan family. (See *Exhibit 2* for a time line.) His father rose in business to become the chief executive of a leading Italian bank. Moves to Austria and back led to a succession of larger villas and greater family comfort. The middle child (with a younger brother Giorgio and an older sister Silvia), Castelli remembered "lots of pretty girls, tennis, swimming, and things like that." Schooled in Austria, he developed a great fondness for literature, especially German, and sports. When not reading current novels (in English, French, German, and Italian, his first language), he was skiing in the Alps or mountain climbing in the Dolomites. He said: "I worried about being small, especially when I was younger. Therefore, I indulged in sports. I wanted to be, if small, strong. It has obviously played an important role in my life."

After four years at the University of Milan, Castelli graduated with a law degree in 1924 "without great enthusiasm. I was really more interested in literary cultural pursuits." Not wishing to practice law, he accepted a job with an insurance company in 1931. He recalled the circumstances of his employment.

> My father had a great deal of local influence, directorships and so on. I was totally reluctant. But my father's friends were very lenient and did not ask me to do anything. It was a bad situation. After a year I wanted to leave . . . go abroad and study comparative literature. My father said he would support me if I would first try business abroad. He arranged a job for me with the same insurance company, but in Bucharest. I agreed . . . went to Bucharest . . . still disliked my job intensely but got involved with a group of amusing people. I found the social situation very lively.

It was in Bucharest that Castelli met Ileana Shapira, daughter of a very wealthy Rumanian industrialist. They were married in 1933. After marrying, Castelli traded jobs—insurance for banking—and in 1935 moved to Paris, aided by his father-in-law. He recalled, "We had more than a comfortable life . . . and banking somewhat interested me, as it related to art and literature. As a young idealist, I did not really want to work. But from my father I did absorb what for him was a puritan work ethic and for me, an interest in economics."

Paris was exciting for the Castellis, . . . ("great parties . . . interesting people"). One new friend was René Drouin, an interior and Art Deco furniture designer whose wife was from Bucharest. In 1939 Drouin persuaded Castelli to become his partner in a gallery that would show furniture, objets d'art, and paintings. The financing came from Castelli's father-in-law. The Galerie René Drouin occupied an elegant space on the Place Vendôme, sharing a garden with the Hotel Ritz, next door to the fashion house of Schiaparelli. Castelli recalled, "I started this business without any idea of what I was doing. I did, however, have a certain feeling for bizarre objects, serendipitous things." Ileana was the Castelli who had spent the most time in museums. But her husband did know Leonor Fini of Trieste, a member of the Paris Surrealist group that also included Max Ernst, Pavel Tchelitchew, and Salvador Dali.

The opening exhibition was dominated by Fini and the Surrealists. In fact, no paintings were even shown. It was all fantasy objects, armoires with wings, mirrors with hair carved in wood, unusual sculpture. Castelli remembered, "Le tout Paris came . . . very chic. Thank God the war came before I turned into God knows what."

When the war broke out, the Castellis moved to the Shapira summer villa in Cannes. After France fell, the family (which now included three-year-old Nina) fled to escape Nazi persecutions of Jews. They migrated to the United States by way of Algeria, Morocco, and Spain, arriving in New York in March 1941. Shapira, already in New York, set them up in an apartment on Fifth Avenue until the townhouse he had purchased at 4 East 77th Street was remodeled for his family. The Castellis occupied the fourth floor.

In the meantime, wanting to do something both practical and intellectual, Castelli entered Columbia University and studied for a graduate degree in economic history. He joined the Army in 1943, gained U.S. citizenship in 1944, and was sent to Bucharest as an interpreter for the Allied Control Commission. While there, he located his sister Silvia and found out that his parents had died for lack of proper medical attention during the war. The news hit hard. He had lost touch with his family during the war. Ileana recalled: "Leo admired his father tremendously. Ernesto had a high position, was kind to and loved by everyone. He was an ideal for Leo."

On leave in Paris in 1945, Castelli discovered that the Galerie René Drouin was still open and showing a group of new artists—Kandinsky, Dubuffet, de Stael, Mondrian, Pevsner—but no one was buying art then. When he returned to the United States in 1946, he went back to Columbia University but did not finish the economics degree. Again, his father-in-law set him up in business—this time in a sweater factory—but as he recalled, "The only useful thing I did, when I was occasionally there, was fold sweaters during a rush."

After the war, however, Castelli did not want to depend on his father-in-law and the remains of the once-great Shapira fortune. He began to act as an agent in New York for Drouin's gallery and others. He would receive rolled-up Kandinsky paintings from the artist's widow and usually sell them to the Baroness Hilla Rebay, director of the Guggenheim Museum.

On a trip to France to sell the Shapira villa in Cannes, Castelli decided to end his partnership with Drouin. Because his father-in-law had put up the money for the gallery, Drouin split with Castelli some of the gallery's inventory—a Léger, three Dubuffets, a Kandinsky, and a Pevsner. Today, these works are worth many millions; unfortunately, not all are in Castelli's possession.

NEW YORK ART SCENE
AND THE CASTELLI GALLERY

When Castelli arrived in New York, his Paris reputation—news of his gallery (albeit short-lived) and his first show—had preceded him. Thus introduced, he quickly became involved with the very small New York art world. Castelli described the situation:

> I had a great enthusiasm for art. It was like a religious experience, not mystical at all, but once I got involved it became an important cause. Artists and writers had always been my heroes. The intellectual exercise of their work, not unlike great generals or statesmen, excited me. I liked getting to know these important people. They were my friends and I believed in them.

Jackson Pollock, Willem de Kooning, Franz Kline, Mark Rothko, Robert Motherwell—second-generation Abstract Expressionists—were all befriended by the Castellis. Parties at the Castelli home, gatherings at The Club (a bar/hangout on East Eighth Street in Greenwich Village), and summers in the Hamptons (the de Koonings stayed with the Castellis one whole summer) solidified their relationships. Castelli also developed friendships with important dealers/collectors such as Julian Levy, Peggy Guggenheim, and Sidney Janis, the art scholar turned dealer. With Janis, he organized his first New York show in 1950, a comparison of French and American artists. He also spent much time at the Museum of Modern Art (MOMA), furthering his education.

This relationship with the art community led Castelli to help with a show, held in 1951 in Greenwich Village on Ninth Street. He spent $600 to produce an advertising flyer and to buy white paint to clean up the building (even today he continues to give each of his exhibitions a "fresh start" by applying a coat of white paint to gallery walls before the opening of a new show. He is given credit by many for inaugurating this custom. The show included all the local artists, famous and unknown, and was a rousing success. Alfred Barr, the renowned curator of the Museum of Modern Art, and other major figures were impressed not only with the breadth and quality of the art shown but also with the efforts of the organizers, mainly Castelli.

About this time some of Castelli's friends encouraged, virtually demanded, that he become a dealer. But he was reluctant. He recalled, "Besides the fact that I considered it ungentlemanly, I didn't have the courage to become a dealer at that time." He did, however, continue to trade pictures on a small scale, which provided a moderate income and kept him involved in the art world. Much of this was done with Janis, who with Castelli's encouragement began showing the most important European artists and later the American Abstract Expressionists. This pairing brought visibility and new credibility to the Americans and helped escalate prices of their work. Castelli was satisfied with the arrangement, which provided him with a modest income and Janis' MOMA connections and knowledge. There was even talk of a partnership.

By 1955, however, the relationship had changed. Working as an agent for Janis, Castelli would scout art works and potential clients. When he brought in a picture and Janis sold it, Janis would take 10 percent as a commission. In the mid-1950s, Castelli brought in a Klee that was sent out to a client who already had on consignment another Klee from the Janis gallery. The client purchased Castelli's Klee and returned the other to Janis. Janis felt he had lost out on a sale because of Castelli's painting and took an additional 10 percent commission (charging a total of 20 percent of the sales price) from Castelli as compensation for the foregone sale. This was an arbitrary action, done without Castelli's approval or consent. When Castelli questioned him on this, Janis replied that he had lost a Klee sale of his own because the client wanted Castelli's painting instead; therefore, he lost out on 10 percent. It was not the idea or the reasoning that upset Castelli, but the fact that Janis had done it without consulting him. It was also difficult to accept what amounted to a 100 percent increase in the service charge. Castelli did not like terms and conditions arbitrarily dictated by someone else. Also at this same time, partnership talk ceased because Janis decided to keep the business in the family, saving it for his sons. Castelli stated:

> Since this thing with Janis couldn't go on, I lost my security. I had to do something to earn a living [Castelli was no longer connected with the textiles business] and stay in touch with the art community. Also, the environment was changing quickly. Prices were going up, to the point where I could not afford to buy. I *had* to become a dealer. It was the only way to stay in touch. Yes, it was a bit distasteful and I was apprehensive, but not because I was worried about the financial risk. I had no money to lose. My fear of failure was associated with feelings and pride. But I challenged this fear by doing it.

In matters pertaining to his career, Castelli was an empiricist. He stated, "If you examine my career over 30 years, you would find everything that I have done has been extremely tentative and has depended largely on whatever circumstances I was surrounded by and good or bad decisions that I made." For example, even though the decision was made in 1955, Castelli did not open his gallery until 1957 at the age of 50. Unsure how to begin, he went to Europe to explore the climate there and sell a few paintings to raise capital. He was certain about two things, however. He did not want to represent artists from an earlier period. While the Abstract Expressionists were his friends, they were all connected to other galleries and he did not relish the idea of raiding. He would give them shows, but he wanted to embrace new horizons, new trends. Having always been interested in the importance of art history, Castelli saw this possibility as a way to make his own impression on history and thus become an equal of his heroes.

He also decided to incur as little initial overhead as possible. Therefore, the first Castelli Gallery was located in his apartment on 77th Street. On February 1, 1957, the Castellis had their first show, a comparison of well-known European and American artists. Some works were borrowed, but most were from their own collection. Some of the pieces from the Castelli collection were from the group he received from Drouin when they split up the gallery inventory.

Johns and Rauschenberg

Of all the artists Castelli came to represent, two names stood out: Jasper Johns and Robert Rauschenberg. Castelli first saw Rauschenberg's work in the Ninth Street show in 1951, but had been most impressed with Rauschenberg's 1954 "Red Show," which Castelli referred to as an "epiphany." Castelli's other memorable event was the first time he saw a Jasper Johns painting. Ileana is quoted as saying that Castelli was so awestruck after returning from a show where a Johns painting was exhibited that he sat and talked about it for hours. He knew he had found something very different (*Exhibit 3*).

He was at Rauschenberg's apartment looking at paintings when he discovered that Johns lived downstairs. Castelli was so excited that he asked Rauschenberg to introduce him. The next moment Castelli was in Johns' studio, amazed by a room full of wonderful works. On the spot he offered to represent Johns, who accepted. Johns' first show, in January 1958, was the sensation of the art world and sold out quickly. Rauschenberg's first show with Castelli, however, was a flop. But Castelli supported Rauschenberg's cause and stuck with him. This vote of confidence was vindicated in 1964, when Rauschenberg won the International Grand Prize for Painting at the Venice Biennale, the first time in its history that an American had won. This enhanced not only Rauschenberg's international reputation but the price of his paintings.

MANAGING RELATIONSHIPS

"Each one of my relationships with artists is different and individual, just like the artists' personalities," Castelli remarked during an interview. This statement was clearly demonstrated during the next few minutes as he answered phone calls. Besides the many languages he used, Castelli used a distinctly different tone and style with each call to an artist. One conversation was bubbly and carefree; another was stern and fatherly.

Castelli also pointed out that the business was much different in 1986 from the 1950s. "Back then it was a shoestring corner store operation. Now, it's a supermarket." Castelli was probably the first dealer to put his artists on a monthly salary or stipend. "I tried to give them not only confidence, enthusiasm, and moral support, but also eliminate the worry of paying the rent."

> When I see something of Jasper Johns, for example, that I particularly find impressive, I go off the deep end . . . but then his new paintings are sometimes very, very difficult to accept . . . the fullness is marvelous, but you then don't

know what the content is. Jasper came out with what was certainly at [one] time really bizarre: he introduced out of the blue that cross-hatch motif. Everybody asked themselves "what the heck is that?" I just stood there and said, well let's hope for the best.

What happened is that a great collector came in, saw the painting and says "wonderful, how much is it? I'll buy it." This was Johns' first vote of confidence for the crosshatch . . . There is always somebody who comes to the rescue, some incredibly enthusiastic collector who has been waiting for a Jasper Johns painting for the past years and never got one. Then, a painting comes along which I consider really difficult or bizarre, and the collector comes in and sees it and says can I have it!

Regarding his relationships with collectors, Castelli remarked:

I have never picked up the phone and said, "Look, I have this special painting here now and I think you should buy it." I have never solicited the collectors. They have learned to be after me; some phone every day. Perhaps I would have done better if I had cultivated them, but I trust them to trust my good taste and support my artists' work.

Castelli had turned the tables: collectors came to him, not vice versa.

In addition, Castelli recognized early on the importance of creating a network of dealers throughout the United States to provide a broader audience for his artists. He commented: "It was financially better to sell for less profit than to have the art lying around unsold in New York. The art needed to be spread around, and every means was good. If I am guilty of propaganda, so were the apostles."

Values

Susan Brundage, who started working at the gallery in 1972 and whom Castelli called "my right hand" (see *Exhibit 4*), had this to say about Castelli Gallery and her boss:

This place is like a little museum. It records, preserves, and disseminates information and has continuous exhibitions. Many people pass through these doors every day. We are beset by more requests than we can accommodate because we have important artists from all the important periods of the last 25 years.

The gallery is certainly well organized and runs like an official business. Leo delegates a lot of authority; everyone has his or her specific tasks and responsibilities—it's very democratic. I'm accessible as the practical person, I'm sort of the resident complaint department. If [artists] want something, they can ask me; if they don't like the way things are going, they can also call and complain. They know if they talk to me, whatever they say or want will get back to Leo. I'm an expediter: I make their requests heard and they get done. Leo is always open to new or differing opinions and viewpoints.

Leo has never compromised on doing things for or spending money on his artists. He is generous to the maximum. This is one of the reasons why the artists respect him and have stayed with him. Leo also has great faith in his artists and their ability to create and will help them do whatever they want. Loyalty is very important to him. He always comes through and does what he says he will do. Therefore, the artists have confidence in him. Leo is also uncritical. He sees his role as the ultimate, unquestioning supporter or patron.

He has even commissioned public works by his own artists. Many times he might like to say "no," but he doesn't. And the smart people know to go to Leo if we have been firm on a price or have said no to a request. He enjoys being the person to say "yes." It's not that his is the ultimate veto; it's more like the ultimate give-in. Because of his personality, Leo is never sorry that he made something possible or gave somebody money or said yes. He has created close bonds with the artists. It's a very familial relationship.

It is very important, of course, to be able to sell the work. In this respect, Leo sees that it is his job to get the art out into the world, to place it with good collectors and museums. Some galleries might make more money, but none places more contemporary art.

I think one reason for the success of this gallery, besides the fact that we have very important artists, is that Leo made the gallery itself important and the center of a lot of activity. The gallery is the focus; not just a few artists. Castelli Gallery is high-profile and people are attracted to it. You can see this as a problem with some of the new galleries that are low-profile and with just a few major names. If they lose that name artist, they're in trouble. Therefore, you work at promoting yourself—your gallery—which differentiates you from the competition. The artists also enjoy the prestige associated with the gallery name. Leo does an interview at least once, sometimes twice a day. He makes himself and the gallery very accessible to the media. Castelli Gallery has cultivated an important image through Leo, and vice versa. He is as famous as his artists. The gallery is an embodiment of him, and I don't think he has any intention of its continuing after he is gone. I certainly don't expect it to.

Another reason for Leo's success goes back to his placement of priorities. He is more interested that the art gets sold and placed with good collectors than in squeezing the last ounce of profit out of a sale. [Unlike some dealers who use their galleries as a culling tool for their own collections, Leo did not keep the best paintings for himself. He has also passed up opportunities to buy back works of his artists and to make a quick profit.] I've often seen him take less on a sale if it meant a better placement. And rather than diminish the artist's profit, he deducts the discount from his commission. Most artists know this and appreciate it. [Jasper Johns gave Leo's son a very valuable drawing for his twenty-first birthday. Another artist once gave Leo a Maserati he had won.] Similarly, he has consistently maintained good relationships with his network of dealers in other regions by providing them with quality work, work that could easily have been sold here, which also reduced his profit.

EXHIBIT 1 Leo Castelli 25th Anniversary Lunch, February 1, 1982, The Odeon, New York. *Standing left-right:* Ellsworth Kelly, Dan Flavin, Joseph Kosuth, Richard Serra, Lawrence Weiner, Nassos Daphnis, Jasper Johns, Claes Oldenburg, Salvatore Scarpitta, Richard Artschwager, Mia Westerlund Roosen, Cletus Johnson, Keith Sonnier. *Seated left-right:* Andy Warhol, Robert Rauschenberg, Leo Castelli, Ed Ruscha, James Rosenquist, Robert Barry. (Source: *Gentle Snapshots*, Bischofberger. Zürich, Switzerland. Reprinted with permission.)

EXHIBIT 2 LEO CASTELLI *Time Line*

Birth	1907
Earns law degree	1924
Joins insurance firm	1931
Moves to Bucharest	1932
Marries Ileana Shæpira	1933
Moves to Paris	1935
Forms Drouin Galerie	1939
Moves to New York	1941
Joins U.S. Army	1943
Gains U.S. citizenship	1944
Father dies	WWII
Organizes Ninth Street show	1951
Decides to become a dealer	1955
Opens Castelli Gallery	1957
First Jasper Johns show	1958
Makes history at Venice Biennale	1964
Receives New York City Mayor's Award of Honor	1977
Celebrates 25th anniversary of gallery	1982

EXHIBIT 3 AT HOME WITH JASPER JOHNS' "FOOL'S HOUSE," 1975. (*Jill Krementz*) (Source: *Gentle Snapshots*, Bischofberger. Zürich, Switzerland. Reprinted with permission.)

EXHIBIT 4 STAFF OF THE LEO CASTELLI GALLERY, MARCH 1982. *Standing front row left-right:* Betsy Cahen, Mimi Thompson, Debbie Taylor, Patty Brundage, Michelle Dreyfuss, Mame Kennedy. *Back row left-right:* Susan Brundage, Terry Wilson, John Good, Tom Pelham. (*Glenn Steigelman*) (Source: *Gentle Snapshots,* Bischofberger. Zürich, Switzerland. Reprinted with permission.)

The Videogame Industry

The videogame, a curiosity that first appeared commercially in 1970, spawned an industry whose 1983 revenues of $10 billion were greater than the record and motion-picture industries combined. Videogames have elicited reactions ranging from interest in their potential educational and medical applications to worry about their contribution to delinquency and moral decay. One view on the industry was expressed by Ronald Reagan in March 1983 in a speech at Walt Disney's EPCOT (Experimental Community of Tomorrow) Center.

> Many young people have developed incredible hand, eye, and brain coordination in playing these games. The Air Force believes these kids will be outstanding pilots should they fly our jets. The computerized radar screen in the cockpit is not unlike the computerized video screen. Watch a 12-year-old take evasive action and score multiple hits while playing Space Invaders, and you will appreciate the skills of tomorrow's pilot.[1]

WHAT IS A VIDEOGAME?

The videogame married two key pieces of modern hardware: the computer and the TV set. The videogame industry included several distinct businesses covering both hardware and software applications.

Videogame Hardware

There were three basic types of hardware. The first was dedicated game-playing equipment designed for public places or specialized facilities such as restaurants or arcades. These machines carried retail prices of about $2,000 to $3,000 and were typically owned and operated by specialized distributors who divided game profits with the proprietors of specific locations. A second type of hardware was for home use, such as the Atari (VCS) or Mattel (Intellivision) game consoles. Third, nondedicated hardware,

This case was prepared by Associate Professor John Kao.
Copyright © 1985 by the President and Fellows of Harvard College. Harvard Business School case 9-486-011.

including mainframe and personal computers, could be programmed for videogames.

The following describes the "anatomy of a videogame":

> What goes on inside a Pac Man arcade game—or any video arcade game, for that matter—that manages to turn a color video screen into an addictive adventure?
>
> Perhaps not surprisingly, the inside of an arcade game, with its single main logic board bearing dozens of circuit chips, resembles the electronic section of a personal computer. In fact, the Z-80a microprocessor chip that operates the game is used as a central processor by Radio Shack, Sinclair, and numerous small-business microcomputer systems. Unlike a general-purpose computer, which has the flexibility to execute a wide variety of tasks depending on what programs are loaded into it, an arcade game's computer is a dedicated system. Serving as a responsive intermediary between humans and video screen is its only duty. Freed from the necessity of dealing with data from a keyboard, human-oriented languages, mass-storage devices such as disk drives and links to a printer, a video arcade game can employ integrated circuits (Pac Man has 84 on its main logic board) to create more detailed video images, versatile animated characters and complex sound effects.
>
> The images on an arcade game's video screen are generated by two integrated circuit chips known as character ROMs. These read-only memory chips are permanent repositories for the program instructions defining the boundaries of screen images and their relative positions. Each chip stores 4,096 words of instruction. One chip provides the instructions for displaying the maze and the blockshaped figures that travel through it. The other contains the details needed to redraw these blocks into Pac Man and his four pursuers.[2]

Videogame Software

The software side of the business involves the computer program creating the videogame scenario. It could be: (1) a dedicated piece of computer memory contained in an arcade game; (2) a dedicated piece of memory in the form of a game cartridge, which can be plugged into a game-playing machine; or (3) a diskette or cassette. A typical game cartridge consisted of packaging plus a computer ROM (read-only memory). Typical manufacturing costs were around $6.00, while the cartridge itself retailed for $25 and $45.

But what actually was a videogame? It could be compared to a miniature movie; their similarities prompted some industry experts to dub California's Silicon Valley "Hollywood North." Videogames had characters, a plot, special effects, and a soundtrack. Some even had dialogue by way of speech synthesis technology. Unlike films, however, videogames were participatory. By pressing buttons, manipulating control levers or "joysticks," or rolling "Trak-ball" controls, players entered the videogame's action and influenced its outcome. As Sudnow and others point out, videogame practice led to a phenomenologically complex set of skills.[3]

Videogames employed numerous themes. Classic examples included Space Invaders, Pac Man, and Donkey Kong. In Space Invaders, rows of alien creatures attempted to land on a planet, which the player defended with a laser base. In Pac Man, cute little creatures chased a Pac Man character around a maze. If Pac Man ate "power pills," he could turn the tables on his pursuers and eat them. Donkey Kong presented the player with a skyscraper that a small video man had to climb to rescue a "fair maiden" from an uncooperative gorilla that hurled balls of fire at the video man.

Recent videogames were remakes of entertainment products popularized in other media. Atari reportedly paid $21 million for the rights to make the movie *E.T.* into a videogame.[4] Disney Studios' feature film *Tron* and its videogame came out at the same time. Other adaptations included games based on the films *Star Wars, Return of the Jedi,* and *Rocky,* the TV shows "Mash" and "Nine to Five," the characters Cookie Monster, Snoopy, and the Pink Panther, and the rock group Journey.[5] As one industry executive put it, "They've licensed everything that moves, walks, crawls, or tunnels beneath the earth."[6] (See *Exhibit 1.*)

Individual videogames had both arcade and home forms. Successful arcade games were often later sold in home versions, as with Pac Man or Galaxian. Journey's Escape videogame was the first to reverse the sequence. Another example of videogame product extension involved a report that MCA-TV acquired the rights to the videogame Donkey Kong for development as an animated children's TV series.[7] Joint ventures between entertainment companies such as MCA and Atari supported this trend.[8]

Videogame Trends

Videogames became a public-policy concern in the 1980s. Their habit-forming nature caused a number of municipalities to pass ordinances either prohibiting adolescents from arcades during school hours or outlawing the games entirely in public places. Several countries, notably Taiwan, completely banned the games out of concern they were a waste of time and a corrupting influence on youth. Numerous examples of petty theft by children or spending lunch money on videogames were reported in the press.

Another issue was product safety. Arista released videogames based on the horror films *Halloween* and *The Texas Chain Saw Massacre.* Others marketed X-rated games. As of 1985, no research existed on the psychological effects of videogames or protracted game playing. A conference on videogames sponsored by Atari and the Harvard Graduate School of Education, however, yielded a number of impressionistic reports.[9]

In several academic centers, videogames were used experimentally as adjuncts to medical diagnosis, treatment, and rehabilitation.[10] As the basis of new educational programs, they were said to help the development of a variety of cognitive skills.[11]

Another important trend concerned the competitive environment for videogame companies. The life cycle of a successful videogame grew shorter as the field became saturated with product. Technological advancement also contributed to commercial obsolescence. Innovations include new player controls, game architecture, speech synthesis, and 3-D effects.[12] One industry source stated:

> Arcade games of even greater complexity are already in the testing stages. Features include stickless control mechanisms that register hand or eye movements as input; detailed graphics that rival the quality of live video; voice recognition, and voice-synthesis abilities that allow the game to conduct a conversation with the player; and hardware and software that is sophisticated enough to make strategy rather than hand-eye coordination the key to playing the game.[13]

Other predicted innovations included videogames linking computers with optical videodiscs and use of holography for enhanced realism. Designers were said to be dreaming of games controlled not with a joystick, but with eye movements or brain waves.[14]

Technology resulted in ever-expanding uses. Videogames were used to train army tank crews, as aids in flying instruction, and as diagnostic tools in medicine to help brain-damaged patients. Games were also directed toward more specialized markets. Ms. Pac Man, for instance, was allegedly the first game designed for women instead of the usual adolescent male audience. Games reported in development included those targeted to small children and audiences age 45 and older.

THE INDUSTRY

Gagnon cites Willy Higinbotham as the first videogame inventor who in 1958 constructed a tennis game on an oscilloscope screen at Brookhaven National Laboratory.[15] The first widely known videogame, Space Wars, was born on a PDP/1 mainframe computer in 1962 in Cambridge, Massachusetts by a group of Harvard students at the Littauer Statistics Laboratory. Small rocket ships firing laser missiles could be guided around a video universe by players who were to avoid such hazards as "heavy gravity."[16] However, the first commercial videogame, Computer Space, was not released until 1970. Commercialization depended on the significant drop in price of integrated circuits in the late 1960s.

Atari

In 1972 Nolan Bushnell, an electronics engineer and former employee of Ampex Corporation, founded a company called Atari with $500 in capital. The word "Atari" comes from the Japanese strategy game Go and is a polite way of telling the opponent, "You are about to be engulfed." Atari's first product, a video version of the game of ping-pong, generated $3 million in sales in its first year.

The next few years saw many new entrants into the industry. One major competitor, Midway, licensed videogames designed in Japan, including Space

Invaders, Galaxian, and Pac Man. Pac Man itself deserves some special attention. Estimates counted 7 billion coins that by 1982 had been inserted into some 400,000 Pac Man machines worldwide, equal to one game of Pac Man for every person on earth. U.S. domestic revenues from games and licensing of the Pac Man·image for T-shirts, pop songs, to wastepaper baskets, etc. exceeded $1 billion.[17]

Bushnell sold Atari to Warner Communications, Inc. for $28 million in 1976. The changeover occurred during considerable internal strife. Emanual Gerard, a Warner executive and Harvard MBA who engineered the acquisition, said, "They [Atari] really had no manufacturing, no sales, and no advertising or marketing expertise. Everything but research was lacking. It was amateur night in Dixie."[18] Dan Valentine of Corporate Management Services, an early Atari investor, put it in another way. "The state of the company in the mid-1970s was absolute chaos."[19]

Under new management, Atari profits mushroomed, so much so that Atari itself, as a division of Warner, ranked in the *Fortune* 500. In 1981, the division was responsible for 50 percent of Warner Communications' operating earnings. It recorded 100 percent growth in its second consecutive year.[20] (See *Exhibit 2*.)

After Warner's acquisition, Bushnell remained for a while as chairman of Atari. However, something reportedly changed in his management style. But so had the industry. According to one expert, "Bushnell started Atari with a 'We're all brothers' attitude, greeting each new employee with a power handshake and a smile. Then competitors began rushing out imitations of Atari's games, some of them very likely gleaned from spies in Bushnell's own plant. Now Atari owns paper shredders and a secret lab in the mountains and it's tough to get any kind of a handshake out of Bushnell."[21]

He did not stay long. There was disagreement whether he resigned or was fired, but the conflict between Warner and Bushnell was unmistakable. "There's a difference between having fun and running a company," said one Warner executive. "Nolan is a creator, a dreamer, a pie in the sky thinker, but he operated in a 'Hey, man,' kind of way."[22]

Warner brought in Ray Kassar, a Brooklyn-born Harvard MBA who had been a marketing executive at Burlington Industries for 25 years, to run the company. His regime was described in the following way:

> Kassar set about changing Atari. "I knew I had a consumer-marketing company, and I had nobody who understood the consumer business," he says. He brought in new people experienced at working in large organizations. He also established normal reporting procedures and financial controls, set specific sales and marketing goals, and tightened security measures to protect confidential information. Kassar put his stamp on the corporate culture as well. "Things were kind of casual here," he recalls. "People didn't work very hard." He made it clear that he expected people to be at work at 8 a.m. sharp, to answer the phones promptly, and to wear ties and jackets instead of T-shirts.
>   Kassar generated considerable resentment. "Ray is very structure-oriented and very elitist" says former Atari executive Gene Lipkin. "If he didn't like what you looked like, he wouldn't talk to you." In time, most of the key executives

from the Bushnell regime left. Kassar also antagonized some engineers who had been treated royally under Bushnell. After a newspaper story quoted Kassar comparing engineers to operatic divas, T-shirts emblazoned with the words, "I'm just another high-strung prima donna for Atari," became popular in the company's research labs.[23]

A heavy turnover in key Atari employees accompanied the change in corporate climate. Some left with entrepreneurial ambitions of their own. Others stayed but were unhappy with the new style. One Atari executive who had begun his professional life at IBM resigned from Atari after six years. He said, "Atari was a whole new world for me. Unlike IBM, it was fun to work there. But when Warner took over, I felt like I was back at IBM. The reason I went to Exidy [another videogame company] was because it reminded me of my early days at Atari."[24]

Since Atari

Other entrants in the videogame business began to make inroads on Atari's market (*Exhibit 3*). The most rapid growth was in home videogame software by new companies employing a "razorblade" strategy—making software for another company's hardware, mainly Atari and Mattel.

One of these new companies, Activision, founded by former recording company executive James Levy and four ex-Atari designers, started with $700,000 in venture capital. In its first year, 1981, it had sales of $6.2 million, $66 million in 1982, and anticipated revenues of over $170 million in 1983. It earned $744,000 in 1981, $12.9 million in 1982, and anticipated $22 million to $24 million for 1983.[25] Unlike many of its competitors, Activision did not rely on external sources of financing beyond its initial venture-capital infusion. It also did not license videogames from outside sources.

Activision exuded a distinctive philosophy directed at building involvement and motivating creative people. According to Levy, "the guys who design games are not [just] engineers or programmers. They have as much creative talent as any performing artist or author."[26] Activision heavily promoted designers as part of the product. The game instruction booklets carry pictures of the designers and tips about how to play the games. The company reportedly received several thousand letters a day addressed to individual designers. Designers were sometimes recognized and greeted by fans in public areas.[27]

Imagic, another Atari spin-off, was founded by William Grubb, former marketing vice president for Atari, in June 1981. It shipped 2.5 million cartridges in its first seven months of production.[28] Imagic allowed its nineteen designers to earn bonuses up to $1 million if a game earned more than $50 million at wholesale (three to four million copies).[29] Its three top designers created six of the first seven games. They, along with the company's president, anticipated becoming instant multimillionaires when the company went public. At an estimated $15–$17 per share issuing price, two of the designers would get $6.8 million and the third $11.8 million. The president of the company would own about 14 percent of the shares worth more than $34 million.[30]

Other firms, including large ones like Twentieth Century Fox Film Corporation, General Foods, Coleco, Paramount Pictures, CBS Inc., and Milton Bradley, as well as smaller start-ups, also threw their hats into the videogame business. They were attracted by the explosion in sales volume of videogame cassettes (*Exhibit 4*).

Promotion budgets increased markedly. According to *Fortune*, $200 million would be spent on videogame advertising in 1982, mainly for TV; 50 percent by Atari and Mattel alone.[31] Promotion budgets for individual games told the same story: Parker Brothers spent $4.5 million to advertise the Empire Strikes Back videogame and $5 million on Frogger.[32] The business also became riskier and the stakes higher: a losing game could cost at least $150,000, while a hit could earn up to $100 million in sales.[33]

But success was difficult to predict. Videogames were described as "a hits-driven" business (*Exhibit 5*). Ten percent of game titles accounted for 75 percent of sales.[34] Five games popular in arcades before they came into the home, including Pac Man, sold over five million copies.[35]

Competition led one industry expert to dub the state of the industry as "software wars." In early 1983 about 400 videogame titles were available and 200 were in preparation.[36]

Moreover, the competition for videogames included other entertainment products. Given the similarity between videogames and films, it was reasonable to assume some cannibalization of sales. This became particularly significant for the videogame industry when the film industry had a banner year, as in 1982 with *E.T.* and other films. Reports of increased spending for record albums in 1984 suggested another source of competition for the consumer entertainment dollar.

The Shakeout of 1982

In late 1982 investors in Warner Communications Inc. suffered a loss of about $1.1 billion in the market values of their shares. The reason? Atari's sales in both home video and arcades were far below expectations due to fierce competition, a recession, and disappointing product quality.[37] Its widely touted E.T. cartridge, for which it had paid substantial licensing fees, sold well below expectations. Warner lost almost half its market value in a few days as its shares slid from $51.875 to $35.125 in December 1982. Following on the heels of Warner's decline, Mattel also reported bad news: a fourth-quarter loss.

Another distress signal came from the arcade segment of the industry. In 1981 players put an estimated $7 billion in quarters into arcade videogames. Machine sales increased from virtually nil in 1978 to about $900 million in 1982, representing about 450,000 units at a price of $2,000.

Business Week reported in 1982 that a shakeout among arcade operators was already underway and indicated that due to distributor overstock, sales would be flat in 1983.[38]

Despite the reverses of late 1982, the industry still remained a juggernaut. It generated over $10 billion a year in revenues. An estimated 15 million U.S. homes had home videogame machines, representing a sixth of all U.S. households with TV. The market for consoles and games was about $3.8 billion for 1982.[39] Industry sources estimated that another ten million consoles or game-playing home computers would be sold in 1983. Thirty million game cartridges were sold in 1981, 65 million in 1982. Industry officials estimated that 1983 sales of game cartridges would approach 110 million units at a retail cost of about $2.4 billion.[40]

The shakeout of 1982 was viewed philosophically by industry leaders. Said one, "It will take the industry nine to twelve months to go through this purge and stabilize. But the thing that fortifies us is that technology and creativity can unlock the market again."[41]

REFERENCES

1. RONALD REAGAN, remarks to students and guests during a visit to Walt Disney's Epcot Center, March 8, 1983, from the Administration of Ronald Reagan, U.S. Government Printing Office.
2. STEVE DITLEA, "Inside Pac Man," *Technology Illustrated,* January 1983.
3. DAVID SUDNOW, *Pilgrim in the Microworld* (New York: Warner Books, 1983).
4. ALJEAN HARMETZ, "Makers Vie for Millions in Home Video Games," *New York Times,* January 13, 1983.
5. Ibid.
6. Ibid; see also Tim Ferris, "Solid State Fun," *Esquire,* March 1977.
7. "MCA–TV Acquires Rights to 'Donkey Kong' Series," *Daily Variety,* May 11, 1983.
8. "MCA Unit and Atari Join in Videogame Venture," *Daily Variety,* May 8, 1983.
9. FOX BUTTERFIELD, "Video Game Specialists Meet at Harvard to Praise Pac-Man, Not to Bury Him," *New York Times,* May 24, 1983.
10. WILLIAM LYNCH, "TV Games as Therapeutic Interventions," a presentation for the American Psychological Association's symposium: "Rehabilitation of Post-traumatic Brain-damaged Patients," Aug. 24–28, 1981, Los Angeles, California.
11. DIANA GAGNON, "Arcade Videogames" (unpublished manuscript).
12. DITLEA, "Inside Pac Man."
13. Ibid.
14. TEKLA PERRY, CAROL TRUXAL, and PAUL WALLICH, "Videogames: The Electronic Big Bang," *IEEE Spectrum,* December 1982.
15. STEVEN BLOOM, *Video Invaders* (New York: Arco Publishing, 1982).
16. Ibid.
17. COLIN COVERT, "Video Gamesmanship, The Rise and Fall of Atari," *Detroit Free Press,* August 1982.
18. PETER W. BERNSTEIN, "Atari and the Video-Game Explosion," *Fortune,* July 27, 1981.

19. Ibid.
20. FERRIS, "Solid State Fun."
21. BERNSTEIN, "Atari and the Video-Game Explosion."
22. Ibid.
23. Ibid.
24. BLOOM, *Video Invaders*.
25. ANDREW C. BROWN, "Cashing in on the Cartridge Trade," *Fortune,* November 25, 1982.
26. DAN DORFMAN, "Is the Video Game Fad Cooling Off?" *St. Louis Post-Dispatch,* September 19, 1982.
27. "The Riches Behind Video Games," *Business Week,* November 9, 1981.
28. PERRY et al., "Videogames: The Electronic Big Bang."
29. THOMAS HAYES, "Imagic Scores in Video Games," *New York Times,* November 22, 1982.
30. PETER NULTY, "Why the Craze Won't Quit," *Fortune,* November 15, 1982.
31. HARMETZ, "Makers Vie for Millions."
32. JEANNETTE DE WYZE, "The Inter Workings of Videogames," *The LA Reader,* August 20, 1982.
33. "The Video Game Explosion," *New York Times,* December 7, 1982.
34. Ibid.
35. HARMETZ, "Makers Vie for Millions."
36. LAURA LANDRO and SUSAN FEENEY, "Fierce Competition in Video Games behind Dive in Warner Stock Price," *Wall Street Journal.*
37. "Arcade Video Games Start to Flicker," *Business Week,* December 6, 1982.
38. NULTY, "Why the Craze Won't Quit."
39. BROWN, "Cashing in on the Cartridge Trade."
40. "Arcade Video Games Start to Flicker," *Business Week.*
41. BLOOM, *Video Invaders*.

EXHIBIT 1 THE VIDEOGAME INDUSTRY (Reprinted with permission of Lucasfilm Ltd. Source: Parker Brothers.)

BECOME A JEDI MASTER
WITHOUT EVER LEAVING HOME.

In the STAR WARS® JEDI ARENA™ perfecting the skills needed to become a JEDI MASTER takes concentration and practice.

Use your LIGHTSABER to direct the attack of the whirling SEEKER. But stay alert, your adversary can attack at any time. So follow your instincts. In no time at all you'll be a JEDI MASTER, ready to go saber to saber against any opponent who dares to do battle with you.

Play the STAR WARS JEDI ARENA home video game. Alone or head-to-head. The challenge awaits you.

® TM & © Lucasfilm Ltd. 1982. Parker Brothers authorized user.   © 1982, Parker Brothers, Beverly, MA 01915

EXHIBIT 2 WARNER COMMUNICATIONS: SUMMARY STATEMENT

Years Ended December 31 (000s)	1982	1981	1980	1979	1978	1977	1976	1975	1974	1973
Operating Revenues:										
Consumer electronics	$2,008,805	$1,227,135	$512,743	$238,066	$177,947	150,327	$35,541	$ —	$ —	$ —
Recorded music and music publishing	752,317	811,257	805,732	725,323	617,068	532,359	406,062	313,787	291,653	235,992
Filmed entertainment										
Theatrical distribution	338,635	439,897	869,647	433,746	261,329	253,574	221,649	202,333	275,497	152,718
Television distribution and production	355,453	315,278	299,287	175,944	131,687	99,599	63,540	53,582	43,499	56,744
Direct response marketing	445,927	359,401	—	—	—	—	—	—	—	—
Publishing and related distribution										
Domestic operations	88,848	84,185	72,005	74,948	55,103	52,235	48,407	40,189	45,698	40,795
Foreign operations	—	—	—	—	—	—	—	21,803	32,967	35,877
Total operating revenues	$3,989,985	$3,237,153	$2,559,414	$1,648,027	$1,243,134	$1,088,094	$775,199	$631,694	$689,314	$522,126
Operating income (Loss):										
Consumer electronics	$328,288	$286,553	$69,929	$6,293	$(2,677)	$(6,144)	$174	$ —	$ —	$ —
Recorded music and music publishing	58,656	85,014	82,902	81,706	92,557	84,041	68,299	50,212	46,921	41,576
Filmed entertainment	101,796	24,748	60,832	117,570	79,914	57,990	42,227	41,704	57,677	31,093
Direct response marketing	26,158	30,979	—	—	—	—	—	—	—	—
Publishing and related distribution										
Domestic operations	12,518	14,867	10,782	18,073	9,561	7,197	5,504	(2,009)	9,725	6,669
Foreign operations	—	—	—	—	—	—	—	(2,642)	(14,600)	(491)
Total operating income	527,416	442,161	224,445	223,642	179,355	143,084	116,204	87,265	99,723	78,847
Unallocated (Expenses) and Income										
Corporate general and administrative expenses	(75,446)	(58,991)	(41,983)	(35,350)	(30,217)	(25,127)	(21,706)	(17,884)	(17,893)	(11,707)
Interest expense	(96,314)	(69,643)	(36,217)	(42,884)	(33,267)	(27,428)	(20,464)	(19,557)	(24,754)	(16,702)
Dividend, interest, and other	29,244	51,666	44,946	19,615	12,918	12,742	13,559	13,538	11,399	14,032
Total unallocated expenses, net	(142,516)	(76,968)	(33,254)	(58,619)	(50,566)	(39,813)	(28,611)	(23,903)	(31,248)	(14,377)
	384,900	365,193	191,191	165,023	128,789	103,271	87,593	63,362	68,475	64,170
Provision for income taxes	(122,089)	(138,700)	(154,100)	(55,965)	(46,592)	(36,057)	(29,724)	(17,587)	(27,355)	(22,159)
	262,811	226,493	37,091	109,058	82,197	67,214	57,869	45,775	41,120	42,011
Gain on sale of 50% of cable operations (less applicable income taxes of $44,352)	—	—	—	91,680	—	—	—	—	—	—
Income from continuing operations	257,811	226,493	137,091	200,747	82,197	67,214	57,869	45,775	41,120	42,011
Discontinued operations	—	—	—	—	5,224	3,867	3,693	(137,471)[a]	5,540	1,282
Net income	257,811	226,493	137,091	200,747	87,421	71,081	61,562	8,304	16,660	16,293
Preferred dividend requirements	—	—	—	(22)	(383)	(1,118)	(1,265)	(1,467)	(1,584)	(1,591)
Income applicable to Common and common equivalent shares	$257,811	$226,493	$137,091	$200,725	$87,038	$69,963	$6,297	$6,837	$15,076	$14,700

53

Illustration by Art Suddeth

The expanding universe of video games. Experts calculate that the big bang occurred about 1972, and since then, the industry has grown to include dozens of companies, some of which are depicted as asteroids on the "screen" above. The size of each asteroid corresponds roughly to the size of its company. Overlapping or touching asteroids represent subsidiaries or joint endeavors; for example, Atari is a multibillion dollar subsidiary of Warner Communications and Midway worked with Disney to produce a game based on the movie Tron.

Atari's growth over the past 10 years has been impressive—from a $500 investment in 1971 to a company controlling 70 percent of the $10 billion video games market—but perhaps more remarkable still has been the rate at which it has spawned other game companies. Former Atari employees have founded such companies as Activision, Imagic, and Videa; on the screen, those companies that split off earliest have naturally "traveled" farther from Atari than those formed recently.

Each spaceship in the drawing represents a video-game
designer or executive whom Spectrum *discusses in this special report. Spaceship trails show the person's movement from company to company. For example, one ship flying from Atari to Activision and back to Atari represents designer Larry Kaplan; flying from Atari to the edge of the screen but turning back is designer Allan Alcorn.*

The tendency of spaceships and their cargo of ideas to shuttle from asteroid to asteroid has displeased many an asteroidal satrap, leading to the barrage of lawsuits and accusations represented here by puffs of smoke. Of course, some designers have left the industry completely, as shown by the ships leaving the "screen" for hyperspace.

Companies represented by light-colored asteroids are involved primarily in video games, whereas darker asteroids show companies with other main missions. The asteroid marked with a "?" represents the company that Joe Keenan, Nolan Bushnell, and Mr. Alcorn, three of the founding figures of Atari, intend to form when their contract not to compete with their former company expires in October 1983.

EXHIBIT 4 A HEADY FUTURE FOR SALES OF VIDEOGAME CASSETTES (Source: *Business Week.*)

1979	100,000 units	1982	1,200,000 units
1980	200,000 units	1983	1,800,000 units
1981	750,000 units		(est.)

EXHIBIT 5 THE VIDEOGAME INDUSTRY (Source: *Electronic Games* magazine.)

☆ Most Popular Videogame Cartridges ☆

This Month	Last Month	Game	System	Manufacturer
1	1	Pitfall	Atari 2600	Activision
2	2	Donkey Kong	ColecoVision	Coleco
3	—	Ladybug	ColecoVision	Coleco
4	12	Venture	ColecoVision	Coleco
5	—	Defender	Atari 2600	Atari
6	3	Donkey Kong	Atari 2600	Coleco
7	8	Zaxxon	ColecoVision	Coleco
8	5	Demon Attack	Atari 2600	Imagic
9	—	Megamania	Atari 2600	Activision
10	—	E.T.	Atari 2600	Atari
11	10	Berzerk	Atari 2600	Atari
12	—	Raiders of the Lost Ark	Atari 2600	Atari
13	14	Star Master	Atari 2600	Activision
14	—	Turbo	ColecoVision	Coleco
15	6	Frogger	Atari 2600	Parker Brothers

☆ Most Popular Computer Programs ☆

This Month	Last Month	Game	System	Manufacturer
1	2	Pac-Man	Atari 400-800-1200	Atari
2	1	Star Raiders	Atari 400-800-1200	Atari
3	8	Centipede	Atari 400-800-1200	Atari
4	3	Castle Wolfenstein	Atari 400-800-1200, Apple II	Muse
5	5	Choplifter	Atari 400-800-1200, Apple II	Broderbund
6	—	Protector II	Atari 400-800-1200	Synapse
7	—	Gorf	VIC-20	Commodore
8	7	Missile Command	Atari 400-800-1200	Atari
9	4	Jawbreaker	Atari 400-800-1200	Sierra On-Line
10	—	Frogger	Atari 400-800-1200	Sierra On-Line

☆ Most Popular Coin-Op Videogames ☆

This Month	Last Month	Game	Manufacturer
1	1	Donkey Kong	Nintendo
2	2	Tron	Bally/Midway
3	3	Zaxxon	Sega
4	5	Dig-Dug	Atari
5	10	Donkey Kong, Jr.	Nintendo
6	4	Ms. Pac-Man	Bally/Midway
7	6	Robotron	Williams
8	—	Tempest	Atari
9	9	Joust	Williams
10	—	Centipede	Atari

The Videogame Design Process

The videogame industry depended on game designers who combined creative artistry with technological sophistication. A typical game could take from 6 to 18 months to complete.

The design process resembled the creative people who carried it out. David Crane, a well-known and idiosyncratic designer, put it this way in a *Wall Street Journal* article: "Most of the time we're joking. Only one out of 50 crazy ideas will ever become anything. A tree falls down, try to get out from under it—obviously, nothing will come of that. But that's how we come up with the original game ideas."[1] This same article stated:

> Each designer has his own particular work habits and creative techniques. David Crane always starts by creating visual images after thinking of an idea for months—or getting struck by one overnight. He rushed back from a Chicago business trip to start work on the game Freeway after he saw a befuddled man trying to run across busy Lake Shore Drive in rush-hour traffic.
>
> Mr. Miller, on the other hand, starts with concepts. "There's a lot of discussion among the designers about what might make a good game, and we have a list of maybe 40 to 50 ideas," he says. "Yet most of the games we do aren't on the list. They come about because a designer gets inspired."
>
> Armed with an idea, Mr. Miller does some rough sketches of what he wants the playing fields of a game to look like, and he writes a brief description of how it is supposed to play. Then he retires to the mostly unfurnished living room of his nearby home, gets comfortable in a padded rocking chair, and spends days alternately staring out the window at trees and painstakingly writing an initial 10 to 20 pages of detailed computer code on small sheets of green paper.
>
> "Writing code for me is like writing English," Mr. Miller said. "I'm fluent in about a dozen computer languages." Each of Mr. Miller's late games had about 2,000 to 3,000 separate instructions which were eventually "burned" onto a computer chip to provide the look and playing features of the games.
>
> The designer spent two months writing and rewriting computer codes, producing about 200 pages of handwritten notes, and a five-foot stack of computer printouts. Then, after getting suggestions from other designers, he programmed his work into Activision's main computer to generate mountains, tanks, and other visual features and colors on-screen. For the next two months, he worked on playability, making the video and audio features of the game challenging without being impossible.

This case was prepared by Associate Professor John Kao.

For the last two months, Mr. Miller and his colleagues played the game for hundreds of hours to debug and polish it. "After I finish a game, I really hate it, and I don't want to see it again for months," Mr. Miller says.[2]

Atari came up with its own way of dealing with the creative process. One industry historian recalled, "Many of the best times occurred not in Sunnyvale, but at Atari's think tank in Grass Valley in the Sierra foothills, where Nolan Bushnell, founder of Atari, sent his brightest employees to consider the company's future. Hot tubs, pot, and private shuttle flights between the two valleys were the modus operandi there—or so legend has it."[3] One designer described Grass valley as "a place to dream up new ideas in a very unstructured work environment. It's very imaginative. Most of Atari's best ideas came from there."[4] Nolan Bushnell spoke about Grass Valley in these terms: "The basic architecture for everything came from there. Oddly enough, the engineering department at Atari was constantly sniping at the Grass Valley operation, and vice versa. They basically detested each other. According to the Sunnyvale crew, Grass Valley was full of prima donnas who couldn't make anything work—which was true in part, but they happened to be good technologists. Excuse me—great technologists."[5]

Bushnell, who planned a comeback in the videogame business when his noncompetition agreement with Atari expired, commented on Atari's design process: "Atari's done everything right in manufacturing and marketing. But it's done poorly in designing. Their current equipment is obsolete because it was designed nearly eight years ago and hasn't changed at all." Atari's approach, as he saw it, lay in creating better games and graphics for more exciting games. But that was not a strategy, declared Bushnell. "That's 'innovate me some more like you did last year' and that's wrong. They should be doing what I'm going to do."[6]

David Sudnow described the creative environment at Atari in the following terms:

> There I was on the Atari premises, and here were these rather speedy and excited young guys and gals in jeans and sneakers with Rembrandt prints and psychedelic posters in their offices, pianos and guitars lying about, Bartok coming out of this room, the Stones out of that, more TV sets going at once than in ten Sears, Roebucks put together, more technology and color and instruments and charts and sounds and knobs and controls and computers of every conceivable description than you'd ever see under one roof outside Silicon Valley, programmers literally sleeping in vans in the parking lot so they'd stay close to their consoles. And with the enthusiasm and animation any corporate manager would give away his American Express card for, they're laying out the lovely little grammars of these microworlds for me, speaking with such expertise and command and exhilaration as we went through the rundown of strategies and angles and hints, I figured myself in the presence of an artist's colony of the first magnitude, Black Mountain of the eighties, everyone working their brains off, chipmunks chipping away colors, movements and sounds into a whole marvelous assortment of new instruments.[7]

Lee Hauck, a noted game designer with Gremlin Industries, had his own point of view on the game design process:

He learned what didn't work—brainstorming sessions, for instance. "They've been absolute disasters. Games by committee are like most things by committee." He had a concept of what made a good game designer. "A lot of them come from computer disciplines. But they might come from other places, too, like people who write cartoons." The ability to work within the limitations of the medium is critical. "A movie screenwriter probably wouldn't work out, because in movies he doesn't have the problem of making it run on cost-effective hardware. Anything you want to do in a film you can do. But here it's gotta be achievable at low cost."

Hauck said Gremlin has a number of company game design groups. "But mainly we're looking to our programmers to supply ideas. If anybody even looks like he has an aptitude for games, we give him his head, let him do whatever he wants for a while." He estimated that ninety-five percent of such efforts hadn't succeeded. "But you only need a few winners to justify it. The trouble with creativity is that you can't teach it and you can't schedule it."

Hauck had strong convictions about those things that historically had fueled his own creativity. "I'm a big believer in the subconscious. The times when I've created the best is when I'm working the hardest doing the most. Going to seminars, reading books. Listening to jazz. Talking to people. Walking around arcades. The more inputs you can cram into your subconscious, the more it works for you, and pretty soon the ideas start coming."[8]

Alan Alcorn, one of Atari's original designers, felt that constraints stimulated creativity. In his words, "you get more juice out of a lemon when you squeeze it."[9]

According to an article in *Business Week* on the videogame design process:

Ideas begin in brainstorming sessions, normally held somewhere away from the company. No idea is too far-fetched, because no one knows what crazy idea will set off sparks in someone else and ignite the next hit game. "We talk about a Halley's comet game, for example," says Siu Kuen Lee, an Atari designer, "that would show a black screen and once every 76 years a light would flash across." This may sound far-fetched, but so did a multisegmented worm—an idea that led to one of the top games of 1982, Centipede.

Ideas can also come from other games, noted Larry Kaplan, a vice president at Atari. "To write a good game is difficult. It takes a long time, a lot of test marketing."

Robert Brown, vice president of engineering for Starpath in Santa Clara, California, said, "One way we choose games to design is by seeing what categories are popular in coin-op [arcade] games and trying to develop something in that category that is a new twist."

Game ideas also come from movies—directly, as when Disney got in touch with the Midway Manufacturing Co. of Chicago, a Bally subsidiary and asked it to design a game based on the movie *TRON*. "It gets to the point where you can't get through a movie without thinking, "Boy, that would make a good game," observed Bill Adams, director of games development for Midway.

Game ideas also come from real-life situations, particularly sports. "Sports games are easier to do," said Bob Whitehead, cofounder of Activision, "because they are well defined. A more original game has to evolve, so it takes more time."

Reality can also present a pitfall for a game designer, because mistakes are obvious. At Atari, a game nicknamed Foul Ball reached the marketing testing stage before anyone discovered that the designer, who did not understand the rules of baseball, was treating strikes as balls.

Some designers start with a picture rather than a concept for game play, then think of ways to interact with their graphics.

"I got interested in drawing pictures," said John Perkins, who designed Artillery Duel for Astrocade, Inc., Columbus, Ohio. "I started out with a desert and put cactuses all over it, then I drew a hill and put rocks on it, then trees. The idea for the game, shooting over the mountain, evolved as a way to interact with the scenery."

One complaint of game designers who left Atari is that too many game ideas were originating in the marketing department. "A videogame is a creative thing, like an artist with a palette full of colors," said Mr. Alcorn, who is still under contract to Atari, but on the inactive roster. "The artist has control of the medium; I can smear paint on a canvas, and it's not going to look like a picture. Take a marketing guy, someone who is nontechnical and doesn't understand the medium, he tries to design a game, and it's inefficient."

One example of a marketer's idea for a game, Mr. Kaplan says, is Polo, designed by Carol Shaw, a former Atari designer who is now with Activision. Mr. Kaplan related, "Ray Kassar [president of Atari] was into cosmetics. 'Hey,' he said, 'cosmetics is a $4 billion industry. Why can't we get a piece of that with videogames?' Warner commissioned clothing designer Ralph Lauren to come up with a perfume and put his name on it and call it Polo. They had a line of cosmetics and wanted this Polo cartridge as a come-on in the stores." The perfume was not a hit on the market. The videogame was not sold.

If marketing people cannot always identify a good game, engineers are quick to admit that they cannot either. Engineers often love games that the public hates, and are bored by games—like Pac Man—that the public loves.

After ideas are generated and a priority list is drawn up, designers choose or are assigned an idea from the list. Perhaps half of the ideas are eventually attempted as games, says Lyle Rains, an Atari vice president for coin-op. Half of those or less are completed, he says and half again are produced.

Graphics artists become involved, doing storyboards for game ideas and working with designers to develop the graphics that will be put up on the screen. In the early days, artists were not necessary—paddles and a ball did not take much artistic ingenuity—but game graphics today have much more detail. Some programmers are artistically talented and will design their own graphics, and this can work very well, because they know the limitations of the system. But Roger Hector, president of Videa and a graphics artist, says it is difficult to find people who are both technically competent and artistically creative. The solution lies in a team approach.[10]

VIDEOGAME DESIGNERS

In a review of videogame designers, the editors of an engineering industry publication wrote:

> The videogame industry is a test bed for engineering design in which there is no cookbook to design from. The research-and-development cycle must be kept short—under six months. Designs are personal. Designers admit they sometimes cannot read each other's code or even each other's schematics.
>
> According to industry sources, there were only 100 full-time videogame designers, and of those, only about 20 in the United States were considered superb.[11]

What made a good videogame designer?

"You have to be a good engineer," said William Grubb, president of Imagic. "You have to have specific knowledge of that microprocessor you're working with and that comes from formal education and experience; it takes time to learn the idiosyncracies of the system. And you have to be able to combine art with engineering, to be able to understand what is fun, what will titillate your markets. Not every engineer used to thinking logically has that ability."

Donna Bailey, who designed Centipede for Atari . . . agreed, saying, "There's a lot of trendiness and pop culture that goes into games. Many programmers have trouble with that so they can't do games."

According to an Atari promotional videotape, a designer had to be an engineer who was also an artist and a musician. "You can't do games if you are a scientist type; you have to think artistically of what the computer can do," one Atari designer said. "I'm creating a world in which my game will live."

People moved into the games industry from many engineering places—automotive, electronics, instrumentation, larger computer systems, defense, and semiconductors to name a few. Many engineers joined the industry straight out of college.

Game designers were difficult to stereotype. "This industry takes all kinds," said Alan Alcorn. "You must have the ability to work with some very perverse people, because the best take strange forms."

On the one end, he said, are people like Steven Jobs, . . . president of Apple Computer. "He showed up on our doorstep, and the personnel lady said we should either call the police or hire him, because he's brilliant," Mr. Alcorn recalled.

Harold Lee, who designed the first game on a single chip for Atari, "came out of the hills of Los Gatos dressed in leather like a Hell's Angel and said he was going to work with us," Mr. Alcorn continued. "He drove a chopper to work and drank Ripple wine."

On the other end of the spectrum were people like Robert Brown, a former Atari employee and executive vice president of Starpath. He had a Ph.D., was bespectacled, and a very straight guy, Mr. Alcorn noted.

Once designers got into the games industry, it was hard to imagine them doing anything else. Brian Johnson, a designer with Fox Video Games, said, "I've thought it might be fun to come back in the next life as a rock 'n' roll singer, and videogames seemed as close as I'll get to that in this lifetime."

Were videogame designers the new generation of pop stars? Activision promoted its designers heavily. Jim Levy said he considers game designers "rock stars."

Atari, on the other hand, never willingly released the names of its game designers, some said for fear that they would be hired by another company. The Atari designers liked a little recognition, so they often buried their names in their games. It took work and memory that would have been used for additional game features, but they considered themselves artists, and artists signed their creations. Atari used to review games and take the signatures out; they have stopped that policy.

Designers learned to hide their tracks and beat the censors anyway.

Larry Kaplan, Atari vice president of product development, said he designed Superbreakout for the Atari 800. After a certain sequence of keys, the screen displayed: "I love Suzie and Benji too." He listed other signed games for the Atari VCS: Adventure with Warren Robinett's signature in a secret room; Yars Revenge with Howard S. Warshaw's initials appearing at one point and ending the game; Defender with the attackers turning briefly into Bob Polaro's initials very late in the game; and Missile Command, with Bob Fulop's initials appearing if the player loses the game immediately in game 13.[12]

Perhaps the most divergent approaches to dealing with and motivating creative people were those of Imagic and Activision.[13] Imagic stressed team projects and market testing. Designers wrote computer motion and control programs, but graphics and sound effects were created by other specialists. Imagic also emphasized interaction between marketing and design staff. Product development made use of collective brainstorming sessions followed by concept testing, in which storyboards and game descriptions were produced and tested with a group of young players. Activision, on the other hand, stressed the independence of the creative designer. Fewer than ten nondesigners had access to the design lab. Each designer was responsible for all aspects of game creation, although designers frequently consulted with each other.[14]

Many other philosophies existed about how to select and motivate talent. For example, Namco, a Japanese videogame company, had an unusual approach to finding the people it needed. It advertised in magazines for reformed juvenile delinquents and grade-C students. Masayo Nakamura, president of the company, stated, "For game designers, the knowledge acquired in school is not so helpful. I want people who think in unusual ways, whose curiosity runs away with them, fun-loving renegades."[15]

On the topic of creativity, Nolan Bushnell stated, "I believe that there is no real correlation between hard work and good results. I think good work is an effective blend of leisure and work. You need leisure for perspective and work for execution, but all execution and no perspective will give you a bad product. I want all my engineers to have that perspective, even more than I want them to work hard—which may be a funny thing to say."[16]

An important trend in videogame design rested with the increasing sophistication of frameworks aimed at explaining the psychological phenomena common to all videogames. Chris Crawford of Atari described key variables in terms of pace, endowing the computer with the ability to produce "reasonable behavior" in response to human opponents, and limiting the information that is available to the player.[17] Malone of the Xerox Research Center spoke of variables such as the meaningfulness of game goals, the uncertainty of outcomes, the multiplicity of goal levels, the randomness of the program, the use of hidden information revealed selectively, fantasy, surprise, and appeals to curiosity.[18] Definitive studies on videogame psychology awaited the next generation of research.

The future of videogame design may be profoundly affected by new technology. Reports indicated that software to help players design their own games is now available. One such product, The Arcade Machine, was a software package for the Apple and Atari home computers that retailed for $59.95. A "shape creator" developed visual images in various colors. The program also created "explosions" and defined the playing field through a routine called the "path creator." Time limits and target scores could be altered. A "load save" feature allowed the weary game designer to break for food and sleep.[19]

REFERENCES

1. STEPHEN J. SANSWEET, "Designers Are Stars in Video-Game Field; Some Get Fan Mail," *Wall Street Journal,* January 19, 1983.

2. Ibid.

3. STEVEN BLOOM, *Video Invaders* (New York: Arco Publishing, 1982).

4. Ibid.

5. Ibid.

6. DAN DORFMAN, "Is the Video Game Fad Cooling Off?" *St. Louis Post-Dispatch,* September 19, 1982.

7. DAVID SUDNOW, *Pilgrim in the Microworld* (New York: Warner Books, 1983).

8. JEANNETTE DE WYZE, "The Inner Workings of Videogames," *The LA Reader,* August 10, 1982.

9. TEKLA PERRY, CAROL TRUXAL, PAUL WALLICH, "Videogames: The Electronic Big Bang," *IEEE Spectrum,* December 1982.

10. "The Riches Behind Video Games," *Business Week,* November 9, 1981.

11. PERRY et al., "Videogames: The Electronic Big Bang."

12. "Creating Video Games That Score," *Business Week,* April 4, 1983.

13. Ibid.

14. STEVE LOHR, "Japan's New Nonconformists, Technology Spurs Change," *New York Times,* March 8, 1983.

15. Ibid.

16. BLOOM, *Video Invaders.*

17. CHRIS CRAWFORD, "Design Techniques and Ideals for Computer Games," *BYTE,* December 1982.

18. THOMAS W. MALONE, "What Makes Computer Games Fun," *BYTE,* December 1981.

19. ERIK SANDBERG-DIMENT, "The Imaginative Path to Designing Games," *New York Times,* May 24, 1983.

George Lucas (A)

At age seventeen, weeks before the end of his senior year in high school (whether he would graduate was still too close to call), George Lucas was seriously injured in a near-fatal auto accident. On his way home from studying, he was broadsided after an illegal left turn by a friend's Impala. Lucas' Fiat Bianchina rolled five times before smashing into a walnut tree on his family's ranch. Rollbars, installed months earlier, kept the car from flattening, and the racing seat belts, anchored to the floor with steel plating, failed—miraculously snapping at the base—allowing him to be thrown from the roof. Lucas stated:

> You can't have that kind of experience and not feel that there must be a reason why you're here. . . . I realized I should be spending my time trying to fulfill it. . . . The fact is I could never have survived that accident if I'd been wrapped around that tree. . . . Actually, the seat belt never should have broken, under any circumstances. . . . All of this affected me seriously. . . . The accident made me more aware of myself and my feelings. . . . I began to trust my instincts. I had the feeling that I should go to college, and I did. I got the same feeling later that I should go to film school, even though everybody thought I was nuts.
>
> I had the same feeling when I decided to make *Star Wars*, when even my friends told me I was crazy. These are things that have to be done, and I feel as if I have to do them.[1]

One of three children and an only son, Lucas was a disinterested student who had a D+ grade average. "I lived for cars, summer vacations, and shooting out windows with BB guns."[2] Fragile even before the accident—5'7" and thin—some classmates referred to him as a "nerd." Diabetes kept him out of Vietnam. He did, however, enjoy fantasy—comic books and later TV— curled up with his black cat Dinky. Home life was easy if not stimulating. His father, a prosperous merchant of a stationery and office supplies store in Modesto, California, spent more time with the business and part-time walnut ranch than at home. Lucas, Sr. was a firm believer in old-fashioned virtues: Be true to yourself, work hard, and be frugal. But he thought his son never paid any attention. He recalled, "Scrawny little devil . . . never listened to me. He was his mother's pet. Always dreaming."[3] Lucas recalled, "Before the

This case was written by Research Associate Lee Field, under the supervision of Associate Professor John Kao.

Copyright © 1986 by the President and Fellows of Harvard College. Harvard Business School case 9-486-070.

accident I never used to think. Afterward, I realized I had to plan if I was ever going to be happy."[4]

During a two-year stint at Modesto Junior College, Lucas discovered special effects filmmaking. "We did trick animation, ran our movies backwards."[5] With the help of cinematographer Haskell Wexler, a friend from his race car days, Lucas entered the University of Southern California (USC) film school. Classmate John Milius said of Lucas, "He played with the concepts; he was free. He felt he was going to change everything and make the greatest art."[6] Before graduation in 1966, Lucas went to Warner Bros. for a six-month internship.

> From my point of view the film industry died in 1965. The day I walked onto the lot was the day that Jack Warner left and Seven Arts took over. The industry had been taken over by people who knew how to make deals and operate offices but had no idea how to make movies. When the six months was over, I never went back.[7]

THE FILM BUSINESS

The movie industry has had a volatile history. Its golden age began in the 1920s and culminated in 1946 with 4.1 billion tickets sold. The introduction and popularity of television, however, helped the industry into a 30-year slump which hit the bottom in 1971 with 820 million box office tickets sold. But the industry picked up in the 1970s when hits such as *Star Wars, The Empire Strikes Back, Raiders of the Lost Ark, Jaws,* and *E.T.* each grossed more than $100 million (see *Exhibit 1*).

Nonetheless, the industry was still plagued by problems: Production costs were accelerating faster than revenues. In 1975 the average film cost $3.1 million to produce; by 1981, the average cost had risen to $10 million. After marking expenses and distribution fees, a $10 million film needed $30 million in box office revenues to break even. The production cycle often ran as long as 24 months for feature films. During that time two potential hazards awaited a new film's release. First, movie audience tastes might change, and second, a similar film by a competitor could be released first and lessen the impact of later releases.

The odds of success (here defined as achieving a return on investment of 15 percent) were poor. Statistics showed that six out of ten movies made lost money, two broke even, and two were profitable. Only one in every 250 films was a blockbuster. Movie-making was, therefore, a speculative business.

Movie-making was sequenced in distinct phases: preproduction, production, and postproduction. During preproduction, a team of people necessary for the project was pulled together, a script developed, the production process planned, and the cast and crew hired. These tasks were handled by studio executives and/or the film's producer.

During the production phase other temporary employees were hired—office help, technicians, and other talent groups—who were tightly scheduled and used (and paid) only for the time needed. The film's director was the key to this segment of production; he or she coordinated all the work teams and managed the creative people.

Postproduction involved new technical people—editors, sound technicians, and special effects experts. The finished product could depend on many variables: the intent of the director; the influence of the producer; or the involvement of the financial backers. In recent years, some films have been prescreened to sample audiences with different endings or effects and finished depending on the most favorable audience response.

Even before a film could be made, however, someone had to put together and contract the four key elements necessary for success in the film business:

1. A network of creative people to produce the product
2. Production controls
3. Access to the distribution channel
4. Financing

This role of "deal maker" was played by many different people—some were major studio executives, others independent production companies, agents, directors, producers, or star actors. Managing relationships with all the potential key players in a deal was the critical attribute of a successful dealmaker.

Two major changes had occurred in the movie business since World War II. Spiraling costs and the risks of production led to a conservative attitude at most major studios. And most major studios sought deep-pocket financial support. As of 1985, five of the eight major studios had been acquired by conglomerates; the others had either diversified independently or arranged additional private and public financial backing.

A PROMISING YOUNG FILMMAKER

In 1967 Francis Ford Coppola, respected director of films such as *The Godfather* and *Apocalypse Now* and himself a USC graduate, hired Lucas as an assistant for *Finian's Rainbow*. As director Roger Corman had done for him, Coppola took an interest in promising USC students and paid them with experience. The following year Lucas was allowed to film a documentary of Coppola directing *The Rain People,* and he repeated the format by documenting Carl Foreman making *McKenna's Gold*. Impressed by Lucas' technical ability, Coppola brought him in as a founder of American Zoetrope, a San Francisco-based production company intent on establishing a northern California film center to counterbalance Hollywood and its southern California power.

The friendship and collaboration grew. Coppola produced and helped Lucas obtain funding for his first feature, *THX 1138,* released in 1971 by Warner Bros. A remake of a student film festival winner that Lucas had made while at UCS, the story was a grim view of the future, filmed in the unfinished BART subway tunnels in San Francisco.

While Lucas enjoyed total control during the creative process, this was not the case for the finished product. Executives at Warner Brothers, who thought *THX 1138* was "unreleasable," ridiculed the film and gave it to an in-house editor to salvage. Only four minutes were cut, but Lucas, deeply hurt and insulted, remarked, "It was a very personal film. . . . I was completely outraged."

Many critics, however, recognized Lucas' potential. Kenneth Turan in a *Washington Post* review of April 17, 1971, saw Lucas' strength as "a very personal vision" that could "transform a collection of cheap effects into a visually gratifying science-fiction film." *Newsweek* (April 3, 1971) described the movie as "an extremely professional first film." *THX 1138,* however, with lackluster studio support, failed at the box office. Lucas commented on this experience:

> I realized I had to make entertaining films or back off and release through libraries. I didn't want to struggle to get $3000. It was too limiting and I didn't want my wife to support me forever. I decided to make a rock 'n' roll cruising movie.[8]

Called *American Graffiti,* the film was released in 1973, and produced by Coppola. "We cooked up a lot of good stuff together," remarked Coppola, "and on a certain type of movie, it would be great."[9] Once again, there were differences with the Hollywood powers, this time Universal Pictures. Even after the studio cut the film, one executive still refused to release it. Only Coppola's bluff tactics saved *Graffiti.* As the story goes, Coppola jumped up at the studio screening, checkbook in hand, and offered to buy the movie on the spot himself if Universal did not want it. He also chastised the executives for being cruel and insensitive after this boy had "put his heart" into this project. Flush from his *Godfather* success, Coppola turned the tide. But Lucas and Coppola also had some philosophical differences. Lucas recalled, "He (Coppola) wanted to be a mogul. I wanted to make more movies and help young filmmakers develop. But first I'd build a solid base for financial security."[10]

THE STAR WARS SAGA

Seven million dollars in personal profits from *American Graffiti* was the start, and it also bought Lucas some time. For three years, eight hours a day, he worked on a science-fiction saga called *Star Wars,* a romantic fantasy adventure laced with the mythic themes of good versus evil and a young man's coming of age. Lucas initially had problems securing a backer. He remembered the time spent writing as excruciatingly painful and difficult. For ideas and relaxation, he read books by Jung and Castaneda's *Tales of Power.* The financial success of *American Graffiti,* however, (cost: $750,000; two-year gross: $50 million) convinced Twentieth Century Fox to invest in Lucas' *Star Wars* script. Released in 1977, it added close to $12-million net profit ($40-million paper gross less taxes and profit sharing for cast and crew) to the Lucas bank account. When ancillary rights such as videocassettes, television rights, books, licensing, and merchandising were taken into account, *Star Wars* would eventually become a billion-dollar product.

Rather than retire to a life of coupon-clipping, however, Lucas determined that the best investment he could make would be in the sequel to *Star Wars,* the second film in a projected trilogy, called *The Empire Strikes Back.* Lucas used savings and $15 million in theater prepayments as collateral for the $30-million budget. Because he had retained all sequel rights to *Star Wars,* Lucas was able to negotiate a very favorable agreement with Twentieth Century Fox for *Empire.* Lucas' pretax profits from *The Empire Strikes Back* (1980 release) were $51 million.

With a secure financial base, Lucas made the last of the trilogy, the 1983 release, *Return of the Jedi.* Initially called *Revenge of the Jedi,* Lucas subsequently renamed it, at considerable expense, when he realized that "Jedi are not vengeful." It was made at a cost of $32.5 million, funded internally, through Lucasfilm Limited, a corporation he had founded to handle all filmmaking operations as well as R&D, contract work for other filmmakers, and new businesses. By 1981, Lucasfilm Limited had relocated all operations and corporate headquarters to Marin County in northern California. Besides film rentals, Lucasfilm had other important sources of revenue including merchandising profits, since it controlled the rights to licensing of all *Star Wars*-related products. With the release of *Return of the Jedi* and ten years after Lucas' personal *Star Wars* saga began, he was anxious to move on to other things.

Between *The Empire Strikes Back* and *Return of the Jedi,* Lucas originated the story for Lucasfilm's production of *Raiders of the Lost Ark* (1982 release) in conjunction with director Stephen Spielberg. He also coproduced the 1984 sequel, *Indiana Jones and the Temple of Doom.* Other Lucasfilm activities included creating special effects for films such as *Star Trek* and *Back to the Future,* developing a high-tech ride at Disney World, producing further Indiana Jones sequels with Spielberg and designing videogames. Lucas also admits that two other trilogies based on *Star Wars,* set in a time prior to and following the original, may someday be made.

LUCASFILM LTD.

Five years after *Star Wars,* Lucasfilm Ltd. had grown from 40 to 400 employees, with a $16 million annual overhead. Yet, Lucas repeatedly insisted that he did not like business; nor did he like having his business in

Hollywood. After completing *The Empire Strikes Back,* in May of 1978, Lucas bought the 1,882-acre Bulltail Ranch in Marin County, California, north of San Francisco. During the next two years he purchased an additional adjoining 1,100 acres; total cost was around $3 million. Skywalker Ranch, its new name, was intended to be a movie think tank, not a studio.

One of Lucas' pet projects was Industrial Light and Magic (ILM), located at the ranch, which had state-of-the-art special effects equipment and artists. ILM did work for Lucasfilm and other quality film companies. In 1980 Lucasfilm had operating revenues of $350 million. Its main products were *Star Wars* and *Empire* and the newly emerging licensing fees and royalties from *Star Wars*-related merchandise. Profits from the films and merchandising subsidized the ranch's operating expenses.

At this time, Lucasfilm headquarters was located in Los Angeles in a converted warehouse near Universal Studios. Charles Weber, chief executive officer, had managed Lucasfilm's growth into a successful mini-conglomerate. Weber, who thrived on growing businesses and being in Hollywood, ultimately clashed with Lucas over the future of the company. Lucas, who had gladly given Weber complete business control, now wanted headquarters and control located in Marin County, with him. He wanted the business to fund his movie ventures, not vice versa.

Lucas agonized over the problem but ultimately decided to centralize all operations at Skywalker Ranch, fire Weber, and cut the size of the business staff. Only 34 of the 80 L.A. employees were invited to relocate. But Lucas offered generous cash settlements, six months severance pay, and vocational counseling for terminated employees. Bob Greber, former chief financial officer, became chief operating officer, while Lucas assumed the role of president and chief executive officer.

VALUES AND PRIORITIES

> A lot of the stuff in there is very personal. There's more of me in *Star Wars* than I care to admit. I was trying to say in a very simple way, knowing that the film was made for a young audience, that there is a God and there is both a good side and a bad side. You have a choice between them, but the world works better if you're on the good side. It's just that simple.[11]

"The key to his success," said one of Lucas' associates, "[is] that he cannot be turned from the vision inside his head or corrupted by outside influences."[12] Yet adherence to personal values and priorities has also resulted in professional and financial loss for Lucas. For example, Lucas resigned from the Directors Guild because they fined him for placing Irving Kershner's directorial credit at the end of *The Empire Strikes Back* instead of at the beginning. He also gave up membership in the Writers Guild over a similar dispute. Lucas described his rationale:

> The Hollywood unions have been taken over by the same lawyers and accountants who took over the studios. The union doesn't care about its

members. It cares about making fancy rules that sound good on paper and are totally impractical. They said Lucasfilm was a personal credit. On that technicality they sued me for $250,000. You can pollute half the Great Lakes and not get fined that much. I consider it extortion. The day after I settled with the Directors Guild, the Writers Guild called up. At least their fine didn't all go into the business agents' pockets. Two-thirds went to writers.[13]

His former wife Marcia (they were married in 1969 and divorced amicably in 1983) commented on Lucas' values and creativity: "He is methodical and ritualistic. He loves to feel safe and secure. Any kind of threat would make him so uneasy and uncomfortable he couldn't work. Even when he's silly, nothing is simply a fun moment. Everything gets logged."[14] Not surprising, the word most often used to describe Lucas is "serious."

Asked if Lucas believed in The Force (from the *Star Wars* movies, a universal power originating from faith), Marcia remarked, "I think deep down, part of his subconscious believes in it."[15] Lucas himself, admitting to his own belief in a "destiny of sorts," said, "I'm trying to set up an alternative filmmaking that allows me to do what I want, within certain parameters. We're trying to make a company that will respect the personality and individuality of filmmakers."[16]

Lucas was not known as a man of leisure. In Marcia's words: "You've heard of nine-to-fivers. George is a five-to-niner. He's up at five, leaves at five-thirty, and comes home at eight-thirty."[17] Lucas describes his workaholism thus:

> Ever since I was in film school I've been on a train. Back then I was pushing a 147-car train up a very steep slope—push, push, push. When *Star Wars* came along in 1977 I reached the top. I jumped on board and it's been downhill ever since. I've had the brakes on trying to stop the train on this steep slope, with the wheels screeching all the way. It's been work, work, work.[18]

His favorite fairy tale was *The Ant and the Grasshopper,* a story of an ant who could move bigger loads than a grasshopper because it worked harder and had confidence. Lucas continued: "I took the day off yesterday. I saw dailies at 9:00 a.m., had a meeting from 10:00 to 12:00, saw more film, had another meeting. I worked eight hours on my day off."[19]

Lucas described himself as someone with "simple wants and needs," and Mark Hamill, who played Luke in *Star Wars,* remembered being invited out to dinner and ending up at Taco Hut: "I should have known that George wouldn't go to a place with tablecloths and waiters."[20] Lucas agreed: "Francis [Coppola] accuses me of not knowing how to spend money. Francis is right."[21]

But Lucas has given percentage profit points in his movies to key employees and donated $5.7 million to the USC film school. However, when Coppola was in financial trouble after his $28 million electronic movie *One From The Heart* flopped, his associates were miffed with Lucas for not offering to bail Francis out. "I didn't ask him," said Coppola. "I don't think George is wired that way. Part of friendship is understanding what the limitations are. We're all products of our background."[22]

REFERENCES

1. DALE POLLOCK, *Skywalking* (New York: Harmony Books, 1983).
2. *Time,* May 23, 1985.
3. *American Film,* June 1983.
4. Ibid.
5. *Time,* May 23, 1983.
6. Ibid.
7. *American Film,* June 1983.
8. Ibid.
9. POLLOCK, *Skywalking.*
10. Ibid.
11. Ibid.
12. *American Film,* June 1985.
13. Ibid.
14. Ibid.
15. Ibid.
16. *Current Biography,* 1978.
17. *American Film,* June 1985.
18. POLLOCK, *Skywalking.*
19. Ibid.
20. *Time,* May 23, 1983.
21. POLLOCK, *Skywalking.*
22. Ibid.

EXHIBIT 1 MOTION PICTURE REVENUES

Top Money Makers

1. E.T. The Extra-Terrestrial (Universal, 1982)	$209,567,000
2. Star Wars (20th Century-Fox, 1977)	193,500,000
3. Return of the Jedi (20th Century-Fox, 1983)	165,500,000
4. The Empire Strikes Back (20th Century-Fox)	141,600,000
5. Jaws (Universal, 1975)	133,435,000
6. Raiders of the Lost Ark (Paramount)	115,598,000
7. Grease (Paramount, 1978)	96,300,000
8. Tootsie (Columbia, 1982)	94,571,613
9. The Exorcist (Warner Bros., 1973)	89,000,000
10. The Godfather (Paramount, 1972)	86,275,000
11. Close Encounters of the Third Kind (Columbia, 1977/80)	83,452,000
12. Superman (Warner Bros., 1978)	82,800,000
13. The Sound of Music (20th Century-Fox, 1965)	79,748,000
14. The Sting (Universal, 1973)	79,419,900
15. Gone with the Wind (MBM/United Artists, 1939)	79,700,000
16. Saturday Night Fever (Paramount, 1977)	74,100,000
17. National Lampoon's Animal House (Universal, 1978)	74,000,000
18. Nine to Five (20th Century-Fox, 1980)	66,200,000
19. Rocky III (MGM/United Artists, 1982)	65,763,177
20. Superman II (Warner Bros., 1981)	65,100,000
21. On Golden Pond (Universal/Associated Film Distribution, !981)	63,000,000
22. Kramer vs. Kramer (Columbia, 1979)	61,734,000
23. Smokey and the Bandit (Universal, 1977)	61,055,000
24. One Flew Over the Cuckoo's Nest (United Artists, 1975)	59,204,793
25. Stir Crazy (Columbia, 1980)	58,408,000

Note: United States and Canada only. 1) Figures are total rentals collected by film distributors as of Dec. 31, 1982. 2) Figures are not to be confused with gross box-office receipts from sale of tickets. Source: *Variety*.

Jerry Welsh

When I came to American Express, I was a college professor, a Russian language and literature and comparative government scholar. I came to American Express because I was too stupid to realize you couldn't do that. I had three kids ages ten, eleven, and fourteen. I couldn't afford to send them to college.

They've been very good to me at American Express. My salary has increased five times in three years. Would I be tempted to go out on my own? Yeah, but I've scaled down my life. I don't want to scale up my life. I would go to a smaller place. Not a company, but out on my own. I don't want to make any more money. I want to scale my life back. That's partly because of my own value system of being a teacher. The only ideas I want to get have to do with the betterment of the world today. Whether I'd do it alone or with someone else, I don't know. At American Express, one of these days my string will run out. That's the way it should be. I think if you're sensitive to yourself and if you're truly yourself and with all your vulnerabilities you will become irrelevant over time, more baggage than you are an asset. I think I'm slowly becoming that and before long the cart will tip over and I'll go and do something else on my own. Not to make money, just to do something else.

You've got to remember I was 35 years old when I came to New York. If you had told me I was going to do what I'm doing now I would have said you're crazy, you've lost your mind. But I realized I had to change my life, so I changed it. I did not know what I was doing and fell into a very lucky situation. God was good to me and that was that. I don't have a very literate explanation for all this.

BUSINESS PHILOSOPHY

There are a couple of false dilemmas. One is the risk vs. risk-aversion false dilemma. There is no safety net in any corporation. Trust me. They will bag your happy ass. And the more visible the mistake is, the quicker they'll do it. There *is* no safety net. If you're hiding behind one of the pillars, that's one

This case was prepared by Associate Professor John Kao.

thing. But if you try to get visibility in the corporation, what you better do is have 33,000 employees under you. The minute you make a bad move you're *gone*. They don't fire you that day, but as my friend here said, you are gone. As you say in the South, when somebody cuts your throat with a razor you don't know it 'til you try to turn your head and it rolls off.

The next false dilemma is freedom vs. constraint. The idea that you're not free inside, but you're free outside is foolish. Unless you are well funded from your family or from an illegal business, you are not free. They've got the stranglehold on you, the banks or whoever has the purse strings. The Golden Rule is he who has the gold, makes the rule. Now inside you're as free as you want to risk, assuming you're in the right department. They'll let you go until you make a bad move and then you're gone. This stuff about you've got to be free to fail, that's just bullshit. Are you free to fail in brain surgery? Hey, let's try to get 60 percent successes. Come on. If you're one of the 40 percent you'll sue, or your heirs will sue. Nobody is free to fail.

Supervisors are not stupid. Their job is to say, "O.K., you've got a great idea. Do this, this, and this, you forgot to do this, get that done and do it." One of the things a corporation is not, is levels of idiocy. There are people there who make sure you mind the store. Are you going to be completely free? Of course not. You won't be free anywhere you are, with the blue box, with American Express' name, with 150 years of a franchise, with a $23 billion company at its current stock price. Do you think they're going to let you and me run loose in the tulips? No way. They'd be nuts if they would do that. Ted Turner wouldn't let you run free either. With Ted you'd be doing it Ted's way. With us you'll do it our way. Of course, if you're in a company with level after level of stupid people who shuffle papers, just quit.

Here is this guy Steven Jobs. What a tremendous thing he did. But he's gone. All he's got is money. He can't even get arrested. Ted Turner wanted to buy CBS. He goes to the investment bankers in New York. Why do all of them want to get in? Why don't they say, "I've got my money, I want to stay out." Why do they want in? Because that is where the power is ultimately, in these big organizations. Do you know how little $50 million is? It's nothing. There are plenty of people who have $50 million. They cannot get arrested. They can't get in the paper, they can't get an idea going, they can't get scope. That's really what I want to say, it depends on what scope and what stage you want to work on. You want a few bucks, make a few bucks. There are people in corporations making a few bucks. Go out and make a few bucks, that ain't going to make you happy. Look at Donald Trump. What does Trump talk about in interviews? Does he talk about buildings? Hell no. All he talks about is disarmament. Getting the Russians to talk. What does Ted Turner talk about? Ted Turner wants to be Secretary of State. They don't make entrepreneurs Secretary of State. I have trouble with the old entrepreneur thing because I'll tell you frankly, most people don't want to do it. You want the rocking chair kind of deal which is a lot of motion, no danger. Nobody wants to get his ass shot off.

In a big company there are a lot of things going on. It is not a laboratory. In a laboratory you have one variable. Look how many variables are swimming around American Express. How many advertising campaigns do we have? How many things are going on in the economy? You never know whether anything works or not. Everybody thinks the Statue of Liberty was a big success. Hell, let's say it was. The business went up. Was it because of that? I don't know, do you? We don't know. Let's say that was the reason. Then let's say that makes me great. Are you ready to say that? I'm ready to say it. I'm great. Now, if the business doesn't go up, does that mean it didn't work? O.K., let's say it didn't work. I think Project Home Town America, which was a much bigger idea than the Statue of Liberty, did not "work" the way the Statue of Liberty did. Some people think it failed. I think it was a brilliant success so the hell with them. So you can't tell. Sure you know when it's a disaster, but you can't tell on an incremental basis what works. Take "Do you know me." Does it work? Well something out there is working. We're going to do an advertising campaign that's going to blow everybody away in about a month. Blow them out. It's going to change the way everybody looks at advertising in America. And the point is, half the people will say, "God damn that Welsh. It's going to be a disaster, noncommercial, it's not going to sell anything. It's counterintuitive that it will sell anything." Trust me, it sells *everything*. Can I prove it? No. So, you just run as hard as you can until somebody gets you.

MANAGEMENT STYLE

I do not believe in general management. And I will urge you never to believe in it. It's like believing in the concept of perfect father, perfect husband, perfect wife, perfect friend. Let's say I'm a perfect friend. What you really mean is the kind of friend I am is going to be perfect for you. The kind of husband I am will be perfect for you. The kind of father I am, I hope, is going to be perfect for you. I do what I am doing. I do my own work. That's the way I manage my department. I let others do the paper and all of that. When the promotions are up, I don't even know about my fringe benefits, so when I interview somebody and they say to me, hey, what's the dental plan? How the hell do I know what the dental plan is? I have no idea, nor do I want to know. I don't even care. Not because I'm an entrepreneur, I never did care about dental plans even when I was a college professor, so I do not want dental plans. I do not like dental plans. I manage our department by doing what I do best which is the projects that I do. And I surround myself with people who do various projects, so I'll be doing some things with Beth [Horowitz], some things with somebody else, and they'll do things without me. The way I encourage this is to say, "Look, understand something, these standards don't come from me. Your job is not to kiss my feet. That is not your job, believe me, trust me. Who cares?" My satisfaction comes from other things than that, believe me.

So your job is to make a tremendous contribution in terms of the value you add by having great ideas, being a great implementer of ideas, being quick off the block. I like things quick, I like things to happen now. I don't want to wait, I don't want to study them. We've got to have them now, and that's the way I manage. You *know* in our department if you don't make it. We have meetings all the time. If we have one meeting at 11:00 then we want the answer about 3:00 so we have another meeting on the answer. We want to know where it is. "Well, what's the idea?" We have to come up with an idea now. That's what my department does. If we've got a problem, what's the answer, give me your idea. There are many ideas, what's yours? I don't come up with all the ideas. They do. So the thing I want is the idea. Then I want someone to go implement it. In our department, we come up with and implement it. I do my own work. I do the things I think I do best, whatever they are. I'm not interested in trying to get everybody feeling good about their job and their career and their aspirations and my aspirations. Forget all that crap. My aspirations are to be arrested for loitering, I guess. It isn't that your aspirations don't matter to me, it's that my aspirations are my personal business, yours are yours. Your career is your personal business. I'm not going to manage your career.

WORKING AT AMERICAN EXPRESS

My thing at American Express is that I got lucky. I took some risks and they *all* worked, every *one* of them, or I would not be sitting here today. I cannot afford a big mistake, even today. Nor will I ever be able to, and that's fine. That's the way I want it when the end comes, and there's an end for everything. You're thinking about the beginning, I'm thinking of the end. There's an end for all of us, not in the ultimate sense, but careerwise. You change. I'll go down, I hope not in disgrace but I'll go down, or I'll make a big mistake and I'll be gone. We'll cover it up and make it sweet and all of that, but I'll be gone and that will be good. Then I'll start the next phase.

I have developed a bit of a track record at American Express so they believe me a little now, whereas they didn't before. If you come up to my department and you have a brilliant idea I feel about you the same way they felt about me. "This is a brilliant idea. We're going to do it and give you full credit for it but we're not going to do it the way you want to do it. We're going to do it this way but everybody will still know that it's your idea. You will be chief point man. I'm here to advise you and of course be your boss and I'm telling you we're going to do it this way." Because my view is that part of being an entrepreneur or whatever we want to call people who are living by their own lights is that I'm not going down with your methodology. I'm going down with mine. If this room caught on fire right now and everybody was waiting for somebody to come up with an idea, I assure you I'd come up with an idea. The idea is to get the hell out of here through that door. And if someone said, "Nope, I'm going through the other door," I'd say, "No, don't! *This* door." Now I might be wrong but I would want to go down with my own idea. Now, if you want to go down with yours you've got to remember when you get a little credibility, the first idea you might do my way, but everyone knows it was your idea. The second idea you do it your way, the third idea you pass me. It shouldn't be frustrating to you. There is an apprenticeship about things. You have to have a track record.

I have people around me who will actually tell me to go to hell. You absolutely must have people around you from your assistants to everybody who will say, that's wrong, don't do it, you'll die, do not do this, don't. I'm very proud of the fact. People around me either care enough about me or are afraid that I'm going to wreck the ship or something, to say, "don't do this it's a bad idea." When I throw out my ideas, by the time I come to the next meeting they're all there and the bad parts are knocked out.

All of us in our department make changes together. For example, we're going to play croquet in our new building in the corridors. A couple of years ago when I suggested we play croquet in the building, that took them by surprise. But now, everybody is open to croquet so people get more comfortable with change. What can you really learn from an entrepreneur? Live by your own rules, know what the risks are, and know what you want.

The chairman of American Express said, "Jerry, where are all the people who are going to be the next group of people like you?" You can't predict who's going to be what. If you had said to me ten years ago when I was a college professor, "Oh, Jerry, you're going to be this, you're going to be that." I think that's silly. You don't know. Ten of the people here are going to do 50 times what I've done perhaps. How can we tell? How can you groom somebody to be whatever it is you are? There's no way to train anybody to be what you are, whether that's good or bad. Someone steps forward or they don't step forward. If I were my boss I would worry about this problem, but I don't because I understand the process and understand how unforgiving it is. Don't ever think there are any corporate parachutes and all that crap. That's a lie. People who get in trouble with American Express listen to all that stuff. "We will help your career. What's my career path?" The hell out of here if you don't do it right. People don't like to say that. If I fail will I be fired? Well, yeah. That's life. Life is that way. If you put the American Express name on a bad idea and bring that name down, you're gone, you are out of here. That's the way it should be.

I have the same philosophy Bear Bryant did about football which is this. You recruit the smartest people, don't care if they're girls, boys, black, white, green, transvestite, you just recruit the best people. You get rid of mediocrity, ruthlessly. Someone who is mediocre you get rid of. Bag 'em immediately! You take all excellent people. Trust me, these people are going to be pains in the ass. You say to them, here are the limits, don't go around without your clothes on, don't do anything weird that way. You work hard, you be excellent, you add value, I'll take care of you. The way I manage is simply to get rid of mediocre people.

What do I do well? I come up with ideas and ram them through. What am I going to do next year? I have no idea. I'm struggling with that myself.

What I'm certain of though is that it will be more beautiful than what I'm doing now. Absolutely confident of that, maybe I'm wrong but I'm confident. No career plans, I just don't have any of that. I do one thing well. I try to stick to that. I'm not going to try to do things I cannot do. That's a mistake you don't want to make. If you look at people who are really smart, they can do one or two things well. There's nobody who can really do a lot. It's just a myth. Life is not that way.

I would say in graduate school if you had tried to get me to sell Jell-O, I couldn't. I don't care if someone ever said to me, "Is there room in this market for another soft pudding?" There's Country Time, Shake & Bake, I don't care about it. I never cared about it. I came right from there to what I'm doing now. I never did care about it. That's why I was a college professor. How do I motivate people? They know they're lucky to be working on ideas that make a difference in the world. It's one thing to sell Pepsi, it's another thing to sell Pepsi to help people. So I think if you work in my area you're a lucky person.

But, I still make major mistakes. When I go down, and I will, it's going to be with my own problems. Everybody can play their role but with the chances we take, I'm going down in my own little red wagon.

We've come pretty far away in my group from business, I'll admit that we're the counterculture, but this still is American Express. The shareholders are still showing up. Now, we have launched things with no research. We've done all those things, but this is business, I don't need to tell any of you here that we think we've done some very good things for the business. I'm just telling you that in another environment these things could not have happened. Whether that means it's entrepreneurial or intrapreneurial, these things could not and have not happened in other places.

ENTREPRENEURSHIP

To me an entrepreneur is a person who is determined to take his/her destiny into his/her own hands and do it their way, period, with little modification. Are you going to be happy with the rewards? I mentioned people like Ted Turner. They're not happy with the rewards. If I went out and made $5 million today or $20 million, I'd still want to make big projects go . . . and you can't do that with $20 million in Nashville, Tennessee . . . You have to have American Express behind you. Are you that kind of person? Are you going to be happy with the rewards? Don't be what you're not going to be happy with when you get it. O.K.? Understand what you want. Do you want power? Influence? Do you want to be a big mucky-muck, then you've got to lay pipe to do that. If you want to be rich, go to the quickest route to get rich. The people who say they want to be rich usually want something more. All of them come back, they want to do something, they want to be Tom Wyman, (former) president of CBS. They criticize Tom Wyman but, they all want to play golf with him. I don't want to do that, but some do.

I will tell you how to find an entrepreneur. First of all, risk is one factor. There are many others. Ability to quickly conceptualize problems and come up with solutions, take risks, and say, "Let me be the one. I'll do it." An entrepreneur would know what he'd be saying at Harvard. "Look guys, all this class participation stuff is dragging me down. I'm not too verbal, but I'll tell you what: I'm going to shoot the eyes out of whatever exam you give me, O.K.? So, I'll be showing up sometimes and I'll be out sometimes. But trust me, when the end of the day comes I'm blowing all these people away." How many people do you hear saying that? They don't want to do that. They want to say, "I was within the limits of what's safe for me, I want to be cool."

You can say entrepreneurship is where you take the big risk. But there is no parachute for you anywhere. You're gone. They will get rid of you in five minutes and they should. In Cleveland, in New York, once a year the modeling agencies have open calls. Every time this happens I always forget about it until it shows up in *The New York Times* and breaks my heart again. All of the young girls come in from Cleveland and these modeling agencies open up their doors. You want to talk about cruelty then? You've won every beauty contest in Cleveland, Ohio and you come to New York and they rip your face apart and rip your body apart and they rip you apart. You ain't got it. You're gone. That is what you're going to face, I don't care where you're going. If you want to hit the top, I don't care if you want to go make $100 million, you want to be chairman of American Express, you want to be head of the stodgiest company in the country, you're going to be looking right across at smart people who are going to say, "I'm better than you are." And the thing that nobody wants to face up to, that very few people acknowledge when they talk about risk, is losing your job, losing your little fortune. Who cares about you? You're bankrupt at 25. You lose your job. You'll bounce back. You know how many people have done that? What you don't bounce back from maybe is to put yourself on the spectrum of how smart am I, how hungry am I, how much energy do I have, how much guts do I have. We all got the rest of it. We're all straight on how to do the risk taking but when the time comes to step out and get your ass shot off, there aren't that many people stepping out.

I don't know about entrepreneurs. I don't know whether I'm one and I really don't care if I'm one. Because all I know is that I am doing what I want to do a lot.

The myth of the general manager is something I feel very strongly about. It is a myth that anybody well rounded is O.K. and the more talented you are the more vulnerable and the more eccentric and the more in trouble you are. Voltaire said, "Great minds have great vices." Absolutely right. Show me a person who is well rounded and I will show you a mediocre person. Show me a general manager, and I'll show you someone who is mediocre, who can't do anything. Unless you find general managers this way: If I'm a general manager I'll give you my strengths and surround myself with people with other strengths who are covering my ass. That is what a good general manager does. They aren't people who know a little bit about this, and sit around and analyze. That is what you've got to come to grips with, whether you want to be a "general manager." Everybody at American Express wants to be a general manager. I've never wanted to be a general manager. I think it would be a disaster to put me in as a general manager. I think I would hate to be a general manager. Who wants to do that?

What I'm really trying to say is, the brighter the person the more eccentrically developed they are. That's generally true. And you can never fully round out your flat sides. I have the same flat sides I did when I was seventeen years old and joined the army. I'm the same person I was then, but a little older. I'm the same person. Oh, when I was younger I was really wild, but I'm more soft-spoken now. I just don't believe you round out.

PERSONAL OBSERVATIONS

The tough lessons in life are to realize what your limits are, to look around at the guy next to you and say, hey, that guy is smarter than I am. That guy's got more energy than I do. That guy is better than I am. That's tough. There are about three people at American Express that are clearly smarter than I am. They're not ahead of me but they're smarter than I am. They're not going to get up earlier than I do. They're not going to charge harder than I do. But they're smarter.

I'm very hard-nosed about mediocrity and I'll tell you why. The way to wreck your boat, whether it's in your personal life or in your professional life is to be either mediocre yourself or surround yourself with those who are that way. What you need to do in the limits of human kindness is to get them out of your way. I want them all working for VISA. I want them all to be somebody else's friend. Why? You're just going to spin your wheels trying to make it. An expression in the South is, kick ass and take names. You never can make chicken salad out of chicken shit, you just can't. I wouldn't have said this 20 years ago, but some people don't have it. Don't have the courage. There are some people who just don't have any guts, and they will sink your boat every time. So, within the limits of kindness, you put them on the street and hope that your competition hires them.

I'm a very self-centered person and in not a very good way. There are a couple of reasons for that. One, when you are in a high-intensity environment like the corporation, you have almost no personal life. You see, it's a self-fulfilling prophecy, a circular thing. When you make so many sacrifices in your personal life then of course it becomes very important. Luckily, my kids were almost grown when I came to New York. I was a college professor and I used to do a lot of things with them. Thank God, now they're grown. If I had small kids today, man I'd have guilt trip all over. You just cannot have a family and do this. I haven't. Almost my whole life is my job, and what intermingles in my personal and professional life. Is that bad? No, but it's not going to go on forever either. You have to get comfortable with the idea that you've got phases in your life. You're coming, you're going, you're gone, you're here, you're somewhere else. What happens to people is tragic. You think, "Well Jerry Welsh, boy, after him—après moi, le deluge. Nothing will be after me because I am the ultimate one." That's when you know you're in trouble. After me there will be something different, probably something better. What happens to people is they think they've got to hang on. If I leave, it will all fall apart. That's foolish. When you start thinking that way, you need to quit. I haven't come to that point yet, my personal and professional lives *are* intertwined to the extent that I'm thinking about business, about ideas a lot of my life. Do you think a person like me has a wife? If you asked all the women here, would you marry a person like me? NO WAY.

The Ladd Company

> The company is an amazing mixture that seems to work so well. It is a beautiful recipe.
>
> Joe Graham
> V.P. Business Affairs

In July 1979, Alan Ladd resigned as president of a major motion picture studio. His senior vice president of worldwide production, Jay Kanter, left with him, along with Gareth Wigan, vice president of worldwide production. By late 1979, Ladd had formed his own independent film production company in partnership with Warner Communications, Inc., which had provided financial resources sufficient to produce a series of films and guaranteed both artistic and business autonomy. Others who left vice president positions at the old studio to join Ladd in ownership of the company were Ashley Boone, Bob Dingilian, Leonard Kroll, Sandy Lieberson, Burt Morrison, and Paula Weinstein. Joe Graham left legal work in a talent agency to join the group.

At the former studio, the team had brought in 33 Academy Awards in 1978. They produced *Star Wars* in 1976—the highest grossing movie yet made. They backed a string of five "women's films" in a single year: *Julia, The Turning Point, An Unmarried Woman, Norma Rae,* and *The Rose.* Ladd brought the studio both critical acclaim and plenty of money. The times were magical.

The decision to join Ladd in his new venture did not come lightly to some. Paula Weinstein, vice president—production, told us:

> It was a gigantic commitment for everybody to come here! You've got a year and a half until your product starts coming out, and you don't know how good you are until it starts coming out, and it's a crapshoot business, anyway. It was the toughest year in my life—I never had anything this hard. And as rewarding—the potential for excitement is endless. . . .

This case was prepared by Research Assistant Joanna Barsh, with the assistance of Research Associate Barbara Kaban, under the supervision of Assistant Professor Leonard A. Schlesinger. It was revised by Associate Professor John Kao.
Copyright © 1982 by the President and Fellows of Harvard College. Harvard Business School case 9-482-122.

The opportunity to work with Ladd offered something different to many group members. As Gareth Wigan said:

> All of us, particularly the older ones amongst us, have worked one time or another with groups of people who were more traditionally untrustworthy, back-biting, and less reliable colleagues. How much easier and more enjoyable life is when you don't have to watch for the knife in the back!

Working for "Laddie," to many "the best boss in the industry," was a major incentive. "He is the magnetic force that all the magnets are attracted to. He inspires a great deal of loyalty," said Wigan. "Laddie is the glue that holds us all together," said Morrison. "I'm not interested in life in ever having another boss *ever* than Laddie," said Weinstein.

Laddie had a style of managing creative people. Could he have created a company culture that encouraged better movies, of higher quality and commercially profitable? What was special about the Ladd Company . . . was it a well-run company and a winning ticket?

INDUSTRY OVERVIEW

"It is a business where if you hit it, you hit it big!" said Frank Rosenfelt, CEO of MGM Films. "You really have to love this business," said Alan Ladd. "If you don't, it can tear you apart."

Making movies is a highly speculative business in which the stakes are in the millions. Historically, two movies out of ten make money, two break even, and the remainder lose money.[1]

Successful participants in the industry seem to share some winning factors: access to distribution; a network of people to draw on for ideas, creative input, production, financing; tight control over production; a reputation based on personality and past success. But each movie is considered a unique product, and there is no formula for success. "One day you're hot, and the next day you're cold," Wigan said. "One keeps reading scripts because you never know, there may be that one in a hundred where you suddenly say, 'Oh, God, I can't put this down! I know this one's going to happen, believe me!'"

One writer compared recognizing a great script to chicken sexing. One learns to tell male from female chickens at birth by standing behind a proven chicken sexer for many years. There are no obvious clues. It takes a combination of talent, instinct, experience, and guts to make the decision.

The process of making a movie is complicated, depending on many creative and technical craftspeople. And "like children growing up, at some point films start to assert their own individuality," said Wigan.

---

[1] *Wall Street Journal*, 6/25/81.

Deanna Wilcox, a marketing executive at MGM Films, explained:

> We have such a long R&D process. Making a movie is probably one of the biggest team efforts that you will see. At each point in the line, the product can be enhanced or detracted from by one of the things that comes along in the process.
>
> When you look at automobiles, you see a design from a designer's hands. You *know* what the car is going to look like. When a writer submits a script, you really don't know what it's going to look like. The last thing that comes along in a project is the actual visual representation.
>
> You have to place faith and have a feeling for all those different elements that come to play on that project.

In the 18 months to two years needed to complete the cycle, public taste may change, or the competition may have already released a similar product. Each movie is a substantial financial risk. Burt Morrison told us:

> When a picture fails, it can be catastrophic. Nobody drops $10 million and doesn't gulp twice! There's no business where you can drop money so fast, or make so much money so fast.
>
> We've had pictures we thought would work well that didn't, we've had pictures that we didn't think would work well that did; when you're doing 10 to 12 pictures a year, half of them you're going to lose money on. That's something you have to live with every day.

In 1980, box office receipts were approximately $2.6 billion domestically (see *Exhibit 1*). This figure was shared by distributors, exhibitors, and producers. The 1980 top 10 movies brought distributors almost $461 million in rental fees (see *Exhibit 2*). It is easy to see why the major studios play the "blockbuster" gamble. At one time, multimillion-dollar productions seemed to guarantee box office success. Investing in known stars and stories supposedly reduced the risk of failure. A succession of expensive films that were financial failures, *Heaven's Gate* ($43M), *Raise the Titanic* ($36M), *The Island* ($22M), and others, disproved the theory.

One inevitable result of these fiascos was tighter control over production. Decision-making powers, which used to flow to the all-knowing agent or magical director, might in the 1980s, flow back to the producers who could bring in well-done movies at budget.

Many of the movie companies belonged to conglomerates. Warner Brothers was part of Warner Communications, Inc.; Universal belonged to MCA; Paramount was bought by Gulf & Western. Seven major motion picture producer-distributors dominated the current markets: Columbia, Disney, MGM/UA, Paramount, Twentieth Century Fox, Universal, and Warner Brothers.

Warner supported the Ladd Company. It, in turn, supplied Warner's motion picture distribution arm with a flow of pictures. Independent production companies, or so-called "mini-majors," were tiny compared to the major studios. Yet they planned to release as many movies (7 to 10 pictures a year) and had the same creative manpower. For each finished project, there might be 8 to 10 development deals that fall through, and hundreds of stories turned down. The companies lacked the bureaucratic structure of the larger corporations.

Whether the solution to cost problems was small, tightly run mini-majors or general management principles applied to motion picture divisions of major corporations, industry participants still used gambling analogies to describe their successes and failures. They vehemently asserted that charts and graphs led nowhere; Lady Luck, magic, and mysticism explained events just as well. We were told the words of an MGM executive as he watched his company begin a downturn in 1971: "You give the people what they want, and they still don't come."

MAKING MOVIES

The financial essence of a movie was the "package." According to Joe Graham, "All it really means is that you have enough elements to get the project going. That could be a director, and a star, and at that point, you have sufficient elements to know, after your budget is approved, that you're going to make a picture." With less prominent names, the package might consist of additional elements before the studio committed itself to the deal.

Deal making was a critical element in the movie making, though no guarantee of a movie's success. The deal maker might be an agent who put together a director, star, an idea; an independent producer; or the directors, screenwriters and stars turned moviemakers. Deals determined who would receive what percentage of gross receipts and potential profits, who got the rights to distribute to domestic and foreign theaters, network television, pay television and video. Frank Rosenfelt expressed a representative opinion about producers who concentrated only on the deals:

> That producer is just a businessman. He is the hustler who took an option on a property and talked a director into it, and ran over here to say, "I laid down $3.5M on *Gorky Park* for an option and I have got so-and-so and he is off and running if we like the project." And he is out hustling another deal the same way.
>
> You can become a multimillionaire on the basis of producing one film and in making that one film you have never risked a dime of your own money, but you are a partner in the profits. So, if you do make it, you make it big. It attracts a very different kind of person who is looking to make that big score. He has to be living by his wits all the time.

A film went through three main stages after the package was formed: preproduction, production, and postproduction.

Pulling the team together was the focus of the first phase. The script was developed, production planned, cast and crew hired. The studio executives and producer of the movie carried out two different production jobs. As studio executive, Paula Weinstein said, "I do a very specific job, which was for the company. I brought the project in. I supervised it, helped case it, got all the people committed. I had more of an editorial and judgment call on specific decisions." The producer was directly involved in the project; he or she the boss, responsible for daily production, and, in general, making things happen. No two producers did the same job.

During a film's production, several distinct subgroups emerged: the office people, technical crew, and talent groups. The task was for all to operate efficiently, making full use of the technical resources available and to find creative solutions to the problems that cropped up. The director became an important figure at this stage, coordinating the efforts of the team, motivating people, and driving the team to good performance.

An effective producer developed skills for working with creative people. Those making a movie considered it their "baby"; their egos were completely wrapped up in the project, seeing it as an extension of themselves. "Giving negative feedback," said Bob Cort (executive vice president at Fox), "is as tough as telling loving parents that their new baby has three ears and is monstrous. You can't tell them directly, but you can maneuver them into the right light so they see if for themselves. Laddie told us, 'You don't have to burst into somebody's office and say, "I don't like what you did."'" You try to express it and not let this whole feeling grow. You sit down and talk with the creative people, and don't try to say, 'I'm right and have all the answers,' because he may be right, too."

Gareth Wigan talked about the judgments he made in managing the creative people:

> If things are going well, and the principal individuals are people who like to be left alone, then your personal contact can be slight. It's a question of judging between not nagging and at the same time appearing not to be disinterested.
>
> If things start not to go well—it gets behind schedule, or you don't like the material—then it becomes much more difficult. It doesn't help to be sitting on top of the creative person's back. You can't tell him or her what to do, exactly, and if you're standing there with a stopwatch, it can be counterproductive.
>
> It's very important with creative people to join them, and not to challenge them. It's always easy for them to turn around and say, "You don't understand, you're not a filmmaker."

The pressures of time and money forced the producer to create the constraints that forced the creative people into action. As Jay Kanter said, "There are times when you have to be tough, and times when you have to be supportive. You have to care about what they're doing."

Although conflict was traditional between the filmmakers and the studio, studio executives considered it detrimental to the project. Kanter said, "You have to care about what the creators are doing, because after all, it's our money." Weinstein related the frustrations of having to work with this conflict:

We're the first audience. We're the first totally pro-biased audience they've got, so why not listen to what we have to say? We're only longing for it to work; we're not sitting there with a hammer wanting to see bad stuff. We just paid $75,000 for that day's work—we *want* it to be good.

During production, film footage was printed and viewed daily. In postproduction, the crew was disbanded, editing was underway, and marketing became a critical task. Product roll-out was not totally dissimilar to the roll-out of consumer packaged goods. Sneak previews gauged the film's degree of acceptance. The marketers created an image of the movie through advertising and publicity, type of distribution (location, quality, and number of theaters), and timing of release. They planned sales to secondary markets based on audience reception and predicted life cycle of the movie.

MOVIE PEOPLE

Moviemaking was an ego-intensive business, everybody told us. The common feeling was that normal business practices were not applicable, that the industry attracted participants who were undisciplined, unpredictable, and highly emotional. Bob Cort said, "There is a normal curve for behavior and at the extreme end, there is another behavioral curve just for movie people. We yell and scream a lot. In this industry, there are extraordinary stories about almost everybody you know."

Movie industry participants were intensely competitive. Mike Metavoy, president of production at Orion, said simply, "Everybody wants everybody else to fail. The higher you are, the more people want to knock you off." Cort told us that "it's a zero sum game":

> Although successful films are good for the industry as a whole, it's really more personal than that. Within a studio, one person's success is viewed as everyone else's failure. Even your best friend will not rejoice in your success, because ultimately, it diminishes him.

People rose to power quickly and disappeared as quickly. It was also a business of intense relationships, a very political environment. One industry participant gave us an example of the difficulties this might lead to:

> You have X in a television series that produces an enormous amount of revenue. X knows he is producing that revenue for you, although two years ago he was behind a counter in a supermarket, checking out. He knows he is no different from the other checkers at the supermarket. Lady Luck just shined on him. He has no background to handle this success. He's getting 11,000 letters a week now.
>
> X suddenly begins to act like the worst son-of-a-bitch in the world, the most outrageous behavior you can find. You can throw your $500,000 in revenue per episode out the window, or you can try to cope with X.

In the movie industry everything was accomplished through relationships. The informal network revealed more than the formal network; companies were people-based, not system-based. Doug Stern, a new executive vice president at Fox, told us, "I had to learn quickly who was who. The gossip tells you a lot about what's going on in the company . . . In the beginning, I did the logical thing, but that didn't get things done. I used to write memos, but things happen so rapidly that I began to use the phone. When I came here I wanted to read everything about the business, but there's nothing to read—and whatever you do read is all wrong, anyway!"

Burnout was the common movie people ailment. Laddie explained its origins:

> This business is constantly turning over. You're on a roller coaster ride from the time you wake up in the morning. Basically, this is the largest business of rejection you'll ever find. You are rejecting somebody's project or you don't want to hire that actor, director, or writer. Or that actor, director, or writer doesn't want to do the project you have.
>
> You really have to gear yourself to be very fluid in this business, or you will just burn out. It happens at least once a week where I am saying "No" to one of my closest friends or they are saying "No" to me. And you can't take it personally, or else you'll just end up destroying yourself.

There was another side of the picture. Somewhat tongue-in-cheek, Wigan explained:

> If it wasn't for the movie business, some of us would have to be put away. It is a business that enables people with a certain amount of craziness to function. If I had not gone into this business, but had gone into the more traditional things that my family came from, I would have been a very unhappy person.

For most people, Hollywood retained a certain glamor, a vision of celebrities and nightly parties. As Mike Medavoy said, "It's a business which everyone is attracted to; it's everybody's second business. The shoemaker is also in the movie business; he goes to the movies and says, 'Nah, that doesn't work.'" To the movie people, the business fulfilled their creative needs. Laddie expressed this feeling:

> It can give you tremendous emotional rewards. There are so few ways for a person to leave a legacy behind. This is one business where you can. I've yet to feel that I've made the definitive picture. I've never made a picture where I say if I never made another movie again, at least I'm happy that I did this one. I still feel I haven't come close to that. Obviously, there are pictures I've liked a lot and many that I've been proud of, but yet there will probably never be a picture, no matter if it wins 15 Academy Awards and was heralded as the greatest picture made, when I wouldn't say "I can do better." That's what keeps you going.

COMPANY OPERATIONS

By May 1981, the Ladd Company had grown to approximately 50 people. There were nine vice presidents. Kanter, Wigan, Weinstein, and Lieberson, vice presidents in charge of production, shared responsibility with Laddie for project selection and development. The other six vice presidents had specific functional areas of responsibility (see *Exhibit 3*). The offices in New York and London were responsible for searching out and developing literary material. The people there collaborated with others in the Los Angeles story department in bringing properties to the team's attention.

The team members supervised production out of the London and Los Angeles offices. The studio executives' personal contact with the movie crews depended on several factors: needs and desires of the acting producers, length of relationship with key members of a project, location of the shooting. The studio executives watched the progress of production by monitoring budgets, watching recently printed footage (the "rushes" or "dailies"), and reviewing daily production reports that described the day's activity in detail. The four production vice presidents were in constant communication with a movie's producer, director, and stars; Burt Morrison was in contact with the production's accountant; Leonard Kroll kept in touch with the technical crews.

Ashley Boone's and Bob Dingilian's marketing arm of the company planned advertising, publicity, and promotion for each movie; developed a strategy for the movie's release to exhibitors through Warner's distribution department; tracked the daily box office grosses; and handled sales to secondary markets.

A single movie would simultaneously be in several stages of development: in the story department as an idea, getting treatment into script (see *Exhibit 4*); in Joe Graham's hand as a deal being negotiated; in stages of production; and on the market.

To date, the company had produced and released three movies—*Divine Madness, Outland,* and *Body Heat.* Two films were in production and to be releases in 1981: *Blade Runner* and *Looker.* The company would distribute an independently produced film, *Chariots of Fire.* Four other movies were in the development stage.

In making these films, what separated the Ladd Company from other studios was that the partners considered themselves participants in the production process. Several members told us:

> We refuse to be a bank. We insist on taking an active part. Some people like it, some don't, but it's natural for anyone who comes to us with a proposal to say, "I particularly wanted to come to you" and in certain cases, they mean it. They believe we can make a real contribution.

Laddie's team operated very differently from most studio groups. He said:

> Where we differ from most companies is that, generally, one group makes the movies and another group sells them and they don't even talk to each other. But

that's where we work together. Everybody gets involved. I don't ask Ashley or Bob to read the scripts, but yet if they want to, they are entitled to. It's not only the executives. There are some secretaries who like to read all the scripts and tell you exactly what they think and you listen to their opinions as well as the other people.

Scheduled meetings took place in Laddie's office every week: story meetings, marketing meetings, production meetings, and administration meetings. In addition to formal gatherings, the executives spent most of their time with people: on endless telephone calls, impromptu pow-wows, at screenings, in negotiations, at meals. Decision making took place all the time where people gathered. Though there was one person with primary responsibility for each project, everyone else was involved, able to step in to be the project's spokesman. Wigan said:

> In movie companies, egos are constantly scrambling over each other's shoulders or rejoicing at others' misfortunes. That doesn't happen here. If an error has occurred because I overlooked something, the next time a similar situation occurs, my colleagues are not going to sit back and say, "I bet he overlooks that again." They're going to make sure, either by helping me or checking themselves, that the point is not overlooked.

CAST OF CHARACTERS

At the studio, Wigan, Kanter, and Laddie worked as a triumvirate. Wigan described Kanter as the one who attended funerals and functions, being essentially the group's "elder statesman." Kanter was quietly attuned to Laddie at all times. Before joining Laddie in 1975 at the former's studio, Kanter was a top Hollywood agent. He had represented Laddie's father, had worked with Laddie as a producer, and remained a close friend. He was enthusiastic about the negotiations and financing in deal making. Wigan was highly expressive, attuned to the needs of the creative people he worked with. Before he joined Laddie in 1975 at the studio, Wigan had also been both agent and producer; his relationship with Laddie went back some time, as well.

Joe Graham spoke of Paula Weinstein as a "bundle of energy," moving things along when they slowed down. She was a displaced New Yorker, having had an earlier career in government. In 1973, she moved west and returned to a business she had known since childhood. She joined Laddie at the studio, having learned the trade at an agency and having been production vice president at a rival studio.

Burt Morrison had worked at the studio for 19 years, having switched from a career in accounting at the New York offices of Peat, Marwick, Mitchell. He stepped down as executive vice president of finance and administration in the former studio's film division, to run Laddie's financial and administrative operations. He left behind an enormous network of relationships and responsibilities. Others spoke of him as a "quite intelligent force." He told us he provided a certain discipline for the others.

Graham was "the outsider." He had worked with an agency as an attorney when he met Laddie, Kanter, and Wigan as executives at the negotiating table. A good-humored man, Graham had a passion for flying planes, and he kept attuned to the Hollywood gossip.

Like many others in the industry, Bob Dingilian had always worked in entertainment. He started with the Motion Picture Association as office boy, moved to public relations. After running his own firm, he eventually joined Laddie at the studio as vice president—publicity.

He told us he was a "low-keyed, optimistic sort, not a screaming, raving person," and spoke about the importance of family and friends.

Ashley Boone had also stepped down as the head of a large network at the former studio to join Laddie. He had been promoted to president of marketing and had a reputation now throughout the industry for his management of distribution. During our stay, Boone was caught up in the rush of working out up-to-the-minute marketing plans for *Outland*. We did not see much of him.

Leonard Kroll was responsible for overseeing daily production, having the technical know-how built up from years in the business of making pictures. He was a quiet man, he listened carefully, and worked mainly on his own. He spent his time making sure the production teams worked together smoothly.

MEETINGS

Story meetings took place every Friday and Monday over lunch in Laddie's office. Regular members included Laddie, Kanter, Wigan, Weinstein, Morrison, Graham, and Sara Altshul, story editor. On the day the casewriter visited, Laddie relaxed in his easy chair at the head of the table. Kanter sat opposite in his usual place. Altshul sat on the sofa at Laddie's left, Wigan in a chair to his right. Graham and Morrison sat at the other end next to Kanter.

Story meetings usually had a liveliness that made them fun. Morrison said:

> I guess it's the difference between what they regard as really serious business and the stuff that's important but really not. There have been times when the story meeting is really animated and alive, but other times when minutes go by and nobody says anything. That depends on what's going on and what kind of mood everybody's in.
>
> I sometimes get very impatient with it. I don't like long silences, but that is the way Laddie runs the meetings! I mean, the meeting just happens. When somebody thinks of something to say, they say it. If nobody thinks of anything to say, then, nobody says anything. He doesn't have an agenda or anything like that. It just evolves. You gotta get used to that! It's like what Bob Townsend calls "decision by dissolve." Everything kind of dissolves, and the decision gets made!

At the end of the day, we found everyone wandering back in to Laddie's office to have a drink, talk over the day's activities, and find out what the rest of the company was doing. It was a ritual that Laddie had begun at the studio—a way to wind down with friends. Weinstein told us:

> Where he's really brilliant is that there are no secrets. I have never worked in a company where from day one at the studio, at 6:30 or 7:00, whenever you finished the work you were doing, everybody would walk to his office and talk—which meant he was totally accessible to everyone in the company! Everybody got to be a part of it. And he was with the people he trusted, who happened to be all the people who worked for him. Or else they weren't there.

And Kanter told us:

> At the end of each day, we gather in his office and talk over certain things that came to our attention during the day—things of value in terms of information—that he should be aware of.

IF LADDIE LEFT

We talked with members of the team about Laddie's management style and personality and asked them what would happen if Laddie left for the south of France. Initial reaction included:

BOONE: I'd retire to Cap Cod.

WEINSTEIN: I'd take my money and go move to New York, thank you.

DINGILIAN: I'm not going to lead a charge up a hill. I'll follow Laddie.

WIGAN: The company would change its character and I don't know how it would exist. It wouldn't just collapse, but the advance might be rather dissipated.

It was a difficult question to answer. No one offered to take Laddie's place, though Weinstein and Wigan each suggested forming a collective. Morrison said:

> It's hard for me to see us operating the same way. Jay, Gareth, Joe, Ashley—any one of them could take on the responsibility of running the place. But it's really hard for me to see them holding it together. I think Laddie's personality, range of experience, taste and effectiveness is so generally broad as to hold us all together.
>
> Nobody here wants his job, which is unique in an organization. As much as we like each other, it's hard to see the whole team hanging together without him. I don't know if Laddie realizes what an important role he plays.

Boone compared the company to a wheel. Without Laddie, a chunk of the wheel would be missing. Instead of rolling smoothly, it would roll and clunk, roll and clunk.

Though Laddie was hesitant to talk about himself, he was intrigued by the thought of his absence. He thought of himself as fulfilling a necessary role in the company.

> You move as a team, but by the same token, there are certain decisions that one individual has to make. There has to be one central person who listens to everybody, says "yes" or "no," and is the tie-breaker.
> You can't have everybody doing everything together, with nobody doing one job. There has to be someone everybody can come to and say, "Do you know what's happening?"

ALAN LADD

Alan Ladd was not the kind of boss who "played the part." He said, "I wouldn't like it if everybody called me Mr. Ladd. It would make me feel too old." He was very far from the movie mogul type known to play croquet with employees' heads. Laddie's secretary told us, "He's the greatest! He's different than all the others. He doesn't scream, he doesn't yell, he doesn't throw things, and he doesn't use profanity."

When we met Laddie on that Friday in May, he was wearing a European cut yellow cotton shirt, white chinos, white socks, and black loafers. He was a name that came up in every conversation, a presence. When he was in, he was readily available to anyone who walked into his office.

Laddie was a very quiet man. When he spoke, he spoke so softly, you had to strain to hear. He spent much of his time listening. Weinstein said:

> He encourages you to tell him everything. It's almost like he knows you're going to the bathroom. He knows everything. He encourages you to tell him even when it's bad news, or when you screwed up, or when you're confused, or when you don't know an answer to something. He's the first one to say, "I don't know, let's try and talk this thing through"—and you have a discussion about it.

Kanter followed a similar line of thought:

> You also use Laddie to get a reaction as to what direction you should go in. If you're on the wrong track—he had a great ability to say, "Hey, wait a minute, you're really in an area you shouldn't be in." And you stop and think and say, "He's right."

Everyone, including Laddie, told us who was boss. The ultimate decision maker, the one with the final say, was Laddie. But for people who needed room, who needed to feel challenged, Laddie went about it in a special way. Dingilian said, "There are no orders given, there isn't a dictatorial kind of thing that you *will* do it. There is no guide for you to use or instruction booklet that you must follow. People suggest things; out of those suggestions comes an idea that we can all improve on."

The sense of *team* was overwhelming. It was not merely the result of a profit-sharing plan; it existed comfortably side by side with the notion of Laddie as boss. Weinstein said:

> The potential for excitement is really endless, because everything we do, *we* do! And it is we, for as much as we all put emphasis on Laddie, we did it. Laddie doesn't operate without you. He never thinks of anything as his decision, and we don't think of it as his decision.

Kanter felt the membership of the team was a critical factor to their success:

> We're hard people to replace, because of our interworking relationship. You can find people who could do the job, but I don't know how well they would interact. We don't have an ego problem. I don't guard over what I'm doing and say, "Get away from here, don't read that script!" A lot of time is wasted in this industry by people not wanting other people to be involved. If Laddie called the director who's doing this movie and I'm supposed to call him—I mean it's nonsense—who cares?

The groundwork of company culture was based on a handful of principles that Laddie lived by. He said:

> As long as you trust the people you're working with and feel that they are responsible, then you don't ask a lot of questions. The one thing that would undermine that trust would be if I ever caught someone lying. I just have a thing against people lying. It's always so much easier to tell the truth. . . .
>   Or if I heard them talking in earnest against someone in the company outside the company. I can't tolerate people who bully people. I just know these people so well that I know they wouldn't. . . .
>   You must be emotionally aware of people and what their needs are. Each person is individual, and you have to gauge how much latitude they should have or shouldn't have. At what point should they be cut off or allowed to continue on. As long as everybody understands that nobody is out to hurt them or try to undermine them or take credit for something somebody else did, it's okay.
>   As long as people don't work on the "I" principle instead of the "we" principle, then it doesn't seem to cause conflicts.

Most of the do's and don'ts were unspoken. Team members seemed to know where the lines were drawn. Graham talked about his initiation rites: "As for feeling like the new kid on the block, I don't feel that way. I just feel like I'm still having to learn the way that things are done, because a lot of it's done by vibrations or eye signals and it just seems to fall into place as a result of a family who has worked together for so many years."

Laddie used the day's meetings as examples of his style:

> For example, the story meeting. Joe and Burt were there. They aren't required to be there, because they aren't necessarily part of the process. But no one would say, "What's so-and-so doing here?" That's one of the nice things in the company. There are various meetings with various people and yet that doesn't restrict others from coming. Whoever is there is there.

But it isn't the kind of situation where you can say, "I'm in a bad mood today, so I'm not going to join in." That would be irresponsible. We all have our days when we don't feel great. That behavior would be really unprofessional and not tolerated. It's not said that it is tolerated—one just knows.

By the same token, if Burt says he can't make the administration meeting at 10:00 a.m., you accept the fact that Burt knows what the priorities are in his life. Obviously, there is a business or personal priority that was more important than the 10:00 meeting, so we switched it to 4:00. There is certainly an understanding about that.

If Paula comes in late to the story meeting, one doesn't assume that she was fooling around. You assume that there was a reason for it; that she was tied up on the telephone or she had a meeting that was going on too long. Occasionally, if things get sloppy or lax, you may have to point out how many times someone has drifted in late and that the extra phone call is keeping everybody waiting. It may not even be me who says it.

Laddie spoke about the switch to running his own company:

You don't get caught up in corporate politics, or be concerned about the board meetings. You make your own budgets, and there's a great deal more time I have to devote to getting involved with pictures.

Here you're dealing with only 60 people in the whole organization. I always try to get to know all those people. At the studio, we used to be like a family. There were more people, but the same rules applied.

When you start hiring people you have to take into consideration how everybody will get along with everybody. Everyone has a different personality—some are introverts, some are extroverts, some are highly emotional, some are quite relaxed. It's really a question of how the personalities mesh and you have to make that judgment. You go on instincts. That's all you ever do. You can't really tell how someone will function until they're in the company.

Nothing could be worse for me than to walk into a business—no matter how much money I was making, how prestigious the title—and look around and not want to be with people I'm seeing as I walk through the door.

SUCCESS AND FAILURE

Failure was something the group faced all the time. "If our movie fails," said Dingilian, "I would feel terrible. It's a death in the family." Morrison said, "If you really get yourself emotionally torn up over blowing five million bucks on a film—if Laddie were that kind of guy—he'd be a basket case! He keeps a lot inside. He's a very withdrawn, subdued guy. You can tell he's tense if you know him well, but he never seems really angry at anybody. A lot of that is self-control he imposes upon himself that isn't necessarily healthy."

Successes are, as Kanter told us, an emotional high. "When *Star Wars* was released, we couldn't believe it. It was like we were getting a shot of adrenalin 24 hours a day—which had to end—and then suddenly it was a very big letdown. What I find exciting about this business is, it's a series of ups and downs. Like any emotional high which you're going to feel, you're going to feel some day a very big emotional low."

Laddie saw his role as smoothing out the highs and lows, trying to keep everything in its proper perspective:

> There's no sense letting everybody go to pieces if something is failing, and there's no sense letting everybody be so euphoric that they're not doing their work if something is succeeding.
>
> If someone's doing terrific and is happy you don't come in in the morning and throw ice water all over them. But you have to say at some point, "Stop dining out on that."
>
> Or if something has gone badly, you don't walk in and say, "It's a joyous day, the sun is shining." But if it continues, you have to stop and say, "Hey, this is yesterday's business; let's go on to the next thing."

Sharing successes and failures among the group provided a freedom from carrying the entire burden. Several people were involved in making any major decisions. Although each project was supervised by one individual, she or he did not own it. Laddie never pointed a finger and nobody ever said, "That's my picture."

Sharing success multiplied the pleasure, Wigan said. "The nicest thing about having a birthday party is to have all your best friends around you celebrating. It has to be somebody's cake, and it may be yours, but the real joy is that all your best friends are there."

Sharing failure cuts the pain. Kanter told us:

> If something is failing, we tend to regard it as our failure, not the guy who's working on it—it's a group effort, so we all share this problem. You don't get to the depths as much that way—there's a time when someone in our group says, "Hey, let's cheer up! It isn't all that bad."

The company was in its first year of full production. Would everything they touched turn to gold? "Everybody's watching to see," said Weinstein. "There's enormous expectation because of the collective group; and we have high expectations. We want to be successful! It matters to us beyond just the money, although that's the symbol of it. It matters a whole lot creatively."

EXHIBIT 1 DOMESTIC MOVIE MARKET (000,000)

	U.S. Box Office Receipts	Theater Attendance	Average Ticket Price
1970	$1,429.2	920.6	$1.55
1971	1,349.5	820.3	1.65
1972	1,583.1	934.1	1.69
1973	1,515.8	860.3	1.76
1974	1,879.8	995.7	1.89
1975	2,051.4	1,001.7	2.05
1976	1,934.6	909.1	2.13
1977	2,217.1	993.8	2.23
1978	2,470.5	1,054.4	2.34
1979	2,636.8	1,047.6	2.52
1980	2,568.8	954.6	2.69
1/1–7/31/80	1,556.7	584.2	2.66
1/1–7/31/81	1,654.4	600.4	2.76
Δ 1970–1980	6.0% P.A.	.4%	5.7%

Source: Motion Picture Association of America.

EXHIBIT 2 THE LADD COMPANY

ALL-TIME FILM RENTAL CHAMPIONS—TOP TEN
(figures signify rentals received by distributors from U.S.–Canada market only)
as of 1/82

Title	Distributor	Date of Release	Total Rentals*
Star Wars	Fox	1977	$175,685,000
The Empire Strikes Back	Universal	1975	133,439,000
Jaws	Fox	1980	134,680,000
Grease	Paramount	1978	96,300,000
The Exorcist	Warner Brothers	1973	88,900,000
The Godfather	Paramount	1972	86,279,000
Superman	Warner Brothers	1978	82,500,000
The Sound of Music	Fox	1965	79,748,000
The Sting	Universal	1973	78,963,000
Close Encounters of the Third Kind	Columbia	1977	77,000,000

1980 FILM RENTAL CHAMPIONS—TOP TEN

Title	Distributor	Date of Release	Total Rentals*
The Empire Strikes Back	Fox	5/80	120,000,000
Kramer vs. Kramer	Columbia	12/79	60,528,000
The Jerk	Universal	12/79	43,000,000
Airplane	Paramount	7/80	38,000,000
Smokey and the Bandit	Universal	8/80	37,600,000
Coal Miner's Daughter	Universal	3/80	36,000,000
Private Benjamin	Warner Brothers	10/80	33,500,000
Blues Brothers	Universal	6/80	31,000,000
The Electric Horseman	Columbia	12/79	30,917,000
The Shining	Warner Brothers	5/80	30,200,000
			460,745,000

* Not to be confused with total box office ticket sales gross.
Source: *Variety,* 1/14/81.

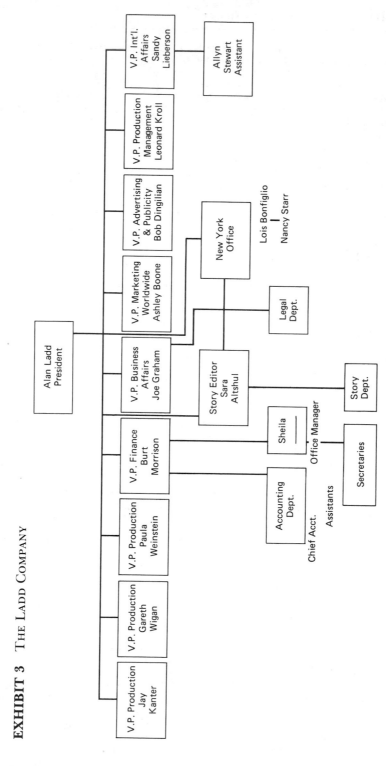

EXHIBIT 3   THE LADD COMPANY

EXHIBIT 4

Title: *THE FIFTH HORSEMAN*

Author: Larry Collins and Dominique Lapierre

Sub by: Interoffice

Via: Sara Altshul

Analyst: Diana Birchall

Elements:

Date: May 11, 1981

Form/Pgs: Novel, 478 pages, pub. Simon & Schuster, 1980

Location: Washington, New York, Libya, Israel, France

Circa: Present

Category: Libyans plant an H-bomb in New York City

Plot: The PRESIDENT of the U.S. gets a message from Libyan President QADDAFI saying that a hydrogen bomb has been placed in New York City and will be exploded in "sixty-three hours from midnight," killing upwards of five million people, unless the President persuades Israel to withdraw from "illegal settlements" taken in 1967. If New York is evacuated, the bomb will go off, as it will if Libya is destroyed. Teams feverishly search the city (the cover story is that a barrel of chlorine gas is missing), and the story of how the Libyans got the bomb and brought it into the city is pieced together. The plutonium came from a·reactor sold to the Libyans by the French; the know-how was obtained through the murder of a French scientist, and the bomb was smuggled into New York on a freighter. An Arab woman, LAILA, and her two brothers, WHALID and KAMAL, are in charge of the operation. When Kamal discovers that Whalid had second thoughts and didn't set the bomb properly, he kills his brother and returns to the city from his upstate hideout. Police detective ROCCHIA shoots him as he reaches the warehouse where the bomb is kept, and it is safely defused.

	Exclnt	Good	Fair	Poor
Characterization			X	
Dialogue		X		
Structure			X	
Uniqueness of Story Line		X		
Uniqueness of Setting (And other production values)		X		

Check One {

Budget: High _____ Medium __X__ Low _____

Windham Hill Productions

> We invented a genre of music, sort of by mistake. Nobody thought it was financially worthwhile to do it. Yet we did it.
>
> Will Ackerman

Windham Hill Productions began modestly in 1976. Will Ackerman and Anne Robinson had met at Stanford University as undergraduates. He was writing music for campus theatrical productions; she was designing costumes for them. After dropping out during her senior year and working at a number of jobs including art teacher and stewardess, Anne wound up as a bookkeeper at The Plowshare, a bookstore in Palo Alto. Will, also a dropout from Stanford, had his own contracting and carpentry business, Windham Hill Builders. The rest, as they say, is music history.

Known locally for his live performances and theatre work, Will was constantly asked by friends to make home-brewed tapes of his guitar playing. So he finally decided to make a privately pressed record. Obtaining $5 from each of 60 friends and fans, he made a record, whimsically called "Search for The Turtle's Navel." For record jackets, Will and Anne used Louisiana prison work song albums and glued homemade covers on top. According to Ackerman, there was never an intention to start a whole record label. As he puts it:

> The sum extent and intent was to sell those 300 pressings. There was no design, no philosophy, no concept behind what we did. It was purely subjective.[1]

* * * * *

> Three hundred records was the minimum order the pressing plant required. I fully envisioned a closet in my house laden with at least 100 extra records for the rest of my life.[2]

---

[1] *Honolulu Advertiser,* "He's Behind the Windham Hill Sound of Music," April 1, 1987.

[2] *New York Times,* "Windham Hill Records," May 4, 1986.

This case was prepared by Associate Professor John Kao.

Echoing this sentiment, Anne said:

> Money was never the objective. . . . We never meant it to be a business. It was an off-the-wall project, like cutting wood for the afternoon.[3]

After considerable debate, Will and Anne agreed to supply several local radio stations with free copies of "Turtle." The response was overwhelming. "Turtle" became a perennial in the Windham Hill Productions catalogue and eventually went on to sell over 300,000 copies. And Windham Hill Productions went on to become an internationally recognized record label, reluctantly identified with the New Age music genre, with several dozen artists, some 50 employees, and 1986 revenues estimated at over $30 million.

NEW AGE MUSIC

Described as "soothing and invigorating" by its adherents, and "Yuppie muzak," "music to wash one's BMW by," and "audio valium" by its detractors, New Age music emerged as an ill-defined musical category in the mid-1970s. Many profess dissatisfaction with the label. Says Ackerman, "I have trouble with 'New Age.' I don't know what it means. If I catch the guy who coined the phrase, I'll strangle him."[4] Furthermore, he stated:

> I am the producer of a lot of these records and I know the emotional depth from which these pieces come. These artists are intelligent, articulate, sensitive, and very creative people. And since I know this, it helps me be less defensive.[5]

New Age music has garnered approximately 2% of revenues from total record, cassette, and compact disc sales of about $4.4 billion. This is roughly equivalent to annual sales of all classical records. In an era where record sales are declining, New Age is a growing segment of the market.

New Age defies categorization. While including artists who rely on the timbral beauty of such traditional instruments as acoustic guitar and piano, it also embraces the high-tech world of synthesizers and advanced recording studio techniques. Known for the pure sound of pianist George Winston, it also includes the electrical sounds of Shadowfax. It sounds like folk, but isn't folk. It has jazz elements, but isn't jazz. Said one critic from *Rolling Stone* magazine, "It doesn't rock, it rarely swings, it's never heavy, you can't really dance to it, and it has precious little soul."[6] Perhaps echoing this genre confusion, one of Windham Hill's only display ads in a trade publication included the words "folk," "pop," and "jazz" crossed out one by one followed by the words "Windham Hill."

[3] *Times Tribune,* "Money Was Not the Motive," May 16, 1985.
[4] *Honolulu Advertiser,* "He's Behind the Windham Hill Sound of Music," April 1, 1987.
[5] *Cashbox* Interview, Will and Anne Ackerman, January 28, 1984.
[6] *Rolling Stone,* March 17, 1983.

Analysts are often at a loss to account for the success of New Age music. However, demographics tell at least part of the story. Studies by Windham Hill show that the average age of its customers is 32, and that they are urban and upscale.

Perhaps in recognition of these desirable demographics, the emergence of New Age has given rise to new radio station formats. In February 1987, Los Angeles' KMET, rated number one in the 1970s for album-oriented rock, became KTWV, the WAVE. Pioneering a new format in radio, the station has no disc jockeys introducing the music. Listeners wanting information about records and performers must call up the station. Audience reaction spans the gamut. One listener gushed that the WAVE "Opens the door to a better tomorrow, reminds each of us that love, empathy, and compassion lead to survival, growth, self-fulfillment and the eventual realization of world peace." Said another, "It stinks. It sucks. I hate it more than life itself."[7]

In recognition of the growing importance of New Age music, the influential Grammy Awards in March 1987 presented for the first time an award in the New Age category. That award went to the Swiss harpist Andreas Vollenweider.

The future of New Age is uncertain. Some feel that New Age will be a major factor for years to come. Others are less certain. A spokesperson for CBS Records was recently quoted as saying, "There is almost a glut of New Age music. I think there's a danger of boredom creeping in."

WINDHAM HILL PRODUCTIONS

Windham Hill gave birth to the whole New Age surge, says James D. Fishel, executive director of the Recording Industry Association of America in New York.

The Windham Hill phenomenon has led to unusual forms of customer behavior. While it is unheard of to hear people asking for a record by its label, i.e., "Give me a record by CBS or RCA," they are prone to do so with Windham Hill products because of their attachment to the brand. It is one of the few companies that has a bin under its own name in prominent record stores such as Tower Records. "People take a chance on any Windham Hill record because they like the other six records they own from the label. That doesn't happen very often," says Fishel. The company also inspires brand loyalty through samplers and multiartist "concert" albums. The success of the company can be measured in numerous ways. For example, Windham Hill albums have long shelf life. Issues that are 10 years old still sell over 20,000 copies a year. The company, according to Ackerman, has never had a losing record, and each project goes into the black on initial orders.

Windham Hill grew slowly. Ackerman gave the company the name of his contracting firm which had been building luxury homes in Northern

[7] *Wall Street Journal*, "Yuppie Radio," June 18, 1987.

California at Sea Ranch and Lake Tahoe. Until 1982, the company had two employees named Will and Anne, and until then neither took a salary. It sold much of its product through unconventional distribution channels such as health food stores, bookstores, and mom and pop establishments. It was only in 1985 that Anne decided to get a receptionist for the office. Describing the development of the company, Will said:

> The evolution was like this: When you start a company you don't care who's what. I was basically doing everything. She (Anne) was doing bookkeeping at a bookstore at the time and she also kept the books for Windham Hill. If I was real busy she'd call the distributors and ask for our payment or send out invoices. Then we hired an employee, then two employees, then there was our first office in Palo Alto. When there were enough employees, it became necessary to ascribe titles. I remember thinking that was a big yuck: I was the president of Windham Hill, Anne was vice president.[8]

See *Exhibits 1* and *2* for more data on Windham Hill's organization and financial milestones.

In 1980, the company signed a distribution agreement with Pickwick, a subsidiary of American Can. Subsequently, Pickwick folded and Windham Hill negotiated a worldwide distribution agreement with A&M records. Although the terms of the deal are not public, Mr. Ackerman has called it the most "enlightened contract ever written in the record industry." Windham Hill retained complete quality and artistic control over its records, the option to create new labels, and the choice of how many or few releases to make in a given year.

A breakthrough for the company came from its association with the pianist George Winston. Ackerman tells the story:

> I originally intended to sign George as a guitarist. I was sleeping at his house in LA and he played me this slide-guitar stuff. I said, "George, this is fabulous, we're gonna do an album." He said, "Great." Then he said, "Hey, do you mind if I play the piano a little bit while you're going to sleep?" That was the end of the guitar album.[9]

Winston's pristine piano improvisations struck a resonant chord. To date, two of his records have gone gold (greater than 500,000 copies) and one has gone platinum (greater than a million copies). By contrast most jazz releases average 50,000 units. It is also striking to note that the production costs of *Autumn,* a Winston release which went gold, are described as $1,720.

In 1986, a management reorganization took place. Anne became president, while Will focused more on working with Windham Hill's artists. Describing this episode, Will said:

> I had to bail out. Last summer we were in a meeting of the board of directors and I just looked over at Anne with a smile on my face and said—not angrily,

---

[8] *Cashbox* Interview, Will and Anne Ackerman, January 28, 1984.
[9] *Rolling Stone,* March 17, 1983.

not bitterly—"I quit." Outside, she asked, "What does this mean?" I said, "It means I am tired of having to shoulder all the personal, emotional, physical, 28-hours-a-day responsibilities of the company. I can't do it anymore." She became CEO and president of Windham Hill. She shouldered an incredible amount of work and responsibility.[10]

Ackerman's current role is to work with artists in an A&R (artists and repertoire) role. As such, he is the final arbiter of taste. He has stated that the criterion for what he records is "Do I cry when I hear it?"[11] He negotiates contracts, creates new labels, and develops new concepts to keep the company evolving. He is working on developing ventures in video, feature films, and book publishing. The job has not been without its pressures. Ackerman is known to joke about his high blood pressure.

As producer, Ackerman, puts his artists

. . . through the wringer because I basically want to know every note and chord change that's going down. It can drive them crazy. We don't like egos here. I don't run a Boy Scout camp, but I won't sign druggies and drunks and schizophrenics. Our guys are eloquent, productive, and can knock them out . . . I have never relied on commercial potential as a criterion, but only whether the music reaches my heart. I never want to proliferate to a large catalog. I know the core sound of what Windham Hill is, and I want to pay homage to that.[12]

*　　*　　*　　*　　*

I'm sure there is a meditative aspect to it. Ours is an intensely profound music that speaks to our audience with remarkable intimacy, from the composer-musician in them. The theme of our label is a return to the natural stable elements of life, not an examination of twentieth century tensions. I like to see our music not as an escape but as a place to go for a while in order to return to the fight.[13]

The Windham Hill company philosophy was recently stated by Ackerman:

Windham Hill is basically a collection of friends. We don't have multiple album contacts. Every artist is free to pick up and go if they're unhappy with us and as yet no one has left. It really is a cooperative environment, not only for artists in relation to the company, but I'd like to think with the people who work for the company. The notion of ethics in business as opposed to getting what you can and moving on has always dictated the way we've done business.[14]

Windham Hill sought to differentiate itself from other record companies in many ways. For example, the packaging differed from industry norms.

[10] *Cashbox* Interview, Will and Anne Ackerman, January 28, 1984.
[11] *Wall Street Journal,* December 13, 1983.
[12] *GQ,* "Mood Music for the Eighties," April 1984.
[13] *GQ,* "Mood Music for the Eighties," April 1984.
[14] *Cashbox* Interview, Will and Anne Ackerman, January 28, 1984.

Anne, who had studied art, designs all the album covers using stark white backgrounds and beautiful color photographs. The covers are double laminated to give them a pleasing glossiness. The albums are also wrapped loosely in plastic instead of shrink wrap. They are also recorded with state-of-the-art digital recording processes, and captured the attention of audiophiles. On the technology front, the company, led by Ackerman, is experimenting with new vinyl compounds, digital technology, new audio tape formulations, and compact disc technology.

The company's business practices also differ from the norm. In the past, Windham Hill used to spend less than 1% of revenues on sales. Currently it spends about 8%, still well below the industry standard of 30%. Sales in 1981 were $150,000 from 50,000 units. Since then the company's sales have more than doubled most years. Sales in 1982 were $2 million; in 1983, $8 million. Sales in 1985 were estimated at $25 million, 1986 sales at $30 million. Ackerman describes this rate of growth as "organic. We have never had to capitalize the business from the day it was started with a few five dollar bills." In addition, the company has never borrowed to finance operations.

As for market research, Ackerman has the following observation:

> We don't strategize about what kind of music the market wants. We believe in what we are doing and it just turns out that there's a market for good-quality music.[15]

Meanwhile, Windham Hill has also diversified. Its contract with A&M allows it to create new labels. It has several spin-off labels including Open Air Records, which features vocal music; Magenta Records, which specializes in jazz; and a reissue label called Lost Lake Arts. Dancing Cat Records is George Winston's own label. Through Paramount Pictures, it has also released a series of music video cassettes. Windham Hill also was the first product on a new video technology made by the LaserDisc Corporation in Japan. When asked about fans who "felt betrayed" by Windham Hill's movement into newer, nonacoustic musical areas, Ackerman said:

> Oh, gimme a break. Windham Hill is nothing if it isn't evolutionary. Part of the reason we're still here, and still vital, is that we have evolved, and aren't still doing solo guitar records of the folk derivative type.

The Windham Hill roster has included guitarist Ackerman and de Grassi, Michael Hedges, Mark Isham, Scott Cossu, Daniel Hecht, David Qualey, Bola Sete, Basho, and the electric group, Shadowfax.

The success of Windham Hill has spawned competition. Recording industry giants MCA, RCA, and CBS are creating New Age labels. Recently, Alex de Grassi, Ackerman's cousin, and Liz Story left Windham Hill for RCA's competitive label, Novus Records, headed for a time by former

---

[15] *New Age,* "Windham Hill, a Business with Heart and Style," July 1983.

Windham Hill executive Steve Backer. And Shadowfax has gone to Capital Records.

WILL ACKERMAN

Born in West Germany, Ackerman was an orphan who came to the U.S. at age nine as the adopted son of Robert W. Ackerman, a specialist in Old English philology at Stanford University. Attending prep school in southern Vermont, Will did odd jobs at nearby Windham Hill Farm, a country inn where he washed dishes and learned the fundamentals of carpentry. When his family returned to California in the 1960s, he attended Stanford, majored in English, considered working towards a Ph.D. but instead dropped out to become a contractor and carpenter. In his words:

> I remember coming up against a paper for Comparative Religions that was filled with all kinds of room to b.s., but I couldn't squeeze out another word. I was absolutely blocked. I took it as a sign. I went to my dad and told him I was dropping out. He sat there stunned for a while—I didn't know whether he was going to cry or kill me. Instead, he reached for the telephone and, right on the spot, submitted his resignation to the university. He got a big smile on his face and said, "I'm kind of sick of this place, too."[16]

In 1977, Ackerman and Robinson married. Speaking of his relationship with Anne, Will said:

> We are the best friends in the world and the best business partners that could ever be. I am obviously somewhat expansive, and sort of like, "Well, we are going to start a winery!" And then Annie, rather than being a downer is, instead of going "Ya how the hell you gonna do that?" she'll say, "Great, how do you want to do that, how's that going to work, how do you see that thing working?" Then she is so competent at detail work and figuring out how the budget is going to be arranged for that and what investment can come out of where. She enables me to do these things, and then she participates in it too.[17]

Describing the nature of their relationship, Anne Robinson says:

> We are the kind of people who say, "Here's a goal, when I get there I'm going to know I got there," or "I'm making a rational decision." Will will probably tell you that he has never made a rational decision in his life and in a way I believe that's true for both of us. I think we got somewhere and realized we were there, and we said, "Oh, that's very interesting—so this is what I do." You could blame it on a lack of planning. You could say that it's lack of vision. I like to believe that it's belief in it so much that wherever it takes you is OK and that you have the skills to deal with whatever it's going to hand you when you get there. Because I think if you ponder something too much, you're going to lose the life of it. It's just going to stop breathing on you. We always made decisions just, "What does it need?—great. Let's do it."[18]

[16] *Cashbox* Interview, Will and Anne Ackerman, January 28, 1984.
[17] Michael Ray and Will Ackerman, Interview, 1984.
[18] Michael Ray and Anne Robinson, Interview, 1984.

Despite the dynamism in their partnership, they were divorced in 1982. Robinson, who has remarried, said the following:

> It was hard to draw the line between self and work. You lose the things that make a marriage work. Even if you're in a wonderful business, you have to work at the marriage too. If the business hadn't been so successful, we might still be married. We put a tremendous amount of energy into the business and kind of forgot about the rest of our life. We trust each other so very much, I can't imagine doing this without him. There was never a question of continuing despite the divorce. The financial split is vaguely 50-50.[19]

Today, she and Ackerman remain good friends, in addition to remaining sole owners of their company. She is remarried to a one-time Outward Bound course director, now working on a Ph.D. at Stanford's School of Education. Raising a family, she says, is "not realistic for now. The downside is I'm not home much. I'm very committed to this."

For the past three years, Ackerman has been working part time on building a house in Vermont. He claims to still feel most at home in New England.

> It's a different way of life up here. I read. I take walks. And I'm always working with a chain saw or a hammer or something. That's the one thing I love. When I'm at home in California, all I can do is sit around on the phone and make deals and all that other crap. . . . Frankly, this business of my turning into a big executive is all a joke.[20]

See *Exhibit 4* for further thoughts of Will Ackerman on music, business, and creativity.

THE ORGANIZATION

In describing Windham Hill's organizational objectives, Will has said, "We are very serious about trying to run an enlightened business. We're interested in the long run, and in the long run the way you treat people is important."[21]

The company has an executive committee which serves to recommend decisions to Anne and Will. It meets every three to four weeks and includes Anne, the company's controller, and all VPs including operations, marketing, and international. It deals with major issues, serving to inform, come to decisions, set policy, and operate as recommending body.

The company also has a marketing committee including representatives from promotion, publicity, sales, marketing, operations, international, and A&R. Before a release hits the street, this group formulates marketing plans and decides on advertising placement.

---

[19] *Savvy,* "Here's to You Mrs. Robinson," September 1987.
[20] *Inc.,* "The House That Windham Hill Built," August 1987.
[21] *New Age,* "Windham Hill, A Business with Heart and Style," July 1983.

As of January 1988, Windham Hill had 50 employees, including Will and Anne. These included corporate headquarters in Palo Alto, marketing in Los Angeles, and regional managers in Chicago, New York, and Europe. See *Exhibit 3* for more information on the company's people and organization.

When asked "What's different from the good old days?," Jim Cahalan, VP of operations, focused on new personnel systems such as formal job descriptions. Each new position now carried a detailed job description with defined reporting lines and descriptions of the nature of routine work to be carried out. The company's employee review process was described as thorough. Reviews take place 3, 6, and 12 months after a hire or transfer to a new position, and then annually thereafter. The company also believed in sharing its success through salary levels and bonuses above average for the industry. All employees were 100% vested in the company's profit sharing and pension plans after three years of employment. In addition, there was an informal system of discretionary bonuses administered by Anne and Will.

The company was now looking for the most highly trained professional individuals to fill jobs. It now rarely advertised for job candidates but did believe in personal referrals. In the old days, people "wandered onto the scene." According to Jim, functional managers in such areas as accounting, sales, and shipping had little or no formal experience. The company developed its own unique approach to business management. It was a style described as "refreshing," but as systems became more complex the limitations of people became evident. The growth of the organization outstripped the ability of people to grow with it. For example, accounting took a quantum leap in complexity, and the solution involved hiring a more competent person above the original employee. It was impossible to teach someone to be a CPA on-the-job. The company's management style in the past consisted of taking responsibility for doing it yourself. Everyone would listen in. Anne's office was in middle of the office with no acoustic privacy. One could literally hear what was going on. Things somehow jelled, but it took time for formal communication systems to catch up as the company got larger.

Many old timers dropped out amicably as jobs became more sophisticated. Some didn't want to take additional responsibility. They never really wanted the job but because they were the oldest employees they had the opportunity. Some left to go back to small business. Employees were encouraged to get training to upgrade their skills.

The company was described as rewarding honesty both in business transactions and internally. Such behavior might be lauded at staff meetings. Said Cahalan, "Mistakes are OK. It's what you learn from them that's important. There is not a lot of the CYA attitude. It's very refreshing; there are no stresses from politics."

What were the core values of the company? Jim Cahalan detailed three:

1. Honesty and integrity in doing business. This went beyond business transactions, and included quality in the relationship between Windham Hill and the end user, providing a high-quality product in terms of music, packaging, and mechanism of delivery. In Cahalan's words, "We don't beat

customers over the head with hype. We respect their intelligence. We're honest and tell them what the music is about."

2. Striving to be innovative. Said Cahalan:

A lot of us are the kind of people that throw away the directions and figure out how to put something together ourselves. We don't take anything for granted, but we don't set out every morning to reinvent the wheel either. We examine our ideas and traditional practices. We don't feel bad about deviating from common wisdom except with technical areas such as generally accepted accounting principles. Often we come up with a creative solution—i.e., our alternative sales department which gets bookstores to stock product. We recently designed a package which fits our cassettes into foamcore, shrink-wrapped book-sized packages suitable for stocking at B. Dalton's. As another example, the industry thinks radio promotion is critical—i.e., getting your record played on the air. We think of promotion as more holistic; touring, getting local press articles, publicity. We don't see any boundaries between publicity, promotion, sales, marketing, and artists which exist in normal record corporations. All those elements sit down together. This is now institutionalized by the way our marketing committee works. This doesn't happen at other record companies. These functions don't mesh. At times they work at odds with each other. We also look for other outlets for promotion, which are unusual by industry standards.

3. Monitoring quality. Quality is important, in terms of manufacturing, production standards, artistic standards, and the quality of the interaction between company and its customers.

Cahalan also emphasized the importance of human resource practices. In the early days, we were small and had no formal review process, no system for evaluating salaries. Everything was done on a personal concern basis by Will and Anne. As things got busier, it was tough to rely on personal concern. The wisest policy is to pay higher than standard and to reexamine compensation frequently because of growth. Some positions were getting evaluated three times per year. The biggest mistake that largest companies make is to underpay their support staff. What they get is what they deserve: high turnover, poorly trained people causing problems when people perceive you as being unprofessional and inept. The company's review process is also a way of evaluating management, getting a feel for how they are doing.

If I were a public relations person, I might be scrambling to get any kind of coverage. I'd bring a lot of old habits forward. It takes supervision and education to change habits. Even though we seek highly professional people, we don't like to hire from within the record industry. People carry their bad habits. For PR we have a good book publicist. Our business has a lot of parallels with the book industry. These hiring practices help us to stay on the original track.

THE FUTURE

From November 30 to December 4, 1987 Windham Hill held its first set of off-site planning meetings in Napa Valley north of San Francisco. The purpose of this meeting was to set objectives for the year. One manager called the meeting "a definite milestone, a way of saying goodbye to the old one-room company."

Reflecting on the impact of growth, Jim Cahalan remarked:

As we grow, there will be inevitable compromises and some problems. It will be harder to find the right people with the same set of values. Each person doesn't get the same kind of holistic view of the company right from the start. Positions become specialized. The company hires because of specific needs. Jobs are very busy right from the beginning. The company needs to sit them down and tell them. There is nothing like letting things soak in from being around the key people. People will feel more distance from the founders and the mission. We will need to develop formal systems to accomplish this. Ultimately it's inevitable that people are going to feel more distant.

Will said:

It never occurred to us that we were really starting a business. Had that concept been something we discussed, in fact, I don't think we'd be here now. . . . We broke every rule there was because basically we had no idea what the rules were. But we are now moving from the entrepreneurial stage to the management stage as a company. It is a very cutthroat business, and we are now a very managed company.[22]

Reflecting on his changed role in the company, he said:

All of the things I'm saying about the initial phases of Windham Hill I need to temper now in that I need to objectify at this point, I need to create trends, I need to see the direction of the label, I need to think of balance in the catalogue.

Both Will and Anne were adamant about the importance of maintaining challenge. Anne said:

The day that it ceases to be of interest to both of us is the day we are really gonna bag it. Jokes aside. The day that it ceases to be interesting and a challenge is the day we are going to say, "There is no life-blood in it for us, and we can't give it any, so we better get out of here."

And Will said:

But as far as holding onto the magic, I guess the death knell for me would be when I became bored and when I didn't feel that by, you know, shouting something down the tube that it wouldn't rattle people. If I didn't feel that I could get on the phone to Jeff Hyman who's our promotion head and say, "Jeff, this tape I've just heard is going to blow you away—you won't believe this," and have Jeff say "God, give me the thing, get it to me, I want to hear it immediately!" As soon as I perceive that I'm not excited anymore and that I can't communicate my excitement down the tube, then I'm going to get worried. Another issue in dealing with the magic is that, magic is going to last only so long. And you've got to change. Change becomes one of the elements in retaining this magic.[23]

---

[22] *San Jose Mercury News,* "New Age Maestros," December 22, 1986.
[23] Michael Ray and Will Ackerman, Interview, 1984.

EXHIBIT 1 WINDHAM HILL PRODUCTIONS

MILESTONES

1976—Windham Hill Productions begins

1978—Will works full time at Windham Hill Productions

1980—the business moves out of the Ackerman house and into a real office

1981—The company incorporates

1982—Will and Anne start paying themselves a salary

1984—Anne hires an assistant

EXHIBIT 2 ESTIMATES OF WHP PRODUCTION REVENUES FROM THE TRADE PRESS

1981—$150,000
1982—$2 million
1983—$8 million
1985—$25 million
1986—+$30 million

EXHIBIT 3 PEOPLE AND ORGANIZATION

Palo Alto

Anne Robinson
Anne's assistant
5—accounting
2—royalty and contract administration
3—art department
2—personnel
2—international
7—alternative sales department (sales to nonrecord store outlets such as
    bookstores, health food. Also includes direct mail)
receptionist
Jim Cahalan—VP operations—general manager
    no marketing—except on marketing committee, not promotion and publicity
Jim's assistant
West Coast regional manager—promotion/PR/sales

Los Angeles Office

12—sales, marketing, promotion, publicity
2—manufacturing and quality control
VP sales and marketing—
assistant
general office staff

Sausalito Office

Will Ackerman
Will's assistant
VP of A&R
assistant
staff engineer/producer
2—clerical

Regional Managers
(Operating out of A&M offices, but paid by Windham Hill)

Chicago
Brooklyn
Dallas
Europe

EXHIBIT 4 QUOTES FROM WILLIAM ACKERMAN (Michael Ray and Will Ackerman, Interview, 1984)

A&S is solely my function at Windham Hill. The criteria for that decision making are as mystical to me as anything else. Either it completely floors you, you have chills, it brings a tear to your eye or it doesn't. And no amount of objectification about, yeah, this guy is touring, he's got a great manager, he's going to be a hit, makes any difference.

* * * * *

I am not a studied musician. I don't read a note of standard notation or tabliture. So everything I do is rather improvisational at least in its conception or inception. Later, I hone it into a piece. But it's usually a matter of my going up into the Sierras. I religiously go up into the Sierras the last weekend before the snow falls or perhaps when the first snow falls, hopefully with a full moon. Go up with a bottle of Wild Turkey, get really nuts and wander around the hills completely nuts and usually three or four good pieces will come out of that. I'm utterly serious!

* * * * *

People are the essence of the whole damn thing. It's building the momentum behind something and getting people excited and organizing them and having this go into a logistical flow that comes out to X number of end results. I love all the people who work for the company. I trust them implicitly. I think that their goals are very similar to my own. I think that the loyalty that we have out of the artists is paralleled by the loyalty we have out of the employees based on some fairly enlightened business relationships, employee to employer.

* * * * *

The objectives were simple. To do the music that mattered to me, that spoke eloquently to me and to package it, to manufacture it in the way that would best indicate the pride that I felt in it.

* * * * *

I expected some science, but experience is that all of the images behind the white coat or any kind of facade that any business puts up is all "a little of this and a little of that." I haven't found any science in anything I've ever done.

* * * * *

I want to work with people who I feel are positive and who will contribute back to this company, who will not be company people necessarily and go out waving the Windham Hill banner, but at least are not malcontents. . . . It all boils down to working with the people you want to work with, who are creative and positive. Who won't just drain you. Who will give you something back, so you can continue giving and appear to be an altruist every now and again. . . . I would say that my greatest talent, and I do see it as a creative talent, is working with people. And warming people up to ideas and getting them excited about it. So in that respect I'm creative, and I guess I'm creative because I do music and all the rest of it. But certainly don't put it in an echelon that is elevated above what I see as the norm in other human beings.

* * * * *

There are no plans. I have a rough idea of where the door goes and then I realize that hemlock tree out there deserves framing, so it needs a window but the stairs are going to go there, and so it's going to have to be a little higher, but I want some light. . . . I mean, that's the way the whole thing has gone, basically.

Catalyst Technologies

I'm sort of a honeybee. I like to fly from flower to flower and pollinate them.

Walt Disney as quoted by
Nolan Bushnell

Nolan walks in the front door with that smile on his face and puffin' on that pipe, and it's like a whirling dervish walked in. People's hair stands on end. Their eyes get like saucers. And they flock around him like J.C. the Man just walked in.

A formal Bushnell colleague

My name is Nolan Bushnell, but I'm not God.

Nolan Bushnell

NOLAN BUSHNELL

Nolan Bushnell, founder of Catalyst Technologies, has been described by more than one observer as the heir apparent to the throne left vacant by the death of Walt Disney. Bushnell has been involved in a wide range of post-1960s entertainment companies whose products and services range from videogames, to domestic robots, to add-on card sets for the Trivial Pursuit game that sported such novel titles as "Vices" and "Rich and Famous." Unifying most of Bushnell's business activities has been the desire to blend technology and entertainment values in startling, new, and unreservedly commercial ways.

Bushnell was born in Clearfield, Utah. He was educated at Utah State and at the University of Utah where he studied economics, engineering, philosophy, mathematics, and business. He spent summers in charge of the games department at a local amusement park. Turned down for a job at Disney, Bushnell moved to Santa Clara County, California, where he worked as an electrical engineer at Ampex.

Late at night, in a home lab carved out from his daughter's bedroom, Bushnell developed a videogame called Computer Space. In 1971, he incorporated himself, first under the name Syzygy, Inc. and subsequently as

This case was prepared by Associate Professor John Kao.

Atari. ("Atari" is a Japanese term from the game of "Go" which roughly corresponds to the concept of "check" in chess.) Bushnell then hit upon the idea for a videogame version of the classic game of ping pong. Pong was an overnight success. The fledgling Atari had sales of over $3 million in 1973 and it proceeded to grow by leaps and bounds as the videogame industry mushroomed.

Bushnell sold Atari to Warner Communications in 1976 for $28 million, a spectacular return on his initial $500 investment in his start-up. His personal net worth at the time was estimated at $15 million. A key condition of the sale bound Bushnell to a seven-year noncompetition agreement. In 1979 he was ousted from Atari because of "management differences."

Bushnell's life-style was fast and well publicized. Divorced in 1974, he took to flying around the country in his Lear jet and sailing on his yacht which sported the name Pong. He bought a 16-acre northern California estate equipped with riding stables, a swimming pool, and tennis courts. He also acquired homes in Paris and Aspen, Colorado. By the early 1980s, his net worth was estimated in the range of $70 million.

Bushnell's first major venture after Atari was Pizza Time Theatre, a concept restaurant chain founded in 1978, which expanded so rapidly that it twice made *Inc.* magazine's list of the 100 most rapidly growing companies. The concept for Pizza Time involved animated robots with names like Chuck E. Cheese, Pasqually, Jasper Jowls, and Madame Oink. Near the dining and theatre area stood the Fantasy Forest Game Preserve—a vast selection of arcade and amusement games. Patrons could play videogames with Chuck E. Cheese tokens while they waited for their pizza. They could also spend real money on an array of merchandise, including Pizza Time Theatre T-shirts, Chuck E. Cheese sunvisors, and theme toys. In 1980, the restaurants grew in number from seven to 88. Half were company owned, the rest were franchises. In 1981, sales were $36 million and the company went public, issuing 1.1 million shares at $15. Company growth continued. By 1982, there were 204 outlets in 35 states as well as Canada, Australia, and Hong Kong. The stock doubled in price. But in 1983, Pizza Times sales ran 20 percent lower in average store sales. Caught in the videogame slump and plagued by customer complaints about food quality, Pizza Time began to hemorrhage money, at a rate estimated by one business periodical as $20 million per month by the end of 1983. In March 1984, Pizza Time Theatre filed Chapter 11.

During this period, Bushnell was involved in numerous other projects in such areas as interactive videodisks and advanced videogame technology. But perhaps his fondest vision lay in the notion of "personal robots," the business of another Bushnell company, Androbot, which was the first company to be included under the Catalyst Technologies umbrella. Bushnell was quoted as saying:

> I'm mad for robotics! . . . Robots are good company. Nice to have somebody around the house. Suppose you're watching a football game on TV and you

don't want to walk into the next room to get your pipe or a beer. You don't want to press a button for one of the servants, either. So you get the robot to do it. And then there's the ego thing. Wouldn't you like someone to come into your room in the morning and say, "O great and omniscient one, are you ready for your coffee?"

Bushnell predicted a "new Victorian era" whose civility and leisure would be a direct result of the home robot revolution. Recommended by Merrill Lynch in the summer of 1983 as a hot new issue, Androbot was in a product development phase and operating at a loss. Caught in the sea of red ink that bathed the consumer electronics industry in general and the videogame industry in particular, the offering was called off.

CATALYST

Nolan Bushnell started Catalyst Technologies in late 1981 with two partners from his Atari days, Larry Calof and John Anderson. Bushnell was chairman of Catalyst, Calof served as Catalyst's president, and Anderson as executive vice president. Catalyst's goal was to provide start-up and development-stage ventures with capital, essential services, management training, and suitable facilities. This would decrease costs, increase speed, and avoid the pitfalls of the business formation and development process. The following comments came from the company's statement of concept:

> It has been the perception of the Principals that, in many cases, the primary reason many start-up and development-stage companies are unable to reach potentials which could be expected based solely on technological criteria, is the entrepreneur's lack of knowledge and experience in developing and managing a business. In many instances this lack of business acumen and experience alone may result in failure but, in any event, will be a source of distraction to the development team and may result in delays of six months or more in the development effort. In high-technology industries such delays often mean the difference between success or failure because companies that first introduce a new technology or product have a distinct advantage in the marketplace.
> The traditional venture capital operating model does not adequately deal with these problems of the start-up or development-stage venture. In that model the venture capital investor provides equity or debt financing to a portfolio company and periodic advisory services, most frequently through representation on the board of directors or in periodic consultation. The day-to-day aspects of running and developing the business are left in the hands of the entrepreneurial group.
> The Catalyst Technologies concept differs greatly from this traditional model, by providing on-site facilities and continuous on-site services and training. Substantially all Catalyst Technologies services and training are rendered in its own facility, which is occupied by the companies using its services. Thus, the Catalyst Technologies facility, located in a 50,000 square foot building in Sunnyvale, California, serves as the incubator for start-up companies. It is intended that these companies will remain in the Catalyst Technologies facility until such time as they are ready to commence manufacturing, a period

expected to be 12 to 24 months, although Catalyst Technologies may continue to provide some services to a company even after it has moved to its own facilities.

The Principals believe that substantial benefits have been and will be derived from the close interaction of a group of very talented technologists under one roof. Although the companies using Catalyst on-site facilities and services remain separate entities, in many instances they encounter common technological and managerial problems in product development and are able to assist each other without the risk of losing control of proprietary information or aiding a competitor. This synergy of entrepreneurial talent with Catalyst experience, services and training substantially enhances the timing and effectiveness of the development efforts of all participating companies.

The Catalyst Technologies approach involves four general categories. First, Catalyst Technologies provides leased space on a short-term basis to start-up and development-stage companies. The space can be customized to the individual company's needs, including office use, product development and assembly of prototypes and preproduction units.

Second, Catalyst Technologies leases or arranges for the lease of equipment for its participating companies. Equipment which is likely to be used by a number of companies, such as test equipment and computers, is acquired by Catalyst Technologies and provided on a time-sharing basis. Specialized equipment is obtained directly for individual companies.

Third and most important, Catalyst Technologies provides extensive management, professional, and office services, consulting and training to its member companies. In addition to normal office services, such as secretarial assistance, telephone and duplicating facilities, the following consulting and training services are or will be provided.

- Accounting and financial statement preparation
- Personnel
- Purchasing
- Material control
- Engineering services (including engineering design)
- Business planning and strategy formulation
- Cash management
- Budgets and forecasts
- Contacts with professional service organizations
  —accountants
  —investment brokers
  —attorneys
  —banks
- Assistance in seeking additional capital
- Marketing and technical assistance
- Assistance in seeking additional management and facilities
- Engineering library

In addition, Catalyst Technologies provides on-site seminars and similar educational programs in order to train the management teams of the participating companies in many of those management skills which will continue to be their individual responsibilities and essential to their continued growth when they leave the Catalyst Technologies facility.

All facilities, equipment and services are provided to participating companies at rates that are generally below prevailing market rates in the area.

Finally, where they believe participating companies offer significant investment potential, the Principals participate in seed capital and later-stage financings for such ventures. The Partnership has been organized primarily to participate in such investment opportunities.

Bushnell described the process in the following terms:

No one has ever done this before because it's easier to simply invest and wait for things to happen. We think that the housing of a group of very talented people under one roof, and providing them with services they need, makes a tremendous amount of difference in product development. We think of the Catalyst as the ultimate incubator, or fertile environment, for the transformation of new ideas into tangible companies producing marketable products. Catalyst provides an environment in which the creative process is fostered and transformed into the productive process. Basically what we hope to accomplish here is to take talented people with good ideas and put them into a framework which can result in economic success.

Which Xerox-type machine do you buy? Well, a technologist can get fascinated with the intricacies and the engineering that go into the machines and spend three weeks making his decision. It'll be the right decision, but he'll spend too much time making it. Our product at Catalyst is essentially to provide the entrepreneurial team with the key to the door. They walk into their office and, lo and behold, there's a desk and a chair and a telephone system that works; there's a full accounting system, purchasing, receiving; there's a stack of papers on the desk; and when the leader gets through signing his name 35 times, he's incorporated, he's got employee benefit plans, he's got insurance, he's got the whole works, he's got his patent-secrecy forms—everything he needs—and he can devote his efforts to the development process as opposed to making mistake after mistake.

As of early 1985, Catalyst Technologies companies and alumni included Androbot; ByVideo, an interactive videodisk point-of-purchase promotion company; Timbertech, a sophisticated computer camp for children; Cinemavision, a large-screen television company; Axlon, which designed an unsuccessful data communications device but is now in the electronic toy business; IRO, a color consultation computer for cosmetology and fashion; and Etak, a company developing an on-board computer navigation system for cars.

LARRY CALOF

"The president's role at Catalyst is less function- than title-oriented. Catalyst is a proprietorship. It's the organization by which we provide the accounting, legal counsel, staff, and other services to our companies. Running it involves making sure we do things like billing and getting leases signed. It's an overall responsibility for administration. This kind of service company is at best a break-even operation. It is difficult to make the service organization profitable, unless you were setting up an incubator-type facility funded by the public sector for small, and not necessarily entrepreneurial, businesses. A lot of cities, for example, are taking some of the areas near universities which are run down, renovating buildings, and renting them out without providing much management help. We're up to something different here.

"How does Catalyst work? Assuming we've decided we're going to go forward with company X, we'll enter into a lease with them—a sublease of our space here. It will cover the space they need and allocation of common area space, basic telephone service and the related equipment, security service, the cost of reception, the Xerox machine, and other general types of services. They'll also enter into an agreement covering direct charges: long distance telephone charges, specific Xerox charges based on the number of copies they run, express mail. They'll probably enter into some sort of equipment lease with us. They can also get equipment from us directly if we have it around. We have scopes and other hardware, but they may need some specialized engineering equipment which we may be able to get for them. Then there will be a management services agreement that covers our providing management services to them—the four of us plus accounting and other general office services.

"We have about 20 people involved in Catalyst Technologies. We've got the management group: the four of us—Nolan, John, Perry, and myself. We then have an analyst level. Right now we only have one analyst, although we typically have had more than that. One is now running a division of Axlon and another has gone over to Etak, which is what we wanted our analysts to do. Since we don't have any other companies in the hopper now, we haven't replaced the people who have moved into operating roles. Analysts spend a lot of time working on business plans for the start-up companies. They look at business plans that come over the transom, that we may have an interest in investing in. They spend a lot of time in day-to-day liaison with the various companies, which is how they end up moving into operating roles. The next level we have is the accounting staff, which depends on how many companies we have. We will have anywhere from four to five up to eight people doing that. This level also involves handling Catalyst Ventures and other administrative matters around here, and accounting for Nolan as well. The rest are building people, the receptionist, and secretaries. At capacity, we have supported 10 companies with over 200 people in them.

"We have done some training and organizational work with our companies at Catalyst but not a great deal recently, primarily because we have shifted from the concept of developing the entrepreneurial engineer into the president, we now prefer to bring in somebody with the right skills and experience. We have worked to develop some skills in our entrepreneurs—accounting knowledge, protecting proprietary technology. We get somebody from our accounting firm or our law firm or just ourselves, and we hold a session for our people and videotape it, so it is available in our library.

"We are the management and the board, when we start one of these companies. When we originally started this process, we brought in a team of engineers, one of them would be president and we would monitor product development and provide general advice. We thought we could make good entrepreneurs. One of the things we found out is that, by and large, engineers or people with big company backgrounds may be pretty good at managing a development group, but they may not be the right CEO. We have made a number of changes in the senior management of our companies.

"When you bring in a professional manager to act as president and chief executive of a company, it can be a terrible ego blow for the founders. When we set up these companies, we said, 'Alright, you're president, but you're not really president. Don't get married to that title because you don't have the skills necessary for that, and we may need to bring in a businessman later to make this successful.' And our person said, 'Oh I understand, that's great.' Then it comes time to say 'You're no longer president.' And all hell breaks loose. So to get around that problem, when we brought in or built an engineering team around an idea, nobody in that team had the title or function of chief executive. We'd have Nolan or Perry or John or me in that role, it didn't matter who. We effectively were operating management and we controlled the company's board.

"Nolan, John, Perry, and I are also general partners of the Catalyst Venture fund. It is a limited partnership funded primarily by institutional investors. The fund is designed to invest, alongside the general partners, in seed-stage Catalyst companies. We each bring to it something a little different because we all have skills in different areas. We start Company A here and Catalyst Venture puts in money. Nolan and the rest of us also put in money personally. Catalyst Technologies provides services, as a sole proprietorship, and money flows back to Nolan. So it's not quite in and out of the same pocket. Later rounds can vary, but the initial positions are equal, to avoid conflict of interest problems.

"We get a management fee which is capped and figured on the basis of net cost. So there's a minimum and a maximum. The maximum is based on asset value. We also have the normal carried interest. Our management fee is higher than most because we have a relatively small fund, a start-up fund. We're not trying to make the service organization a profit center. The profit for us comes from the capital gains we are going to make on our investments.

"We had some early losses. We've got two or three companies that look like they're on a growth curve. The fund has been in existence now for about a year. It was easy to cut out two or three companies in the beginning, and we've done that. We've aggressively written down the value of companies that were going in a direction that we weren't happy about. It's too early to tell about the ones we just started and invested in. If you project the numbers out based on where we are today, I think the fund is going to be significantly profitable, but it is not there yet.

"We're being conservative in doing any further investing in start-ups right now. We do provide our companies with a lot of assistance. When we get to the point where we've got something to show we put deals together for further financing. We have good contacts in the venture business. However, venture financing is tough to get today. In looking at the reasons why, it is necessary to examine the IPO market and the lower levels of current financing. The IPO market and the mezzanine round have disappeared for now. When the mezzanine round disappears, everyone in traditional venture capital has to put their money not only into the companies they've got trouble with, but into the ones that are doing well and need more working capital. They're not yet quite bankable, which would open up other capital sources from Europe, the Middle East, and major institutions here. There's a lot less capital available today, a lot less being allocated for first-round financing of companies by venture capitalists. There are two reasons for that: one, because their money is going to good companies that they wouldn't have otherwise had to finance; two, there are a lot of companies in trouble and that requires money, but more importantly—people, everybody is people short.

"You take a prototypical venture capital firm, five or six partners and 65 investments. Say you get fifteen companies, five in serious trouble and 10 wavering a little bit, and you've got to save them or kill them. That takes personnel. So you've got your staff trying to save what you consider worth saving and then kill a few. When you do that, you don't have people around who can do the analysis, due diligence, *and* spend time preparing to commit time to new companies. As a result, it's been very tough to raise second-round financing, and we've been reluctant in recent months to say we want to commit to a new business if we're going to have to turn to the venture capital community to provide that next round of financing. Right now, we believe that if later financing isn't going to be there, we're going to run into a brick wall. Obviously, these things do run in cycles.

"You've got to be able to fund your companies. We had one last year that we started that we thought had a tremendous amount of promise. It has developed an interactive cable television system, a good idea. We put the money in, got the prototype developed, and then the cable television industry had an awful year. We ran into a brick wall trying to finance it. We found an investor who's going to come in and take over, but everyone's going to suffer a tremendous amount of dilution. You've got to avoid doing that very often. Everybody's still excited about the technology, but you don't want to pour any more money into it unless you can see your way clear to profit. We were the only ones around to finance it, and we decided we weren't going to do it.

"You've got to have the team as well as the product well in place when you go for outside financing, but it's harder to draw the good people out to form these companies during a period of time when a lot of start-ups are going out of business and there's no clear window to leave a reasonably good job to come in and take some high risks. We take our people risks at the beginning of our companies, and that's something we feel pretty good about, because we're here and we can see what they're doing. But you've got to be able to pull people out of secure positions. There are a lot of people wandering around this valley who'd be happy to come in and do something, but are concerned about risks. The good engineers are easily employed, so it's tougher to get them during times when financing is more difficult, compared to what it was a year or so ago. You don't want to lose people, so you've just got to be more careful. Our fund is designed to put in that first $500,000 or

$750,000 and then get out, not in terms of liquidating our position, but not participating in any further financing. We've got our position, we'll take the dilution that we expect, and we go on with it. Then we do another deal. If we get into the situation where we've got to continue to finance one of those companies, then we run out of money. So, we want to make sure we're doing things in a fashion where we have as much assurance as we can that the second round will feed it.

"We've been hurt by Pizza Time and Androbot. The Androbot story rests on the fact that we believed that our underwriters could get us public. And I think that was realistic. When they pulled out, the offering was already oversubscribed at retail. But they didn't want to take it solely at retail. A lot of that had to do with their internal situation. Then part of it was that we were coming out just when Atari, TI, and Mattel announced their enormous losses. It blew the market out. We had been ready to go. We weren't delayed. We followed our time schedule almost down to the day. We cleared the SEC and were ready to go. If we had been able to do it quicker, conceivably we would have been out. Had Androbot been public, the stock may have been down in the dumps, because high-tech stocks went down that way. Androbot certainly had not performed, but it would have had $15 million, and it would have had time to get its products on the market. Instead, when that fell away, Nolan provided the financing and it became a scramble. Businesspeople do better when they can plan and avoid having to act in a completely scramble mode. That really changes the way you do business.

"Finding the people to make it happen is the absolute critical element for our business. One of the problems I think we had in Androbot was not enough engineering talent and not enough management of the engineering team. So we got a long way down the road and were not anywhere near where we ought to have been. I think the other thing we have learned is to look for open niches to create new technologies and new industries, or applications of existing technologies without having to do the kind of basic scientific research which increases market risk. Androbot is a clear example of that risk. ByVideo was another. You get an idea, and everybody says without any reservations it is going to happen. But all of a sudden we find ourselves three to five years ahead of the time that it will happen, either because of cost considerations or technology or markets. Building the market for something new is more difficult than many people expect. Pong and the videogame industry took off so fast that I don't think they provided realistic examples of what it takes to open a brand-new market. I think we have come to a realization that being early can be just as bad as not getting the technology there. I think those are our principal lessons."

JOHN ANDERSON

"I was in financial accounting at Atari. Then I moved into administration and eventually I was vice president of administration there. At Catalyst what I do here is mostly day-to-day administrative and financial operations. I spend a lot of time on financial transactions: banking relationships, managing assets. When you have things wrapped together in a sole proprietorship, you have to keep things separated and trackable. We are either starting or running or closing a business, or trying to figure out what we should do next. So it involves a continual review process. Right now, for example, there are three projects that I am giving a fair amount of my time to, trying to be like a shepherd of the projects. Perry has his projects. And Larry has his. I also act as liaison to the various companies that I have worked in or have responsibility for; I function as the chief financial officer. Our accounting department does the accounting for all the companies as well as Catalyst.

"We're always running out of cash. You're always running out of cash in the future; you always have a need to finance. I figure out the financial strategy. Then I figure out how we are going to get there and how we are going to justify it. Do we wait? Do we raise the price? Can we stretch it that long? Should we take our money now and make sure?

"We have an informal management group. No one runs it. Larry and I organize it. We run Catalyst. Nolan suggests and creates and strategizes the companies. We meet as needed and a lot of our work is done over the phone. Three of the four of us meet quite a bit. We don't sit down on a regular basis—maybe once every two weeks, when there are a couple of critical issues that need to be addressed. The four of us will sit down either here or at Nolan's house or mine. Nolan likes to have breakfast meetings at his house. Ultimately, Nolan makes most decisions, but he has to be informed of the pros and cons of what we are going to do.

"Most of what we do here is Nolan's idea, within some framework. Almost everything we have done here has been an internally generated idea from people who come on our staff, throw out a bunch of ideas, and then go off and form a company around it. Or ideas that we have kicked around on various fronts with various people. The time may be right and we like that person and that project and off they go. A case in point would be IRO. Larry, Nolan, and I were talking about it two years ago. What's hot? What is it that people are spending money on? What's new in the consumer world? What has high margins? People are interested in finding out what colors suit them best. What about the technology requirements? Maybe we could use a computer, we could wave around a wand. Having your colors done with a little bit of technology on some kind of a Mary Kay, Avon, Tupperware party basis—it seemed like a do-able business. We had a lady who'd worked with Nolan for several years who had a good perspective on design and fashion. She was working with another one of our companies called ByVideo. She decided that there weren't any opportunities for her there and wanted to do something on her own. Nolan gave her IRO. He said, 'Here, you got it. Here is what I want it to be. Let's get together once in a while. You need to decide on hardware. We've got to design the color scheme and the software. We have to think about how we are going to market this thing.' Unfortunately, she didn't run it as well as she could have. She's gone now, and we have someone else in charge who is reconfiguring the hardware and software, and getting the marketing effort off to an effective start. We are now making some money on this idea.

"People inventorying is an important concept. People are out there that have certain talents, people in our companies as well. We are able to assemble packages of people. For example, our trivia card project involved our being able to call in three or four strong marketing people, a couple of technologists, and a guy who used to be CEO of one of our companies.

"I'm not sure we have a formal conflict management procedure here. A traditional venture capitalist will go to board meetings and then on behalf of the company, talk to people from time to time. We have the advantage of being in the building; we know everybody who works for the company. We can walk through the room, every day, several times a day if we need, to just see what is going on. Is there a team here? Are they working in the same directions? Are they all off to lunch all day long? Or do they get in late and go home early? Is the guy who is supposed to be in charge, really in charge? Or is he just sitting in his room working on something else? Or is he dreaming about God knows what? All those incidents you don't see unless you are physically there. So our work is a daily process of constantly refining, redirecting, supporting, challenging, advising, strategizing. A lot of it relates to how the Catalyst notion is perceived by the various companies. Some are not very experienced. They may ask us a lot of questions that we may not have the answers to, but we discuss them. Or we bring somebody in who can give us input, from the inventory of people that are around. We are always bending over backwards to serve our entrepreneurs' needs. They don't stroke each other very often. Sometimes it is tough to keep them all happy.

"Our CEOs have autonomy. The companies are theirs to run. But we have an active role as well. 'You know, you don't seem to be really getting to where you are supposed to be going. What are your problems? Some technician isn't doing the job? Why don't you get rid of him?' Then you might suggest that he go talk with one of our other people who is hanging out upstairs with some office space working on their own project. Let's bring him down and pay him some consulting fees for a couple of days and see what the problems are. So Catalyst is constantly shifting, depending on which of its companies has the problems. We follow financials closely, but we don't want to strap a lot of administrative burdens on people. We have a lot of back and forth with our people.

"People look to Nolan for inspiration because he is perceived as having the answers, particularly on technical, marketing, and strategic topics. I am the answer man on financial matters. Larry is the answer man on negotiations and legal matters. Perry, when he is here, is the answer man in operational and marketing situations. Nolan is the ultimate answer.

"We've gotten rid of more than one or two CEOs. It is not easy. Our basic approach is to try to find the right people who can handle the challenge. We also have the pressure of external as well as internal financing, getting outside venture capitalists onto our company boards. We are becoming a little tougher; we will give you some time, but we won't give you forever. We may give less time than we did in the past. If it doesn't work out, we'll put you back in the inventory pool where you'll either be on salary to the company or to Catalyst in addition to retaining whatever equity interest you may have accumulated.

"Let's suppose I was to have an idea on the way to work. OK, I'm going to ask Nolan for $100,000. OK, I am going to move into an office. The first thing that happens is that we all meet the players and come up with a skeletal business plan. I hate the term; but it's needed. I prefer to call them executive overviews. What's the plan? What are we doing here? Who's going to develop the product? How are we going to market it? Lots of work goes to budgeting. What are the time constraints? What year do I plan to get things done in? How many critical tasks are there? What sequence do I have to accomplish them in? Do I have the production capacity? How can I take advantage of internal resources? There are a lot of people here at Catalyst who can be extremely useful to talk with. How are we going to organize all this? Are we going to do this as an R&D partnership? As a sub-S corporation? As a straight corporation? As a sole proprietorship? Then we structure the deal. How much do you own? How much do they? What are you going to keep in reserve? This can take several weeks. Then you come to a focus with a plan. We review the critical tasks. Gradually we work things out and come up with the people we need and the resources which we can't get in Catalyst itself.

"Facilitating internal communications in Catalyst is what we try to do—trying to get people together with other people. You never know who around here might really be able to help you. I spend a lot of my time just developing relationships, telling someone what another person is going to come to see them about. Encouraging someone to go see somebody and talk about what they are doing. Or helping people with their needs. We answer questions, prepare people, head them in the right direction or say, 'I don't know.' Or say, 'That's what you were hired for. You figure it out.' It's a good place to work. It isn't heavily and rigidly structured.

"So we capitalize the company—half ours and half venture funds at a seed level, maybe $60,000. Now we are going to put in a quarter of a million dollars. You don't have to worry about money here up to that amount. You do have to think about marketing expenses. Three million dollars? How do we get it? How much do we need to put in? Where can we get the rest? What should the valuation of the company be? Do we talk to R&D people? To venture capitalists? Almost always it winds up being venture capitalists. Which ones? Larry and I will make introductions, and build relationships. So the venture capitalists come in, stock is issued, people come on board, you get a lot of de facto outside consultants. You like to get good people on board. Then you have to deal with growth. More space. More equipment. We provide what is required. Another PC? Access to a VAX computer? Maybe we have some of that stuff around. Maybe someone is unloading equipment so we can buy it at a discount. What kind of people do you need? Do we have this person around at Catalyst? If not, can we get them?

"Sometimes things are quiet around here, sometimes they're not. But you can always sense the enthusiasm and energy. In part, it comes from just being here and getting the resources and advice you need. Making your own presence felt. We have lots of exchanges, occasionally arguments. We try to make sure that everybody knows everybody else. We used to have monthly meetings. 'Grand Council of Empire' is what we used to call it. All the company presidents would come for beer and to talk about anything. These meetings don't happen as often as they used to. Everybody got too busy for one reason or another. Our process has become a lot more informal.

"This building is full now. It was full before, but in between being full then and now, it was almost empty. Ideally you don't have everyone move out at once. It has happened that a company has returned to Catalyst. They may have moved out too early and then collapsed. One of the reasons they may have collapsed was because of this huge overhead they had to pay every month called rent. If they are here and they can't pay rent, we don't shoot them. After all, it is our money."

Activision (A)

> Creativity springs from human ingenuity. The marketing challenge is to illuminate that creative force and to engage others in its glow.
>
> Activision Annual Report

> You inevitably become who you hire.
>
> Ken Coleman, Activision VP
Human Resources

> Activision is one of the best places to work in the Valley.
>
> An Activision Employee

THE INDUSTRY

Activision was founded on October 1979 amid the hoopla of the exploding videogame industry. Videogames, a result of the marriage of television and computer technology, consisted of three types: coin-operated games, typically played in arcades; cartridges containing computer ROMs (read only memories) inserted into a home game machine such as the Atari 2600 and Mattel's Intellivision systems; and computer software diskettes used on personal computers.

While the first videogame, a basic version of tennis, was said to have been developed in 1958 at Brookhaven Laboratory, it was not until 1970 that the first commercial videogame, called Computer Space, debuted. A few years later, PacMan Fever hit the United States. It has been estimated that PacMan has grossed almost two billion dollars in revenues from the arcade machines alone. Licensing of the PacMan concept has brought an additional one billion dollars. In 1972, Atari was founded by Nolan Bushnell. Purchased by Warner Communications in 1976, Atari's profits exploded to the extent that, as a division of Warner, it qualified for a position in the *Fortune* 500 by itself. In 1983, total revenues from videogames—the sum of coin-operated arcade

This case was written by Associate Professor John Kao.

Copyright © 1986 by the President and Fellows of Harvard College. Harvard Business School case 9-487-059.

game revenues and the sale of videogame cartridges—was estimated at $10 billion, greater than the movie and record industries combined.

Companies and videogame concepts proliferated in the early 1980s as the search for fame and fortune accelerated. Videogames sprung from every imaginable theme, including feature films. Atari, for example, reportedly licensed the rights to the film *E.T.* for $21 million, anticipating mammoth sales of a videogame spin-off. As one executive put it, "They've licensed everything that moves, walks, crawls, or tunnels beneath the earth."

Some new companies concentrated solely on the design and manufacture of software cartridges for home videogame use. They were producers for existing hardware systems developed by Atari, Mattel, and other large firms. (For further information on the industry see "The Videogame Industry" case and "The Videogame Design Process" case.)

THE COMPANY

Jim Levy founded Activision with four established videogame designers who had quit their jobs at Atari to start their own company. Levy was a marketer whose experience included branch manager at Hershey Foods, assistant business manager of *Time* magazine, manager of corporate development for Haverhill's, a mail order merchandising subsidiary of Time, Inc., managing director of Time-Life Audio, manager of direct mail marketing and then vice president of business affairs at GRT Corp., a record producer. The four designers were David Crane, Larry Kaplan, Al Miller, and Bob Whitehead. They left Atari in reaction to a perceived decline in its creative environment and personal desires for independence.

In contrast to hardware-oriented videogame companies, Activision was the first to focus exclusively on the design, manufacture, and marketing of home computer entertainment software. Activision shipped its first product in July 1980. By 1982, the company registered an impressive performance by any standard. Its sales rose from $6 million in FY 1981 to $158 million in FY 1983. Its 15% share of the videogame cartridge market was second only to Atari. Over three years, Activision realized a 123% ROE on profit margins of 14.5%. In the trade press, Levy reportedly described his next financial benchmark as $250 million in sales. Informally, he hoped for billion dollar sales figures in the foreseeable future. By 1983, the company had sold approximately 16 million units at retail prices near $30. On June 9, 1983, Activision went public with an offering of 4.5 million shares at $12. Approximately 1.5 million shares were sold by certain founders and 3 million by the company, which raised $33 million in new capital.

Activision prided itself on quality and creativity. Its products received considerable critical acclaim. Of 23 titles released by March 31, 1982, 14 had sold over 500,000 units (considered a hit), and four had sold over one million units each.

The company expanded on many fronts. Activision went international in

1981—by shipping cartridges to the United Kingdom—and by 1983, sold games in 32 countries. In fiscal 1982, the company began construction of a 92,500-square-foot manufacturing and distribution center in Milpitas, California. Three modern office buildings located in Mountain View, California, with a combined area of 100,000 square feet, served as corporate headquarters. In addition, the company operated five regional design centers, two regional distribution centers, and three sales offices. National retail accounts included Sears Roebuck, J. C. Penney, and Montgomery Ward.

By 1983, profits were such that the company even funded philanthrophic projects. Activision supported public television in the San Francisco Bay Area, and such programs as "Nova" and "Science Notes." Levy explained this activity, stating, "This is more than just corporate commitment; this support comes from each Activision employee. We feel fortunate to be able to share our success with the community."

Exhibit 1 provides financial information.

COMPANY PHILOSOPHY
AND THE CONCEPT OF CREATIVITY

The company believed that its ability to attract and develop talented software designers was an important creative and competitive advantage, allowing it to maintain one of the highest ratios of "hits" to titles released in its industry.

The company saw itself, like a record company, engaged in the creation of "hits" and the management of "stars." For example, one trade journal described senior designer Al Miller as "the Chuck Berry of home video." Designers were given considerable freedom to pursue their creative work without interference from the rest of the organization. The review process at Activision consisted of informal input from fellow designers who chose their own projects, without deadlines or constraints imposed on their work. The company's creative philosophy focused on the individual designer rather than design team. "Great innovations never come from committees" was a universally accepted Activision belief. What made this creative process work, according to one company officer, was the constant contact between Levy and the designers, and the quality and free flow of information.

In contrast to the marketing philosophy of other videogame companies, Activision heavily promoted its designers along with their software products. Packaging included pictures and personal information about individual designers as well as their tips on how to play the game. A large, internal group handled floods of fan mail from people partial to a particular Activision game or designer.

Searching for an optimal creative atmosphere, "designer centers" were set up which separated creative activity from the rest of the company, both physically and psychologically. "Creative Design Managers," analogous to "Artist and Repertoire" professionals in the record industry, were the sole link between people on the creative side and the rest of the company.

This formula for creativity was not shared by other firms in the industry. For example, Imagic, another software design house, placed designers on creative teams, which included a variety of specialists in areas such as graphic design and sound effects. The company employed extensive concept testing and market research, looking for the elusive hit, rather than relying on the "gut" of the individual designer. Imagic designers received input from the marketing department and senior management.

By April 1983, Activision engaged a software design staff of 34 designers; 24 were company employees and 10 were under exclusive, long-term contracts. The company's five design centers, in northern and southern California, New Jersey, and Massachusetts, were supported by an editorial design and administrative staff of 27 professionals. The company expected to expand the number of designers and design centers in the near future.

HUMAN RESOURCES AT ACTIVISION

The Activision management expressed an early commitment to human resources. Ken Coleman came to Activision in March 1982 as vice president of human resources. Prior to that, he had been a personnel officer in the United States Air Force from 1967 to 1972, and at Hewlett-Packard as personnel supervisor/recruiter for 10 years, North European personnel manager, personnel manager for several systems divisions, and finally, as corporate staffing manager. He described the HR role at Activision in the following terms:

> Activision is sort of a schizophrenic environment in that the business culture and human culture are different. From a human point of view, the most important thing is how people are treated on a day-to-day basis. There is a high premium on congeniality. It is not nice, not to be nice. There are many good companies where you can mistreat people while implementing your objectives and get away with it. Not at Activision. It isn't enough to be right, or have the right objectives. The way you implement being right is very, very important.
>
> From a business point of view, Activision is a very organized place, primarily because of Jim Levy. While the organization is not highly structured, there is a constant planning process, a strong sense of business discipline, and a commitment to fiscal responsibility. Things are done right. Jim Levy would say, if you can't do things right, don't do them at all.
>
> In most companies, the human culture and business culture tend to be in sync. At IBM for example, the human and business cultures are fairly formal. Apple is informal from a business and a human culture point of view. Here, we have both formality and informality. We have, for example, a very formal requisition approval policy, a well-designed orientation program, and a performance appraisal system. We have twice-a-year performance evaluations, twice-a-year salary reviews which involve a very formal process. On the other hand, we don't have a personnel policy manual. Formal rules can become crutches. In reality, what you have to do is understand what you are trying to achieve. You want to have a delicate balance between flexibility, consistency, and equity. In order to make this work, training becomes very important. People

have to feel a responsibility for making and keeping the environment special. The culture is determined by how we treat each other on every Monday morning.

Human resources has a fundamental responsibility to ensure that the culture works in terms of communications, employee relations, and activities. The role of human resources is to translate the Activision family, the human culture, as well as our business approaches into daily management practice. We also feel a commitment to share our success with our employees. Our salary program and benefits package are very competitive.

In most companies, human resources has to prove it has value. In most companies, people will allow human resources not to do its job. We didn't have that problem here. It comes from a basic belief that the HR function could and should add value. In fact, I've seen a report of a meeting when the company had 35 people. It said that one weakness was we don't have a professional, strong human resources person. So conceptually, the company knew it needed the function and that it needed to add value.

My charge when I came into the company was based on the assumption that we were a special place to be. We knew that we were going to grow very rapidly. We didn't want to lose our specialness and my responsibility was to make sure that things worked. We had to make sure we hired the right people and that the line managers had the responsibility, not me, of making sure the culture worked. We needed also to fight the "we-they" syndrome that can easily develop in a fast growing situation. "We-they" in the sense of "I've been here longer than you have" and "I know the Activision family better than you do." We had to make sure we had a real personnel function in terms of hiring and training people, and making the system work.

What you try to do is help people understand that a culture is a living, breathing thing that is different today than it was yesterday, and will be different tomorrow than it was today. Each person makes up an important part of that culture and therefore nobody has an exclusive on the right answer. The only thing that's stable is a commitment to certain fundamental values, like people will be treated well, the process will be fair and equitable, people will be open and honest. Past that, it's a moving target. Individuals do different things with it, and you just have to make sure that your reward system—your perks, your promotion, your responsibility systems—do not reward people for incorrect behavior as happens in many companies. It is important to make people believe that you can't gloss over the issues. If you really walk over people, you just can't win.

What helps in human resources is that you have influence through credibility. Over time, people came to understand that it was very difficult to win a battle with me. People learned this because I helped them win things. Jim was helpful also. He forced involvement of the function and did not allow people to do end runs around human resources. He supports me for several reasons. I deliver quality stuff. I have insight. I read people in situations very well. I don't hide anything from him. I haven't given him any surprises. He likes the way I think. I handle pressure and uncertainty well.

It's been important to hire the best people for the HR department; very bright, with lots of self-confidence, who know how to influence people in situations where there tends to be very little absolute right and wrong. I'm convinced that when we had 20 people in the function, we had one of the strongest HR departments in Silicon Valley. And the people in it would say to me that it was the best group they had ever worked with. We are having a gathering of our alumni from our HR department soon. Almost everyone who has left here has gotten promoted elsewhere.

Activision grew very rapidly, from 75 to 375 people in 18 months. It was a very difficult process, and impossible to do perfectly. We learned not to allow our commitment to participative management to influence letting the right or wrong people be hired. That's the only mistake I won't let somebody working for me make. The hiring decision mistake is a very costly one and you don't have to make many of them to have an incredible impact. We probably could have looked for more basic maturity and experience in our people and given up some on talent. We were three to five years light on experience in many areas. People would do things like attacking problems by using more resources. If you'd had more experience, you might not have done things that way. Some people were more prima donna-oriented than they might have been. Some people were a little too much concerned with their own success. We had people 26–28 years old doing 35-year-old jobs. In a fast-growth environment, having a certain amount of maturity and experience is far more important than in a slow-growth environment. You need some stability around you, some pillars to hold on to. If you've got nothing but young people, they may have a hard time getting that stability from each other.

Through this growth process, I've learned a lot about how important the HR function is. In a fast-growth situation, your biggest risk other than the market going sour is with people and organizational structure. Can you MOVE your organizational structure to fit your current size and are you able to hire, move around, and change people to fit where you as a company are? You have to be willing to tackle your people problems promptly. Waiting involves a larger piece of your life in a young company. Somebody might be in the process of doubling his staff in six months and delays could be a real problem. If I were doing it again, I would move faster in terms of moving people around and changing responsibility. If you haven't been in that kind of an environment before, all of your instincts say give the guy another chance, let the situation work itself out. You don't want to overreact. But your growth does not allow you that luxury.

I think the uniqueness of human relations at Activision comes from four things. One is the CEO, who has a fundamental belief that people should be treated with fairness and dignity in an organization. Second is the willingness to support the HR function. Third is the ability to hire incredibly talented people with a common belief in how people ought to be treated, which tends to be a distinctive feature of Activision people. And fourth, a human resources person who understands that the only way HR can have a real impact is to hire incredibly talented people. The thing that I've learned more than anything else is that you cannot underestimate how difficult it is to do human resources. You cannot underestimate what people have to do to make it work.

I've learned two basic things which are important. One, you set up your organization with certain key fundamental values—like commitment to customers, employees, quality of products—whatever those key things are. Everything else must be subject to change. The final thing I've learned involves my definition of a good company. A good company to me is one that's able to take its stated philosophy about people, whatever it is, and day-to-day see that people get treated that way. In a good company, the employee understands the deal. Most companies have the problem of saying one thing and doing another. That confuses people. They don't feel commitment to their organization because you're not being straight with them.

Exhibits 2–5 provide various HR data.

EXHIBIT 1   ACTIVISION, INC. AND SUBSIDIARIES

CONSOLIDATED STATEMENTS OF INCOME

| | Year Ended March 31 | | |
| | 1981 | 1982 | 1983 |
	(In thousands except per share data)		
Net sales	$6,226	$65,987	$157,633
Costs and expenses:			
Cost of sales	2,590	20,829	42,820
Sales and marketing expenses	1,230	13,941	62,346
General and administrative expenses	1,093	5,201	15,339
	4,913	39,971	120,505
Operating income	1,313	26,016	37,128
Interest income	18	244	575
Interest expense	(27)	(155)	(152)
Income before provision for income taxes	1,304	26,105	37,551
Provision for income taxes	560	13,187	18,368
Net income	$ 744	$12,918	$ 19,183
Net income per common and common equivalent share	$.03	$.43	$.64
Number of common and common equivalent shares used in computing net income per share	29,730	30,095	29,987

The accompanying notes are an integral part of these financial statements.

EXHIBIT 1 (cont.)

CONSOLIDATED BALANCE SHEETS

	March 31	
	1982	1983
	(In thousands)	

ASSETS

	1982	1983
Current assets:		
Cash and temporary cash investments	$ 1,380	$ 2,403
Accounts receivable, less allowances for doubtful accounts and sales returns of $1,753 in 1982 and $5,016 in 1983	21,792	22,974
Inventories	6,810	21,186
Prepaid income taxes	—	3,484
Other current assets	178	1,027
Total current assets	30,160	51,074
Fixed assets	1,249	5,204
Other assets	141	181
	$31,550	$56,459

LIABILITIES AND SHAREHOLDERS' EQUITY

	1982	1983
Current liabilities:		
Accounts payable	$ 6,280	$ 9,265
Accrued liabilities	3,039	5,878
Income taxes payable	5,689	7,493
Deferred income taxes	2,243	—
Total current liabilities	17,251	22,636
Deferred income taxes	73	239
Subordinated notes payable to shareholders	550	550
Total liabilities	17,874	23,425
Commitments and contingencies (Notes 10 and 11)		
Shareholders' equity:		
Preferred stock, no par value:		
Authorized: 10,000,000 shares		
Issued and outstanding: None	—	—
Common stock, no par value:		
Authorized: 100,000,000 shares		
Issued and outstanding: 30,146,000 shares in 1982 and 29,696,800 shares in 1983	187	362
Retained earnings	13,489	32,672
Total shareholders' equity	13,676	33,034
	$31,550	$56,459

The accompanying notes are an integral part of these financial statements.

EXHIBIT 1 (cont.)

CONSOLIDATED STATEMENTS OF SHAREHOLDERS' EQUITY

	Common Stock		Retained Earnings (Deficit)	Total
	Shares	Amount		
		(Dollar amounts in thousands)		
Balances, April 1, 1980	28,550,000	$143	$ (173)	$ (30)
Issuance of common stock:				
Employee stock purchase agreements	1,350,000	8		8
Employee stock bonuses	15,000	1		1
Net income for the year			744	744
Balances, March 31, 1981	29,915,000	152	571	723
Issuance of common stock:				
Employee stock purchase agreements	220,000	30		30
Employee stock bonuses	11,000	5		5
Net income for the year			12,918	12,918
Balances, March 31, 1982	30,146,000	187	13,489	13,676
Issuance of common stock:				
Employee stock bonuses	6,500	30		30
Employee stock options	7,800	10		10
Other sales	70,000	140		140
Repurchases of common stock	(533,500)	(5)		(5)
Net income for the year			19,183	19,183
Balances, March 31, 1983	29,696,800	$362	$32,672	$33,034

The accompanying notes are an integral part of these financial statements.

EXHIBIT 1 (cont.)

CONSOLIDATED STATEMENTS OF CHANGES IN FINANCIAL POSITION

| | Year Ended March 31 | | |
	1981	1982 (In thousands)	1983
Resources provided:			
From operations:			
Net income	$ 744	$12,918	$19,183
Add charges to income not requiring a current outlay of working capital:			
Depreciation and amortization	28	154	794
Deferred income taxes	13	60	166
Resources provided by operations	785	13,132	20,143
Issuance of common stock	9	35	180
Total resources provided	794	13,167	20,323
Resources applied:			
Acquisition of fixed assets	207	1,209	4,751
Other	33	99	43
Total resources applied	240	1,308	4,794
Increase in working capital	$ 544	$11,859	$15,529
Increase (decrease) in working capital by components:			
Cash and temporary cash investments	$ (455)	$ 1,325	$ 1,023
Accounts receivable	2,369	19,421	1,182
Inventories	531	6,278	14,376
Prepaid and deferred income taxes	195	(2,438)	5,727
Other current assets	(19)	170	849
Accounts payable	(829)	(5,417)	(2,985)
Accrued liabilities	(496)	(2,533)	(2,839)
Income taxes payable	(742)	(4,947)	(1,804)
Increase in working capital	$ 554	$11,859	$15,529

The accompanying notes are an integral part of these financial statements.

EXHIBIT 2 ACTIVISION (A)

TOTAL EMPLOYEES
ACTIVISION—1/82 to 11/83

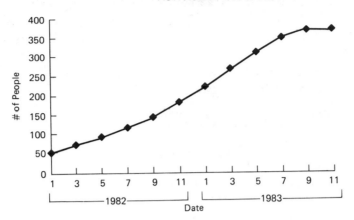

HUMAN RESOURCE FLOWS
ACTIVISION—PART I

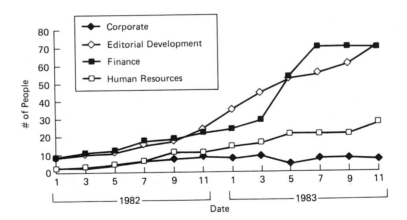

EXHIBIT 2 (cont.)

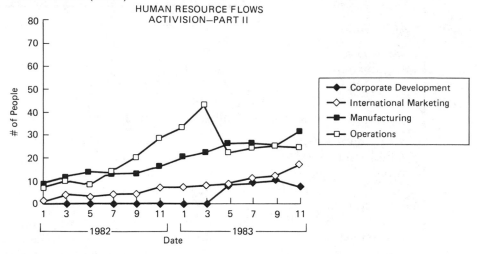

HUMAN RESOURCE FLOWS
ACTIVISION—PART II

Legend:
◆ Corporate Development
◇ International Marketing
■ Manufacturing
□ Operations

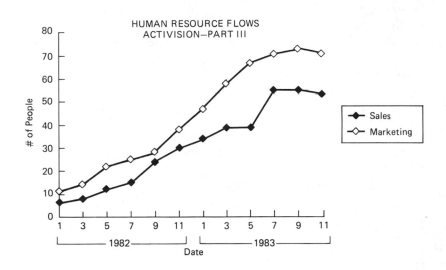

HUMAN RESOURCE FLOWS
ACTIVISION—PART III

Legend:
◆ Sales
◇ Marketing

EXHIBIT 3 ACTIVISION (A)

ACTIVISION

James H. Levy
President

Welcome to the Activision Family!

Activision is a very special place. It was created by people with a dedication to excellence and leadership, a commitment to high standards of business integrity, and a desire for an open, energetic, and creative "home" where the members of the organization really care about each other and enjoy being together.

We've grown very rapidly in a few short years, from a handful of determined entrepreneurs to a much larger organization of determined entrepreneurs. But, this growth and our success has not gone to our heads, and I am always thrilled to see that the spirit of dedication and excitement which existed in the early days has continued to grow as the Company has grown.

This handbook has been prepared to help you "get your bearings" and begin to learn your way around. Don't be concerned if it takes you a while to learn what Activision is all about. You'll find that the Company, the business, and the Family are unlike any others you have ever seen. We are leaders in a new industry and a new revolution in home entertainment, and we are leaders in the way we go about doing it.

So, welcome aboard! We know you will make a great contribution to Activision and to the spirit of the Activision Family.

I look forward to meeting you soon.

James H. Levy
President

JHL:nas

Activision, Inc.
2350 Bayshore Frontage Road
Mountain View, CA 94043
(415) 960-0410 Mailing Address: Drawer No. 7286, Mountain View, CA 94042

EXHIBIT 3 (cont.)

<table>
<tr><td></td><td>CARTRIDGES</td></tr>
<tr><td>DISTRIBUTION</td><td>When you begin working for Activision, you receive six gift cartridges from the "current" selection.

Thereafter, each time a new game is released, Activision Family members receive a complimentary cartridge of that game.</td></tr>
<tr><td>FORM</td><td>You will be given a form during your First Day Orientation.</td></tr>
<tr><td>PERSON TO CONTACT</td><td>Records</td></tr>
<tr><td>PATCHES</td><td>For most of our games, patches are awarded for achieving qualifying scores, as shown in the instruction booklet accompanying the game cartridge.</td></tr>
<tr><td>POSTERS</td><td>Posters for some of our games are printed to be sent to the club members. They are also available to you if you desire to have one for your office or home.</td></tr>
<tr><td>PERSON TO CONTACT</td><td>Consumer Relations</td></tr>
</table>

CONFIDENTIALITY

As Activision continues to grow rapidly, so, too, does the necessity for a continuing flow of information to enable all of us to work for Activision's continued success. Much of this information is also highly sensitive and would be very valuable to our competitors. While not always labeled as "confidential," much of what you run across in your daily activities would be best kept within the Family in order to protect and preserve our position. Two terms are useful in labeling this sensitive information.

- CONFIDENTIAL—FOR YOUR EYES ONLY. To be kept within your confidence and not spread beyond individuals whom you *know* will have the information. Very little information will fall into this category, and most of it will reflect important corporate information which should not be broadly spread.
- COMPANY CONFIDENTIAL. To be retained within the walls of Activision and not revealed to anyone outside of the immediate Activision Family.

When in doubt about whether the information has been published, please do not discuss it outside of the Activision Family and your immediate family. This is true whether the information has been printed yet not marked as "confidential," or if it is information spread by word of mouth.

As our company continues to grow and prosper, all of us want to be able to share in as much knowledge as possible, in order to make the greatest possible contribution to our continued health. This will only be

EXHIBIT 3 (cont.)

possible in an atmosphere where all of us take our responsibilities to Activision and our fellow members of the Activision Family very seriously and protect our confidences. The last thing we want to do is to stop talking to each other.

	UMBRELLAS
SERVICE PROVIDED	Blue Activision umbrellas are available during the rainy season to provide protection for our Family members as they "commute" between buildings.
LOCATION	Lobby, Building 1 Lobby, Building 2
PERSONAL UMBRELLAS	Names are being collected of those Family members who would like to purchase their own personal Activision umbrella.
PERSON TO CONTACT	Office Services

	WORK HOURS
WORK WEEK	Activision was founded upon the concept of providing a progressive, flexible environment for all our Family members. One such progressive policy is our 9:00 AM to 5:00 PM, 35-hour standard work week (there are some jobs that require different hours due to the nature of the position, such as that of receptionist). However, most of our positions require more than a 35-hour work week in order to get the job done. Therefore, we expect our employees to have the dedication and commitment to put in whatever amount of time is necessary to complete assigned tasks.
LUNCH "HOUR"	There is no standard lunch hour at Activision, nor is there a minimum or maximum of time that should be taken for lunch. However, we expect that most employees would take lunch sometime around the noon hour and would normally use 30–60 minutes.

	OVERTIME
NON-EXEMPT	For non-exempt employees, overtime is paid at the rate of one and one-half times the employee's hourly rate if that individual works more than 8 hours in one day or more than 40 hours in one week. Double time is paid if the individual works over 12 hours in one day or works on Sunday or an official Activision holiday.
PROCEDURE	The Overtime Authorization form should be submitted to your supervisor at the end of each pay period for anyone who qualifies to be paid overtime. Overtime will be paid the pay period following the submission of the signed Overtime Authorization form to Finance.

EXHIBIT 3 (cont.)

FORM	Forms are available from the Payroll Department.
PERSON TO CONTACT	Payroll
EXEMPT	Although Activision doesn't pay overtime to exempt employees, we do recognize that often many of our exempt employees put in significant amounts of time above 40 hours a week in order to get the job done. Although we do not have a formal compensatory time-off program, managers do have the flexibility to grant compensatory time off in those situations deemed appropriate.

MORNING MUNCHIES

WHICH MORNINGS?	Mondays and Fridays
LOCATION	Mountain View: Lunchroom, Building 1 Cafeteria, Building 2
WHICH MUNCHIES?	Fresh fruit in season is served on Mondays. Bagels and donuts are rotated on Fridays.
LOCATION	Milpitas
WHICH MUNCHIES?	Coffee cakes, donuts, and fruit are rotated on Mondays. Bagels are served on Fridays.
HOURS	Early morning until they're all gone.
FREE	These munchies are, of course, *free* to all employees. In addition, coffee, cold drinks, and milk are provided free of charge throughout the week.

PERSONALIZED NAMEPLATES

PURPOSE	Office nameplates have been designed to help us to find each other and at the same time give us all a chance to individualize our own nameplates.
NAME CHOICES	You may choose to use your full name, with or without middle initial, or you may decide to use the nickname which you are generally called by. It's up to you.
ARTWORK CHOICES	Now for the fun part. There are three choices to pick from. First, you may choose the box art character for one of the Activision games. Second, you may choose any character, animal, figure, or symbol of special meaning to you. Third, you may choose to leave that space blank. Your nameplate will still look great.
ARTWORK— PERSONAL DESIGN	If you want a design other than an Activision character, you will need to provide a rectangular (more vertical than horizontal and close to the size of 2″ by 4″), camera ready (able to be photographed), black on white background, piece of artwork. This can be hand-drawn in black felt pen, or cut out of black construction paper and pasted on

EXHIBIT 3 (cont.)

white paper, or traced-over coloring book art, or very clean and simple lines on a black-and-white photograph, etc. Please remember that the finished picture basically will be a silhouette. So think about this carefully before you submit your artwork. You'll be notified if your artwork can't be reproduced for this purpose.

TURNAROUND TIME	You should receive your nameplate about a month from the receipt of your request.
FORM	Complete the Personalized Nameplate Request Form and return it to Employee Relations.
PERSON TO CONTACT	Employee Relations

ACTIVISION CALENDAR

1983*

Friday	January 21	Family Affair
Saturday	February 12	Beach Blanket Babylon
Friday	February 18	Family Affair
Friday	March 18	Family Affair
Friday–Sunday	March 25–27	Tahoe Ski Trip
Saturday	March 31	End 4th Fiscal Quarter, 1983
Monday	April 4	Activision's New Year Party (FY 1984)
Friday	April 15	Family Affair
Friday	May 20	Family Affair
Sunday–Wednesday	June 5–8	Summer Consumer Electronics Show—Chicago
Friday	June 17	Family Affair
Saturday	July 2	End 1st Fiscal Quarter, 1984
Friday	July 15	Family Affair
Friday	August 19	Family Affair
Saturday	September 10	Family Picnic
Thursday	September 15	Family Affair
Saturday	October 1	End 2nd Fiscal Quarter, 1984
Friday	October 21	Family Affair
Friday	November 18	Family Affair
Saturday	December 10	Winter Festival
Saturday	December 31	End 3rd Fiscal Quarter, 1984

1984

Saturday–Tuesday	January 7–10	Winter Consumer Electronics Show—Las Vegas

* These dates may change.

EXHIBIT 4   ACTIVISION (A)

1981 INCENTIVE STOCK OPTION PLAN
(As proposed to be amended, with changes shown in italics)

1. *Purposes of the Plan.* The purposes of this Stock Option Plan are to attract and retain the best available personnel for positions of substantial responsibility, to provide additional incentive to the Employees of the Company, and to promote the success of the Company's business.

    Options granted hereunder may be either "incentive stock options," as defined in Section 422A of the Internal Revenue Code of 1954, as amended, or "non-statutory stock options," at the discretion of the board and as reflected in the terms of the written option agreement.

2. *Definitions.* As used hereunder, the following definitions shall apply:

    (a) "Board" shall mean the Committee, if one has been appointed, or the Board of Directors of the Company, if no Committee has been appointed.

    (b) "Common Stock" shall mean the Common Stock of the Company.

    (c) "Company" shall mean Activision, Inc., a California corporation.

    (d) "Committee" shall mean the Committee appointed by the Board of Directors in accordance with paragraph (a) of Section 4 of the Plan, if one is appointed.

    (e) "Continuous Status as an Employee" shall mean the absence of any interruption or termination of service as an Employee. Continuous Status as an Employee shall not be considered interrupted in the case of sick leave, military leave, or any other leave of absence approved by the Board.

    (f) "Employee" shall mean any person, including officers and directors, employed by the Company or any Parent or Subsidiary of the Company. The payment of a director's fee by the Company shall not be sufficient to constitute "employment" by the Company.

    (g) "Incentive Stock Option" shall mean an Option intended to qualify as an incentive stock option within the meaning of Section 422A of the Internal Revenue Code of 1954, as amended.

    (h) "Option" shall mean a stock option granted pursuant to the Plan.

    (i) "Optioned Stock" shall mean the Common Stock subject to an Option.

    (j) "Optionee" shall mean an Employee who receives an Option.

    (k) "Parent" shall mean "parent corporation," whether now or hereafter existing, defined in Section 425(e) of the Internal Revenue Code of 1954, as amended.

    (l) "Plan" shall mean this 1981 Incentive Stock Option Plan, as amended.

EXHIBIT 4 (cont.)

DIRECTOR WARRANT PLAN
(As proposed to be adopted)

1. *Purposes of the Plan.* The purposes of the Director Warrant Plan (the "Plan") are to attract and retain the best available candidates for the Board of Directors of Activision, Inc. (the "Company") who are not also employees of the Company, to provide additional equity incentive to such non-employee Directors and to promote the success of the Company's business.

2. *Stock Subject to the Plan.* Subject to the provisions of Section 8 of the Plan, the maximum aggregate number of shares of the Company's common stock (the "Common Stock") which may be granted under warrants and sold under the Plan is 200,000 shares. The shares may be authorized, but unissued, or reacquired Common Stock.

3. *Administration of the Plan.* The Plan shall be administered by a committee (the "Committee") appointed by the Board of Directors of the Company. The Committee shall consist of three or more persons, who may but need not be directors or employees of the Company, and none of whom is, or at any time within the year preceding such member's appointment has been, eligible to participate in this Plan or any other stock or stock option plan of the Company or any of its affiliates. The Committee shall have the authority, in its absolute discretion, to (a) determine the fair market value of the Common Stock, (b) subject to Section 4 below, determine the directors to whom warrants to purchase shares shall be granted, and the number of shares to be subject to each warrant, and (c) make all other determinations deemed necessary or advisable for the administration of the Plan. All decisions of the Committee shall be final.

4. *Eligibility.* Any director of the Company who is not an employee and who is not a member of the Committee at the time any warrant is granted under the Plan to such director shall be eligible to be granted warrants pursuant to the Plan for a period of six months commencing on the Effective Date of the Plan (as determined in Section 9) below or, in the case of a director who was not a member of the Board of Directors on the Effective Date, commencing sixty days after the date of such director's election, or, in the case of a director who is or becomes a member of the Committee, commencing on the date of such director's resignation from or replacement on the Committee.

5. *Purchase Price.* The purchase price for shares to be purchased upon exercise of warrants granted under the Plan shall be the fair market value for the Common Stock, which shall be the mean of the bid and asked prices of the Common Stock on the date of grant, as reported in the *Wall Street Journal* (or, if not so reported, as otherwise reported by the National Association of Securities Dealers Automated Quotation (NASDAQ) System). The purchase price for the shares may be paid by cash or check.

EXHIBIT 5

PERFORMANCE EVALUATION GUIDELINES

The following information is to assist you in preparing the performance evaluation.

Written performance evaluations are intended first to augment, clarify and summarize the many verbal discussions we all have with the people who report to us. Secondly, written appraisals establish future direction and goals for the individual. The mutual feedback process that a written appraisal offers to us in our rapidly changing environment is invaluable.

Written evaluations are also critical for the formulation and maintenance of an equitable company-wide salary administration program.

COMPLETING THE EVALUATION FORM:

I.   Describe no more than six major responsibilities and give a general statement addressing the performance on each responsibility.

II.   Specify major achievements of the individual and major improvements that the person made since the last review.

III.   Rate the individual in each of the major performance factors and give the individual an overall rating.

IV.   Establish a development plan. (This should be done with the employee.)

V.   Give the employee an opportunity to make comments of his/her own.

NOTE: Since we will be holding salary reviews during June, there should be no salary adjustment associated with this performance evaluation.

CONDUCTING THE PERFORMANCE EVALUATION:

1.   Write your evaluation based on job responsibilities since the previous review.

2.   Discuss the evaluation with your manager before conducting the actual performance evaluation.

3.   Ensure that the individual is notified in advance of the time and location of the evaluation and whether you expect any preparation on their part.

4.   Make every effort to have an uninterrupted discussion. The process, attitude and environment in which the evaluation is held greatly influences what will be "heard" by the reviewee.

5.   Schedule sufficient time for a thorough exchange of information.

6.   Make sure the evaluation reflects what was actually discussed.

7.   Have the individual sign and date the evaluation.

8.   You, as evaluating supervisor, sign and date the evaluation.

9.   Return the evaluation to Human Resources.

Activision, Inc. 2350 Bayshore Frontage Road Mountain View, CA 94043 (415) 960-0410
Mailing Address: Drawer No. 7286 Mountain View, CA 94039

EXHIBIT 5 (cont.)

ACTIVISION®

PERFORMANCE EVALUATION AND

DEVELOPMENT PLAN

general

Name_____ Emp. No._____ Date of Evaluation_____

Date Hired_____ Department_____

Job Title_____ Evaluating Supervisor_____

The purpose of this evaluation is to:
1. Communicate personally, honestly, and frankly on performance improvement desired or necessary.
2. Recognize and comment on exceptional performance.
3. Suggest specific courses of action to help each individual develop in areas of need.

I. POSITION OBJECTIVES: Summarize responsibilities on the job and resulting performance.

Objectives/Responsibilities	Performance

II. MAJOR ACHIEVEMENTS AND/OR IMPROVEMENTS: What specific achievements and/or improvements has this individual made since the last review?

EXHIBIT 5 (cont.)

ACTIVISION®

PERFORMANCE EVALUATION AND

DEVELOPMENT PLAN

management

Name _____ Emp. No. ____ Date of Evaluation _____

Date Hired _____ Department _____

Job Title _____ Evaluating Supervisor _____

I. POSITION OBJECTIVES: Summarize specific job responsibilities and resulting performance.

Objectives/Responsibilities	Performance

II. MAJOR ACHIEVEMENTS AND/OR IMPROVEMENTS: What specific achievements and/or improvements has this individual made since the last review? What progress has been made toward meeting established goals?

Activision (B): Downturn

Later, in 1983, videogame industry euphoria turned into dismay. Atari announced losses ultimately totaling over $1 billion. Numerous corporations exited the business. Industry casualties included Apollo, Data Age, and U.S. Games. Imagic scaled back operations and dropped plans to go public.

In fiscal year 1984, Activision reported sharply lower sales of $70 million and a loss of $18 million or $0.56 per share. *Exhibits 1* and *2* present financial data for this period.

In a somber message to shareholders, Jim Levy explained the turbulence of the industry in terms of five factors:

1. More than $1.5 billion in losses by industry producers in the past year.
2. Delivery, quality, and reliability issues tarnishing the industry's image with retailers, consumers, the media, and the public.
3. Withdrawal of several competitors from the market.
4. Proliferation of incompatible hardware, some plagued by performance problems and some subject to severe price instability, confusing potential buyers.
5. Large quantities of software dumped into retail channels at low prices which clogged distribution pipelines and took sales dollars away from more profitable front-line product.

Stung by dramatic and unforeseen reversal in the videogame market, Activision reluctantly announced its first layoff of employees in late 1983. Three more layoffs followed in March, June, and September 1984. By November 1984 the company had gone from a peak of 369 employees to 136. *Exhibit 3* presents changes in human resource flows for this period.

RETRENCHING

Ken Coleman, vice president of human resources, had the following comments about this turbulent period in Activision's history:

This case was prepared by Associate Professor John Kao.

Copyright © 1986 by the President and Fellows of Harvard College. Harvard Business School case 9-487-060.

In retrospect, we might have hired a few less people. But we never caught up with the growth in the market. Also, we were off in our estimates of what would happen to the business. We've gone through layoffs three or four times in the last year. But how can you plan for what happened? We did exactly what we ought to have done given what we believed was going to happen. I'm totally comfortable with that and would not have done things much differently. The process had strength. This place still has morale, and people are still committed. We handled the downsizing in the same spirit of professionalism and dignity that we handled the growth. We cared about people, we were sensitive to their needs. We had a very liberal severance package. We've done it in a very organized, human, businesslike way. We have not become ruthless in the process.

There's no right way to tell someone he or she doesn't have a job. Any way you do it, it will cause a lot of consternation and unhappiness. There are lots of wrong ways to do it, though, which I think we avoided. The only thing that really matters is that we cared about it. As long as it is perceived that the decision making was fair and equitable, that's what's important.

Basically, Jim and I were involved in the process along with other members of the executive staff. We'd try to get some general agreement on the targeted size of the organization. "If you can have so many people, which ones do you want?"

Very few people would say they were treated unfairly by the company. I spoke to a friend who works at another company. He said, "I just recently interviewed a couple of ex-Activision people and I must give you guys credit. It's incredible how positive they were about Activision. Those people who used to work for you spoke very highly of you, your company, and your organization."

We had to change very rapidly and drastically, and that caused part of the shock. Since the layoffs though, we have tried to say to people that we can't make promises that you will have your job here, but we say that if we're successful, you'll be successful, and we'll treat you fairly. For the last six months, anyone here knows that their job could be eliminated for business reasons. Different people dealt with that differently. Whenever somebody's asked for a commitment or a promise, I say, we can't make one. Jim can't make one. And if that's not OK with you, I understand.

REORGANIZING THE CREATIVE PROCESS

By December 1984, David Crane was the only senior designer out of the original four. Reflecting on company changes in the creative arena, he recalled:

What we used to do was have four or five people together in one room. Everyone worked on their own original concept. Each person benefited from the experience of the people around them. We would badger each other a bit. We had a lighthearted peer review process. That seemed to work with a unique group of people who had already been through the mill. We knew what we wanted and what was good, so we were able to handle ourselves without management around. We would even cover our own costs. We would know not to buy a certain piece of equipment when we could make do with another one. We did that during a time when we could do no wrong. The industry was exploding, and we were far above the rest as far as product quality was concerned.

In the home computer industry of 1985, where it's easy to do things wrong, we don't have the same clear creative line on the industry. Nowadays, computers have more power, colors and picture capacity than videogame machines. It makes it difficult for the consumer to tell that he has a quality product that comes along. I can say, "Come back and I'll tell you what went really quality or if it's just a good picture.

My role at the company now is to represent the qualitative creative review for everyone who works on product design. That kind of review is best done during the development of the product. I am intimately involved in every product that comes along. I can say, "Come back and I'll tell you what went wrong six months ago," that's a waste of time. I can usually see in advance where a person is going wrong. So my general role is to keep a short rein on the quality of the product, yet try not to put my stamp on everything.

Brad Fregger, the former manager of training for the company, and I will be doing a job which is called the CDM (creative development manager). I am not a manager, but I have the creative side. Brad is both, but would be swamped by the size and scope of the organization. We will make up the only CDM in the company. When discussed with Brad, his first thought was, "Why don't you change my title to DM? I said, "Because you have creative input and I don't want to remove 'creative' from your title. I still expect that out of you." Ken will be the overall administrator of the process. [In December 1984, Ken Coleman became vice president in charge of product development.] One thing Jim once told me was that he's seldom seen a person with creative gears who could also administer a process. "You can either search for talent and see it, or be able to administer details: dollars, cents, compensation, and rewards."

We're going to spread out the configuration so if a good idea comes from anybody in the company, it'll filter down and you'll hear about it. I think that is probably the best design arrangement the world's ever seen. We have strong, proven talent and some raw talent all put together in a group organization where we lean on one another and leverage one another. And it will be administered by Ken who is one of those rare people who can work in a managerial situation and never lie to you. He's one of the people who you always know is telling the truth. When you're dealing with a creative group of people, honesty is very important. In order to sit back, create and have fun, we must have confidence that the system will take our product to market, and that we're being treated fairly.

What we have attempted now at Activision is to recapture the flavor of the company's first couple of years. Our best feelings have always come when three or four of us could push our chairs back, stare at a screen and not feel any outside pressure. Just have a look at it and say, "Gee, what should we do now?" There is a lot to be said for the feeling you get from mutual respect in a group.

In the early days of the company, we had five people working in a design center. We found that if you put 10 or 20 people in one room, there is just too much confusion. We would take a group of five and drop them in an office, surround them with a wall, give them an administrator, which was the CDM. He/she was meant as "manager of development of creative product," not necessarily as a creative addition to the product itself. We started design centers as a seeding process and hoped that one of those people would rise to the level of dominance. Then he could be plugged in with another group. The concept was great, but one of the problems was that we were doing it at a time when the best people in the industry were starting their own companies. So, we often got people who had been skipped over by other people who had left to start something of their own.

We had six design centers and now we have one. One of my goals in this environment is to polish the raw talent and give them what they need to become the primo designers of two or three years from now. I've got a lot of good people to work with. Our current approach involves the notion of co-design. I will be working one-on-one with another designer and sharing my time that way. Sort of like a co-authored book.

It's still possible that we'll find out we're wrong. Maybe my best contribution is just to do one piece of a good product. But one piece of a good product does not an industry make. Maybe it can support a company, but we're trying to rebuild an industry. So we need lots of good quality products. It's going to be harder work than I've done for a long time, but it's work that I enjoy and do well, so I'll come in and do it. As long as I can continue to enjoy it, I can make creative decisions. I do it by feel. Ten seconds per decision. That's not so bad.

We don't hesitate to shelve projects either. If I'm two months into an eight-month project and I cannot feel what's it's going to be like at the end, then it's time not to gamble the next six months of your life on it. We'll shelve it.

On the issue of motivation, royalties can be a problem. We've always believed that there is value to group interaction. Nothing destroys group interaction more than individual royalties. "You didn't help me. I helped you." "What's in it for me?" The good game designer is a person who's doing it because he enjoys it. So, we've always felt that overriding all compensation and management issues is the importance of providing an environment in which the designer can do that. I haven't seen any other places that do that well. I've seen a lot of places that reward individual effort, but they have not generated the best quality product that the industry has seen.

Exhibits 4 and *5* discuss two important new products for the "new" Activision.

EXHIBIT 1 ACTIVISION, INC. AND SUBSIDIARIES CONSOLIDATED STATEMENT OF INCOME (in thousands except per share data)

| | YEARS ENDED MARCH 31, | | |
	1984	1983	1982
Net sales	$ 69,981	$157,633	$65,987
Cost and expenses:			
Cost of sales	40,719	42,820	20,829
Sales and marketing expenses	42,016	62,346	13,941
General, administrative and product development expenses	22,197	15,339	5,201
	104,932	120,505	39,971
Operating income (loss)	(34,951)	37,128	26,016
Interest income	1,407	575	244
Interest expense	(66)	(152)	(155)
Income (loss) before provision (credit) for income taxes	(33,610)	37,551	26,105
Provision (credit) for income taxes	(15,600)	18,368	13,187
Net income (loss)	$ (18,010)	$ 19,183	$12,918
Net income (loss) per share	$ (.56)	$ .64	$ .43
Number of common and common equivalent shares used in computing net income (loss) per share	32,143	29,987	30,095

The accompanying notes are an integral part of these financial statements.

EXHIBIT 1 (cont.) ACTIVISION, INC. AND SUBSIDIARIES
CONSOLIDATED BALANCE SHEET
(in thousands except share data)

	MARCH 31,	
	1984	1983
ASSETS:		
Current Assets:		
Cash and temporary cash investments	$7,605	$ 2,403
Accounts receivable, less allowances for doubtful accounts and sales returns of $6,747 in 1984 and $5,016 in 1983	12,815	22,974
Inventories	10,278	21,186
Refundable income taxes	11,900	—
Deferred income taxes	5,501	3,484
Other current assets	1,916	1,027
Total current assets	50,015	51,074
Fixed assets	6,495	5,204
Other assets	211	181
Total assets	$56,721	$56,459
LIABILITIES AND SHAREHOLDERS' EQUITY:		
Current liabilities:		
Accounts payable	$ 4,592	$ 9,265
Accrued liabilities	3,129	5,878
Income taxes payable	—	7,493
Subordinated notes payable to shareholders	550	—
Total current liabilities	8,271	22,636
Deferred income taxes	128	239
Subordinated notes payable to shareholders	—	550
Total liabilities	8,399	23,425
Commitments and contingencies (Notes 10 and 11).		
Shareholders' equity:		
Preferred stock, no par value:		
Authorized: 10,000,000 shares		
Issued and outstanding: None		
Common stock, no par value:		
Authorized: 100,000,000 shares		
Issued and outstanding: 32,691,460 shares in 1984 and 29,696,800 shares in 1983	33,660	362
Retained earnings	14,662	32,672
Total shareholders' equity	48,322	33,034
Total liabilities and shareholders' equity	$56,721	$56,459

The accompanying notes are an integral part of these financial statements.

EXHIBIT 2 ACTIVISION (B)

ACTIVISION STOCK PRICE DATA

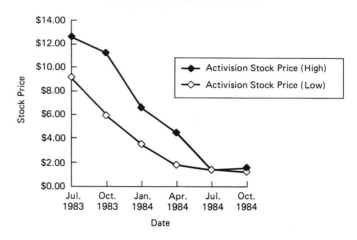

EXHIBIT 3 ACTIVISION (B): DOWNTURN

TOTAL EMPLOYEES
ACTIVISION—9/83 to 11/84

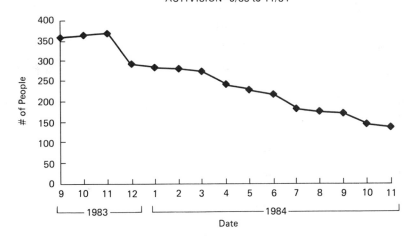

HUMAN RESOURCE FLOWS
ACTIVISION—PART I

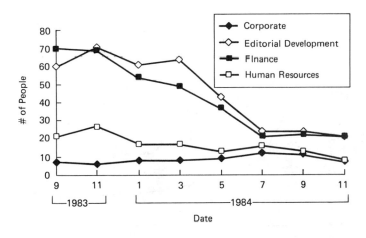

EXHIBIT 3 (cont.)

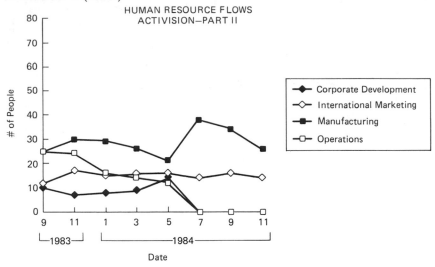

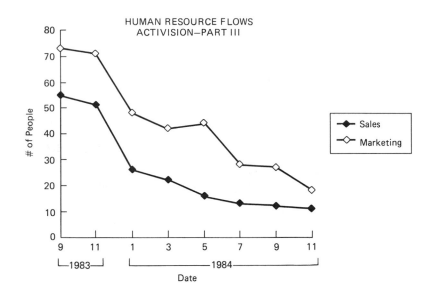

EXHIBIT 4   ACTIVISION (B)

For Immediate Release
Contact: Mike Ayers
(415) 960-0410

LATEST ACTIVISION SOFTWARE PUTS YOU IN THE DESIGNER'S SEAT

MOUNAIN VIEW, CALIFORNIA, NOVEMBER 9, 1984—*The Designer's Pencil* from Activision tackles head-on the issue of "user friendliness." The product, currently reaching retail stores, unlocks the graphic and sound power of the Commodore 64 in a quick and easy format accessible to even the novice computer owner.

Designer Garry Kitchen developed *The Designer's Pencil* so that anyone could experience the creative thrill of software design without having to learn complicated programming procedures. "All you do is tap the joystick a couple of times, and you can experience the immediate satisfaction of seeing a computer execute your commands," he says.

The Designer's Pencil is currently available on disk or cartridge for the Commodore 64. Apple II, IBM and Atari versions will be available early in 1985.

The key to the *The Designer's Pencil* is a new computer language developed by Kitchen which replaces complicated computer instructions. For further ease, the owner needs only a joystick to enter, modify, run and save his programs. Thus reducing the kinds of errors common with keyboard commands.

The user controls two screens. The first is a computer "palette," with more than 80 graphic and musical commands. Choosing from these commands, the user can create graphics and music on the second screen or "canvas." On the canvas, a familiar yellow pencil executes the commands instantly.

Because of this ease of use, Activision says that almost anyone will be encouraged to create something—even those who claim, "I can't draw a straight line with a ruler."

Activision's complete package provides 12 sample "canvasses" which preview some of the many directions the user can take. Simple directions start the user on a new path toward becoming a "software designer" in his own right.

The Designer's Pencil requires absolutely no previous artistic or computer knowledge and is the only product of its type which lets the user create both pictures and sound (or music).

Because of its simplicity and instant feedback, *The Designer's Pencil* offers anyone the ability to have a "personal relationship" with his computer. But Activision says its new software language is also sophisticated enough to attract the computer programmer who would like to create pictures and music without the time, effort and frustration of traditional programming.

Kitchen says, "Because everything is in English, this is the first computer language that really takes the power of a computer and lets anybody play with it, painlessly.

"If you've been delaying buying a home computer because you don't know what to do with it, or you've had some reservations about your own capabilities, you'll have to create some other excuse, because *The Designer's Pencil* has erased those alibis," Kitchen says.

EXHIBIT 5 ACTIVISION (B)

For Immediate Release
Contact: Mike Ayers
(415) 690-0410

ACTIVISION RELEASES GHOSTBUSTERS, THE COMPUTER GAME

MOUNTAIN VIEW, CALIFORNIA, NOVEMBER 5, 1984— Activision, Inc. today announced the shipment of *Ghostbusters, The Computer Game.*

This original computer game, by David Crane, is based on the blockbuster movie of the year. It captures all the visual excitement, music, story and humor of the film, and then adds more: the game play, action and strategy of a compelling adventure.

"A game has to be more than a movie," says award-winning designer David Crane, who created and directed the design of *Ghostbusters.* "We pulled out all the stops to make this a game based on a movie, not a story that resembles a game."

In *Ghostbusters, The Computer Game,* the player is a would-be ghostbuster challenged to start and build a franchise and avert a ghostly disaster of biblical proportions brewing in New York City.

The plot and game play of *Ghostbusters* are marked by a wealth of creative and technical surprises: multiple screens of New York City landmarks; voice synthesis; a detailed map of the city to help coordinate the citywide battle; specially-equipped "Ectomobiles" that comb the streets of New York; custom equipment to nab the best in graphic ghouls from "slimers" to "roamers" to a giant marshmallow man. There is even the hit *Ghostbusters* theme song.

The title is available on disk for the Commodore 64 home computer, and will soon be available for Apple and Atari home computers.

Promotional support for *Ghostbusters* includes television spots on MTV, radio contests in major markets, a four-color in-packed poster for retailers as well as a national print advertising campaign in trade and consumer publications. A four-color full-page ad is appearing in such magazines as *People, Billboard, Rolling Stones,* and *Enter.*

Activision is a leading developer and marketer of entertainment software for home computers.

Editor's Note
Ghostbusters, The Computer Game—Game Play

Activision's *Ghostbusters* begins with a colorful title screen accompanied by a sing-along version of the movie's theme song. As the music plays the player can follow the words as they appear beneath a bouncing ball.

The player opens play with a $10,000 bankroll to start a franchise. The money must be spent wisely to purchase the right Ectomobile (choice of four) and outfit it with the appropriate equipment. This includes a PK (Psychokinetic) Energy Detector, an Image Intensifier, a Marshmallow Sensor, a Ghost Vacuum, Ghost Traps and Bait, and even a Portable Laser Confinement System.

Next, a map of the city appears, with Zuul's horrible temple in the center and Ghostbusters headquarters (GHQ) at the bottom. Red flashing buildings indicate the presence of nasty "Slimers." Other ghosts, called "Roamers," slink across the city on their way to Zuul. The player must plot a course to the disturbances while stopping and capturing Roamers (by crossing their path). When the vehicle arrives at the flashing building, a push of the joystick button brings up a "travel" screen; the player then steers his Ectomobile through the city streets, vacuuming up Roamers with another push of the button.

Scary? The fun's only beginning. At the site of the paranormal activity is a hovering blob of ectoplasm: yes, a Slimer. The player—directing a pair of Ghostbusters—must deposit a trap, power on the pair's negative ionizer backpacks, and use the streams (WITHOUT CROSSING THEM!) to maneuver the Slimer over the trap.

A well-timed push of the button activates the trap and pulls the ghoul in. A miss gets you slimed. Every trapped Slimer earns money for the franchise; every missed Slimer adds 300 dangerous points to the city's PK energy level.

By the way—beware the random appearance of the dreaded Stay-Puft Man. When a MARSHMALLOW ALERT flashes on the bottom of the screen, the Roamers will quickly run to a single spot. The player must immediately drop a dollop of ghost bait—or else the minions of Zuul will gather to form that well-known monolith of marshmallow monstrosity. He will then stomp the nearest building—the damage cost of which could put the franchise out of business.

When the gatekeeper and keymaster finally join at the Temple of Zuul, the final screen appears. If the player has earned enough credits to continue, he must sneak some Ghostbusters into the entrance of spook central. Unfortunately, it is guarded by the huge, gleeful, leaping Stay-Puft Man. If two men get through his legs, the player has won—and earns the right to view the animated finale. The streams are crossed, the portals to the underworld are closed, and the world is safe once again, thanks to the spunk of your Professional Paranormal Investigations and Eliminations franchise.

On My Painting

MAX BECKMANN

Max Beckmann (1884-1950), the great independent among German expressionists, did not attempt to explain his art, nor art in general. *On My Painting* is a beautiful extension in words of the haunting world of his paintings, one of the rare instances in which an artist has succeeded in putting into words the sense not just of his paintings, but of their genesis. It is probably more accurate to call it a prose poem, rather than an essay.

On My Painting was a lecture given by Beckmann at the New Burlington Galleries, London, in 1938. It was published in 1941 by the late Curt Valentin, in New York, and I am indebted to Ralph F. Colin, executor of the Valentin estate, for permission to use it here. Mrs. Max Beckmann, working from the original German manuscript, provided me with a number of corrections, especially in the "Song" toward the end of the text. With the greatest goodwill and patience, she checked and rechecked the revisions, and I offer her my sincerest thanks.

Before I begin to give you an explanation, an explanation which it is nearly impossible to give, I would like to emphasize that I have never been politically active in any way. I have only tried to realize my conception of the world as intensely as possible.

Painting is a very difficult thing. It absorbs the whole man, body and soul—thus I have passed blindly many things which belong to real and political life.

I assume, though, that there are two worlds: the world of spiritual life and the world of political reality. Both are manifestations of life which may sometimes coincide but are very different in principle. I must leave it to you to decide which is the more important.

What I want to show in my work is the idea which hides itself behind so-called reality. I am seeking for the bridge which leads from the visible to the invisible, like the famous cabalist who once said: "If you wish to get hold of the invisible you must penetrate as deeply as possible into the visible."

My aim is always to get hold of the magic of reality and to transfer this reality into painting—to make the invisible visible through reality. It may sound paradoxical, but it is, in fact, reality which forms the mystery of our existence.

What helps me most in this task is the penetration of space. Height, width, and depth are the three phenomena which I must transfer into one plane to form the abstract surface of the picture, and thus to protect myself from the infinity of space. My figures come and go, suggested by fortune or misfortune. I try to fix them divested of their apparent accidental quality.

One of my problems is to find the Self, which has only one form and is immortal—to find it in animals and men, in the heaven and in the hell which together form the world in which we live.

Space, and space again, is the infinite deity which surrounds us and in which we are ourselves contained.

Reprinted with permission of the estate of Max Beckmann, from *Modern Artists on Art,* Robert L. Herbert ed. (Englewood Cliffs, NJ: Prentice Hall, 1964).

That is what I try to express through painting, a function different from poetry and music but, for me, predestined necessity.

When spiritual, metaphysical, material, or immaterial events come into my life, I can only fix them by way of painting. It is not the subject which matters but the translation of the subject into the abstraction of the surface by means of painting. Therefore I hardly need to abstract things, for each object is unreal enough already, so unreal that I can only make it real by means of painting.

Often, very often, I am alone. My studio in Amsterdam, an enormous old tobacco storeroom, is again filled in my imagination with figures from the old days and from the new, like an ocean moved by storm and sun and always present in my thoughts.

Then shapes become beings and seem comprehensible to me in the great void and uncertainty of the space which I call God.

Sometimes I am helped by the constructive rhythm of the Cabala, when my thoughts wander over Oannes Dagon to the last days of drowned continents. Of the same substance are the streets with their men, women, and children; great ladies and whores; servant girls and duchesses. I seem to meet them, like doubly significant dreams, in Samothrace and Piccadilly and Wall Street. They are Eros and the longing for oblivion.

All these things come to me in black and white like virtue and crime. Yes, black and white are the two elements which concern me. It is my fortune, or misfortune, that I can see neither all in black nor all in white. One vision alone would be much simpler and clearer, but then it would not exist. It is the dream of many to see only the white and truly beautiful, or the black, ugly and destructive. But I cannot help realizing both, for only in the two, only in black and in white, can I see God as a unity creating again and again a great and eternally changing terrestrial drama.

Thus without wanting it, I have advanced from principle to form, to transcendental ideas, a field which is not at all mine, but in spite of this I am not ashamed.

In my opinion, all important things in art since Ur of the Chaldees, since Tel Halaf and Crete, have always originated from the deepest feeling about the mystery of Being. Self-realization is the urge of all objective spirits. It is this Self for which I am searching in my life and in my art.

Art is creative for the sake of realization, not for amusement; for transfiguration, not for the sake of play. It is the quest of our Self that drives us along the eternal and never-ending journey we must all make.

My form of expression is painting; there are, of course, other means to this end such as literature, philosophy, or music; but as a painter, cursed or blessed with a terrible and vital sensuousness, I must look for wisdom with my eyes. I repeat, with my eyes, for nothing could be more ridiculous or irrelevant than a "philosophical conception" painted purely intellectually without the terrible fury of the senses grasping each visible form of beauty and ugliness. If from those forms which I have found in the visible, literary subjects result—such as portraits, landscapes, or recognizable compositions— they have all originated from the senses, in this case from the eyes, and each intellectual subject has been transformed again into form, color, and space.

Everything intellectual and transcendent is joined together in painting by the uninterrupted labor of the eyes. Each shade of a flower, a face, a tree, a fruit, a sea, a mountain, is noted eagerly by the intensity of the senses to which is added, in a way of which I am not conscious, the work of my mind, and in the end the strength or weakness of *my soul*. It is this genuine, eternally unchanging center of strength which makes mind and sense capable of expressing personal things. It is the strength of the soul which forces the mind to constant exercise to widen its conception of space.

Something of this is perhaps contained in my pictures.

Life is difficult, as perhaps everyone knows by now. It is to escape from these difficulties that I practice the pleasant profession of a painter. I admit that there are more lucrative ways of escaping the so-called difficulties of life, but I allow myself my own particular luxury, painting.

It is, of course, a luxury to create art and, on top of this, to insist on expressing one's own artistic opinion. Nothing is more luxurious than this. It is a game and a good game, at least for me; one of the few games which make life, difficult and depressing as it is sometimes, a little more interesting.

Love in an animal sense is an illness, but a necessity which one has to overcome. Politics is an odd game, not without danger I have been told, but certainly sometimes amusing. To eat and to drink are habits not to be despised but often connected with unfortunate consequences. To sail around the earth in 91 hours must be very strenuous, like racing in cars or splitting the atoms. But the most exhausting thing of all—is boredom.

So let me take part in your boredom and in your dreams while you take part in mine which may be yours as well.

To begin with, there has been enough talk about art. After all, it must always be unsatisfactory to try to express one's deeds in words. Still we shall go on and on, talking and painting and making music, boring ourselves, exciting ourselves, making war and peace as long as our strength of imagination lasts. Imagination is perhaps the most decisive characteristic of mankind. My dream is the imagination of space—to change the optical impression of the world of objects by a transcendental arithmetic progression of the inner being. That is the precept. In principle any alteration of the object is allowed which has a sufficiently strong creative power behind it. Whether such alteration causes excitement or boredom in the spectator is for you to decide.

The uniform application of a principle of form is what rules me in the imaginative alteration of an object. One thing is sure— we have to transform the three-dimensional world of objects into the two-dimensional world of the canvas.

If the canvas is only filled with a two-dimensional conception of space, we shall have applied art, or ornament. Certainly this may give us pleasure, though I myself find it boring as it does not give me enough visual sensation. To transform height, width, and depth into two dimensions is for me an experience full of magic in which I glimpse for a moment that fourth dimension which my whole being is seeking.

I have always on principle been against the artist speaking about himself or his work. Today neither vanity nor ambition causes me to talk about matters which generally are not to be expressed even to oneself. But the world is in such a catastrophic state, and art is so bewildered, that I, who have lived the last thirty years almost as a hermit, am forced to leave my snail's shell to express these few ideas which, with much labor, I have come to understand in the course of the years.

The greatest danger which threatens mankind is collectivism. Everywhere attempts are being made to lower the happiness and the way of living of mankind to the level of termites. I am against these attempts with all the strength of my being.

The individual representation of the object, treated sympathetically or antipathetically, is highly necessary and is an enrichment to the world of form. The elimination of the human relationship in artistic representation causes the vacuum which makes all of us suffer in various degrees—an individual alteration of the details of the object represented is necessary in order to display on the canvas the whole physical reality.

Human sympathy and understanding must be reinstated. There are many ways and means to achieve this. Light serves me to a considerable extent on the one hand to divide the surface of the canvas, on the other to penetrate the object deeply.

As we still do not know what this Self really is, this Self in which you and I in our various ways are expressed, we must peer deeper and deeper into its discovery. For the Self is the great veiled mystery of the world. Hume and Herbert Spencer studied its various conceptions but were not able in the end to discover the truth. I believe in it and in its eternal, immutable form. Its path is, in some strange and peculiar manner, our path. And for this reason I am immersed in the phenomenon of the Individual, the so-called whole Individual, and I try in every way to explain and present it. What are you? What am I? Those are the questions that constantly persecute and torment me and perhaps also play some part in my art.

Color, as the strange and magnificent expression of the inscrutable spectrum of Eternity, is beautiful and important to me as a painter; I use it to enrich the canvas and to probe more deeply into the object. Color also decided, to a certain extent, my spiritual outlook, but it is subordinated to light and, above all, to the treatment of form. Too much emphasis on color at the expense of form and space would make a double manifestation of itself on the canvas, and this would verge on craft work. Pure colors and broken tones must be used together, because they are the complements of each other.

These, however, are all theories, and words are too insignificant to define the problems of art. My first unformed impression, and what I would like to achieve, I can perhaps only realize when I am impelled as in a vision.

One of my figures, perhaps one from the "Temptation," sang this strange song to me one night—

Fill up again your pumpkins with alcohol, and hand up the largest of them to me. . . . Solemn, I will light the giant candles for you. Now in the night. In the deep black night.

We are playing hide-and-seek, we are playing hide-and-seek across a thousand seas. We gods, we gods when the skies are red at dawn, at midday, and in the blackest night.

You cannot see us, no you cannot see us but you are ourselves. . . . Therefore we laugh so gaily when the skies are red at dawn, at midday, and in the blackest night.

Stars are our eyes and the nebulae our beards. . . . We have people's souls for our hearts. We hide ourselves and you cannot see us, which is just what we want when the skies are red at dawn, at midday, and in the blackest night.

Our torches stretch away without end . . . silver, glowing red, purple, violet, green-blue, and black. We bear them in our dance over the seas and the mountains, across the boredom of life.

We sleep and stars circle in the gloomy dream. We wake and the suns assemble for the dance across bankers and fools, whores and duchesses.

Thus the figure from my "Temptation" sang to me for a long time, trying to escape from the square on the hypotenuse in order to achieve a particular constellation of the Hebrides, to the Red Giants and the Central Sun.

And then I awoke and yet continued to dream . . . painting constantly appeared to me as the one and only possible achievement. I thought of my grand old friend Henri Rousseau, that Homer in the porter's lodge whose prehistoric dreams have sometimes brought me near the gods. I saluted him in my dream. Near him I saw William Blake, noble emanation of English genius. He waved friendly greetings to me like a super-terrestrial patriarch. "Have confidence in objects," he said, "do not let yourself be intimidated by the horror of the world. Everything is ordered and correct and must fulfil its destiny in order to attain perfection. Seek this path and you will attain from your own Self ever deeper perception of the eternal beauty of creation; you will attain increasing release from all that which now seems to you sad or terrible."

I awoke and found myself in Holland in the midst of a boundless world turmoil. But my belief in the final release and absolution of all things, whether they please or torment, was newly strengthened. Peacefully I laid my head among the pillows . . . to sleep, and dream, again.

Creating Video Games That Score

One Startup Stresses Team Efforts, Another Creative Freedom. Both Are Winners.

In one corner of Imagic Inc.'s Los Gatos (Calif.) headquarters is an area nicknamed "the zoo." Inside, behind locked doors, are Imagic's 30 video-game designers, most of them young men in their 20s. There are few rules in the zoo. Designers work any hours they choose. Some dress in shorts and T-shirts. One wears three earrings.

Activision Inc., in nearby Santa Clara, has a similar lab. It, too, is a distraction-free haven for game designers. Fewer than 10 nondesigners have access to the lab. No memos are ever delivered to it. The telephones there don't ring—they simply flash a small light.

If Imagic and Activision pamper their designers, it is with good reason. These small, elite groups are at the heart of the companies' product development efforts in the video-game software business, a cash mill that generated $1.4 billion in sales last year and may top $2 billion this year as game machines and home computers proliferate. Unlike other leading competitors, such as Atari Inc., these two stunningly successful startups rely entirely on internal development for their game ideas. But their approach to game design could hardly be more different.

Arts and sciences. Reflecting nearly opposite philosophies of product development, Activision tries to give individual designers as much creative freedom as possible, while Imagic emphasizes team projects and market testing. Says James H. Levy, Activision's president: "Creative businesses aren't factories. To be successful, you must deal with and live with uncertainty and surprises. If you try to make it too predictable, you squeeze all the life out of it."

Imagic comes at it from the other side. "Product development is not one artist creating something all by himself," says President William F. X. Grubb, who, at 38, is the oldest member of Imagic's management. "Here, the designer is more like an orchestra leader."

Activision's 31 designers, for instance, choose their own projects with no interference from the marketing department. In fact, Activision does no market research on a game until the designer is completely finished. "Market research will kill as many good games as bad ones," says Levy. Instead, during the game design process, which typically takes about six months, a designer constantly tries out new ideas on his fellow designers and on Activision's creative-development managers. These managers serve as sounding boards for ideas and as liaison with the rest of the company.

But for the most part, design at Activision is a one-person process. Each designer is responsible for all aspects: selecting the idea, writing the computer programs that control objects on the screen, and adding sound and background graphics. Activision managers believe team projects cut creativity. "Very few novels are written on an assembly-line basis," says Thomas M. Lopez, vice-president for editorial development. Says designer Steve Cartwright: "I wouldn't want to let someone else do my work. I'm the only one who will put in enough effort to make it right."

Toothpaste to the rescue. Cartwright has designed several of Activision's hit games, including Megamania, and has just finished Plaque Attack, set for release this summer. Rather than have the player fire missiles against a spaceship, this game calls for shooting a jet of toothpaste to defend a set of teeth against advancing columns of hamburgers, French fries, and ice cream cones. Cartwright spent months revising his original idea. "You go through hundreds of different combinations. There's a fine line between something that's challenging and something that's frustrating."

Throughout the long process of designing a game, Activision officials avoid imposing deadlines. "Time pressure makes the designer take short cuts," says Lopez. "It could turn a mega-hit into an average game. The game might lose that indescribable something that tickles neurons in millions of people."

At Imagic, designers write the computer motion and control programs that form the heart of the game, but in many cases a specialized artist designs the game's graphics, while another adds sound effects. This specialization is made possible, in part, by software tools developed at Imagic that make it easier to program a computer to perform special tasks. For instance, Imagic has developed a program called Da Vinci, which assists in designing graphics, and another called Handel, which helps create sound effects.

Imagic promotes close collaboration between the marketing and design staffs. Marketing managers even sit in on the designers' twice-a-year "game-storming" weekends and sometimes throw out ideas of their own.

The Imagic product development process begins with those weekend meetings. After each one, designers draw up a list of 100 or so game ideas, then whittle that down to 30 or 40, and present these to the marketing department. Marketing produces story boards and game descriptions for each idea and then runs a "concept test" with about 100 teenagers. The results can influence the designer's approach to the game. One game originally involved a mouse trying to pick up cheese while being chased by a cat. Concept tests showed that teenagers preferred a game in which a prince tries to pick up treasures while being chased by a dragon. The designer followed the market feedback, and the game, called Dragonfire, is now a hit.

With Stock Options and Incentives, Top Designers Can Become Multimillionaires

Designer Rick Levine got the idea for his new game, Truckin', during one of his regular 800-mi. round trips on California's Highway 5 to visit his girlfriend. Market research showed children preferred a truck game to a car game. The player learns about U.S. geography as he guides the truck around the country, making deliveries on a tight schedule.

Imagic designers do not have to use all

concept-testing results in their games. "We like to see engineers follow about 80% of the results," says James H. Goldberger, vice-president of marketing. But if concept scores are very high or low, "we lobby very hard," he adds.

Licensing devotees. Most of the half-dozen other leading companies in the videogame software business hew to a product development approach totally different from those practiced at Imagic and Activision. They rely largely on licensing well-known arcade games and movie titles and converting them to home games. Atari's hugely successful Pac-Man, for example, was based on a license from Bally Mfg. Corp.

Coleco Industries Inc. attributes its zoom from zero to 8 million game cartridges sold last year to the "prerecognition" of its games drawn from arcade hits, such as Donkey Kong and Turbo. Releases for 1983 include licensed games based on the movie *Rocky* and the cartoon characters, the Smurfs. Coleco President Arnold C. Greenberg insists: "The real weak area [in home videogame sales] is the multiplicity of nonlicensed titles." But Activision and Imagic disagree; both believe that in the long run, internal development of original games will be the best way to survive.

Until recently, explains Levy of Activision, product development played only a modest role in the game software business. "The consumer developed a voracious appetite that couldn't be satisfied," he says. "To a certain extent, products sold no matter how good they were."

E.T. stays home. The seller's market fizzled last year when supply caught up with demand, and weaker software products no longer sold well. Earnings fell below esti-

mates at several companies, including industry leader Atari, which was hurt by defections of key designers to Activision, Imagic, and elsewhere. One of Atari's most spectacular losers was a game based on a coveted license that seemed like a certain winner: the movie *E.T.* Atari paid $22 million in licensing fees. Thinking it could sell 4 million cartridges, it reportedly produced that many. It sold only 1 million—potential buyers found the game dull.

The supply of movie and arcade properties suitable for conversion to video games is limited, says Levy. "Each year, 100 titles will drive the business," he predicts. "The arcade business can provide 6 or 10 titles a year. Only a half-dozen movies could be the conceptual basis for video games. Where will the other 85 come from? They will be original product designed for the medium."

So far, that thinking has worked, and the payoff for Activision and Imagic has been remarkable. At Activision, founded in 1979, revenues for the nine months ending Dec. 31 topped $100 million. Imagic, which shipped its first product in March, 1982, sold more than $75 million worth of game software in its first year of business. Its Demon Attack won the-game-of-the-year award from *Electronic Games* magazine last year. And in recent months two cartridges from Activision, Pitfall and River Raid, have occupied the first and second positions on the top 10 chart published by *Billboard* magazine. "When it comes to creative games, Activision and Imagic are definitely the leaders," says Michael J. Blanchet, who writes a syndicated column on video games for a variety of papers.

Thoroughbred talent. For the designers, too, the rewards stretch well beyond the freedom of "the zoo" and a phone-free lab. Both Activision's Cartwright and

Imagic's Levine, for instance, receive royalties on games they have designed. And if, as expected, Activision and Imagic go public later this year, both men will become multimillionaires through their stock holdings.

Such incentives have helped Activision and Imagic attract the cream of the industry's design talent, giving them both a big advantage. "Design is the cornerstone of success in video games," notes Arnie Katz, editor of *Electronic Games* magazine. "If you don't have the horses, you can't run."

When Friends Run the Business

In the summer of 1979, Alan Ladd, Jr., Jay Kanter, and Gareth Wigan resigned their top positions in the motion picture division of Twentieth Century-Fox over, among other things, a major dispute concerning the payment of bonus money to production people. After a few months, Ladd founded The Ladd Company, an independent film production group, in partnership with Warner Communications Inc., where Kanter and Wigan continue their creative roles as heads of production.

A couple of things stand out in this simple chronology. First, the people at the top of a large division—which in 1978 had received 33 Academy Award nominations and which had just produced the largest single money-making film in the industry's history (*Star Wars*)—believed that the people involved in the creation of the product were more important than the company. Second, the relationships between the three of them and those people were themselves important to their success. Quite simply, Ladd, Kanter, and Wigan trust each other, and they are friends.

The link between friendship and managerial success, at least at The Ladd Company, is the climate for encouraging creativity that trust creates. Attributes of friendship, candor, lack of competition among individuals, and deep mutual concern become the attributes of a company. The interviews that follow show how these relationships contribute to making effective decisions and allow Ladd and company to motivate creative people in ways that go against such traditional management practices as MBO and performance appraisal techniques.

Readers may ask how the successful management approach at The Ladd Company and the work atmosphere could apply to other management teams, films being so distinct a product. But the work environment of the film industry is not so foreign to any company where creative individuals need to blend their talents and where the goals are unsure, the means ambiguous, and no one has a blueprint.

The success factors Ladd and company have isolated, aside from sheer expertise, should be of interest to peer organizations or professional groups such as architectural and consulting firms, advertising agencies, publishing houses, engineering and scientific groups, and R&D groups even within large companies. Ladd worked as a film agent for Creative Management Associates and then as a film producer for a few years before joining Fox as vice president of production in 1973. In 1976, he became president, Twentieth Century-Fox Pictures. Kanter, for years a top Hollywood agent, produced films for MCA Inc. in London before joining Ladd at Fox in 1975, where he was senior vice president of worldwide production. Wigan began his career in film working first for MCA Inc. and then in his own agency, which eventually merged into EMI Limited, before joining Fox in June 1975, where he was vice president of worldwide production.

These interviews were conducted and edited by Eliza G. C. Collins, senior editor, Harvard Business Review.

Photographs by Bill Aron.

ALAN LADD, JR.

HBR: We'd like to discuss how important close personal relationships are to your work, mainly relationships with people you work with daily but also with the creative people you select to do a film. For instance, you have been quoted as saying that when you decided to do Star Wars you were actually betting on George Lucas.

That's true. I had seen the two movies he'd done—*American Graffiti,* which I was very impressed with, and *THX,* which is a different kind of movie altogether—and I felt that he had extraordinary talent. I get a lot of credit for taking a big risk on *Star Wars,* but the truth is it didn't scare me as much as a lot of other pictures did.

What made the difference?

Lucas himself and the way he explained what he was going to do and how he was going to do it. He said he had an idea about a space picture that was a throwback to all the old movies we grew up on as kids. Because I grew up in this business and saw every movie ever made, or tried to, and have a great love for film, when he said, "This sequence is going to be like *The Seahawk,* or this like *Captain Blood,* and this like *Flash Gordon,*" I knew exactly what he was saying. That gave me confidence he was going to pull it off. I knew from other people and from spending time with him that he was a dead honest person who knew what he was doing.

Was the same true of Ridley Scott? You had seen only his one film, The Duelists, before you chose him to direct Alien. Did you get to know him too?

Yes, I did. But I think, too, you can see a lot in films about directors—what their attitudes are, how they feel. You can look at a film and get a feeling—just an intuition—that the director is not quite sensitive enough for what you're trying to do, or lacks a sense of humor, or seems to back away from confrontation sequences.

So you have to be on your intuitive toes all the time. Isn't that exhausting?

Yes, it is. That's why you really have to love this business. If you don't, it can tear you apart.

Could you describe what tears you apart?

Well, you're constantly dealing with people who have ideas different from your own, trying to make them feel that you're right, or to let them convince you that they're right. So there's a lot of giving and taking. Also, you have to form quick assessments of people and material because you don't have a lot of time. You have to make quick judgments and decisions. For example, how a film is to be marketed: Is this the right way or the wrong way? Should we go out with a picture in 500 theaters or in just 10? Some films lend themselves to a natural course of decisions, but others don't, particularly the riskier pictures like *Julia* and *The Turning Point*.

Then there's always that final moment when you say to somebody, "OK, here's $5 million, or $7 million, or $10 million—do what you want to do." And then you look at the daily rushes, sometimes saying, "Wonderful," and sometimes, "Oh, my God." Finally, it's always frightening to go to the first preview when you show the picture to the people "out there." Every time somebody gets up you think, "My God, are they walking out of the theater or are they going to the bathroom?" And you discover yourself getting up and following people to find out. It's a scary feeling, the 10 or 12 times a year you go to the theater and expose a picture for the first time. All you have to go on up to that point is the reaction you get sitting in an isolated little screening room.

What helps you deal with that pressure?

I think having friends around. For example, when we were still at Fox and we began to have trouble with the chairman and the board, I didn't involve anybody else in it. But I think it showed that my relationship with Jay and Gareth was very healthy. Basically, I had to deal with the corporate problem on my own, but there was someone to whom I could say, "God, was this frustrating! Can you believe this new chart that's coming out?" I need that. I like family. I've been married for over 20 years to the same person.

The relationships between you and Jay Kanter and Gareth Wigan seem important to the work you do. How would you describe them?

One thing that characterized us at Fox, which made us distinct from other companies, was that we ran it much like a family. Our personalities, thoughts, and ideas intertwine. This is a business of collaboration; you'll find that among people who make films, certain writing teams are wonderful together and certain directors work better with certain stars. The creative side is a business of input, discussion, and attitude. It's also a business we all work very hard at. In the mornings, Jay picks up the trade papers and we ride to the office together. Generally, we don't leave the office until 7 or 8 o'clock at night. We sit around and talk and laugh and let the tensions of the day wear off. I guess it works.

Do you see a lot of Kanter and Wigan during the day?

A great deal. We're in and out of each others' offices all the time and of course we're required to do certain social things in the evenings—take a writer, director, or producer to dinner, for example. Then our weekends are filled with business, often previewing pictures, which means we're away for the whole weekend. Working this way could be a nightmare if we didn't have good, strong relationships.

We read volumes of material and we phone to exchange ideas like, "Hey, I read this script; I think it's pretty good." Or if I get the figures on a Fox product such as *The Rose,* and it's doing really well, I'll call Jay and Gareth over the weekend.

You're still getting the Fox figures?

Sure, I left a bunch of films, like children, there; I still want to find out how they're behaving.

Would you call Kanter and Wigan friends?

Oh, absolutely, they're friends. Even if we didn't work together, we'd still be very close friends. There's no question about that. We left many people behind at Fox with whom all three of us are still very close. Last night Joe Graham—who's our vice president of business affairs—and I went out and watched a football game together. And we want the same kind of relationship with anybody who joins us. It's always been my feeling that you work best in a family environment, where you really care about the people you work with. I've just found working that way has always been more productive for everybody.

Would you say the relationships are intimate? Are there areas you feel you can't touch on?

I think we're very close. If something happened to one of my children, I'd certainly tell Jay or Gareth; or if they said, "You seem upset today," I wouldn't hesitate to say, "Well one of my daughters is fighting with her teacher." And they would tell me the same thing. It isn't as if the only things we talk about are work related.

If you had a personal problem, would you feel that you could talk to them without lessening your authority?

I think being able to talk freely is one of the things that makes it all work. And it's not just the three of us, but the same applies to all the people we've worked with in the past. They always felt they could talk to someone about a problem. Even the people who are still at Fox have no hesitation about calling one of us and saying, "Hey, do you mind if we have dinner? I've got a problem." We've always run a very open situation: people aren't suspect if they have emotions.

Does part of the work you do depend on being very close to your emotions—so that you can feel and trust your feelings?

People have always said that I'm very quiet and laid back and seem unemotional. But that isn't really true. Maybe I don't walk around shouting at people or hang up the phone and cry—but it's still a business of emotions. Reading a script, you have to be able to sit there and laugh. If it makes you laugh, you know it must be funny. Or you must be able to cry—if you can't, everything becomes flat. It's crucial to be able to trust your own responses to material.

Did you look for something particular in choosing Kanter and Wigan to work with?

Trust, basically. That's the first thing. Life is too short to work in an environment where you have to worry about somebody stabbing you in the back. You have to be able to trust a person completely.

How can you tell what somebody is likely to do?

Know the person. I've known Jay for a very long time; he was my father's agent. Then we worked together in London producing a lot of unsuccessful movies. Gareth and I worked together too; in fact, I more or less worked as an agent for him. So when Gareth came to Fox it was because I had known him previously. Sandy Lieberson—

he became president of Fox's production after I left, though he left too—and I worked together very closely 20 years ago as agents. I knew I could trust and feel comfortable and safe with him.

What about women?

We've had the same close working relationships with women. Strangely enough, I think half the people at Fox were women—Lucy Fisher, Paula Weinstein, to name two. I knew something about Paula because she dated David Field, and David worked at Fox. I knew from David she was a very trustworthy person.

What does that mean?

That you can communicate with each other, that you care about one another personally, that you can have a good old-fashioned argument without anybody walking out, slamming the door, and pouting.

When conflicts arise, how do you solve them?

It's a collective responsibility to resolve conflicts. We work them out openly, in a healthy manner. I've never gone home at night angry at Jay or Gareth. We might do things differently, but I've never gone home thinking, "They messed up everything; I should have done it myself." It's a business of making mistakes, and we all make them. You don't go in thinking you might be making a mistake, but you sure find out later.

So you don't take personally differences in feelings or opinions about a project—say, choosing a director for a film?

You have to respect those differences. Every Monday morning we have a meeting and discuss the scripts we've read over the week-end. Now one of us might be impassioned about a script, and someone else might hate it. We don't take a vote, but if everybody doesn't hate it, then we'll probably let the person who likes the project take it through the next step. By the same token, we can't expect the entire moviegoing public to like the same movie. Just because I like *Breaking Away* doesn't mean everybody out there is going to like it. Not everybody in the world liked *Star Wars*.

It seems to me enough did! Do the relationships ever become more important than a good business decision? In other words, are there times when preserving the group friendship and cohesion is more important than the price tag on a particular decision?

I don't think the question becomes an issue. If Jay came in and said, "Here's a picture that I'm totally passionate about; I really must do it," and Gareth and others in the company were totally negative, I'd say, "Well, wait a minute. As a friend I'd love to see you do the picture, but you can't put that burden on the rest of the company, because everybody else dreads it." If 50% of the people liked it and I didn't, I'd never say we weren't going to do it. But I don't think any of us would say, "I love it and I don't care that everybody else in the company hates it." On the other hand, the rest would never say, "We'll go along and do this because we don't want to hurt your feelings."

How do you appraise friends? Is that a problem with people who are close to you?

No, I don't think so. You don't sit down and appraise somebody on a yearly or six-month basis. We're not making shoes, where you can say, "Your output's lousy." Appraisal is an ongoing, constant thing that happens when you speak openly and freely to one another. When you feel something's going amiss, you say, "I think you're on the wrong track." But you state it at that time, not six months later when the personnel review comes up.

Do you feel it's necessary to say it at the time because you have to have a clear emotional slate to work with?

Absolutely. The worst thing we can do to ourselves and each other is let something fester inside and bother us. It's better to get it out in the open as best you can. And you try to do it tactfully. You just don't burst into somebody's office and say, "I don't like what you did." You don't send a memo and include it in someone's personnel file.

Isn't the confrontation difficult?

Not if you see it as necessary to the team effort, which it is. One thing that has made all this teamwork succeed is that none of our egos are involved. Nobody's ever said, "This is mine." Everything is everybody's. We all share. Nobody's ever said, "Well, the picture that failed was yours, and mine was the one that succeeded." You just can't say that because I made the decision to go with a film, I'm the one who should be heavily rewarded. A whole team of people—the person who comes in with the terrific ads, the person who develops a wonderful new kind of publicity, the production people—makes something work, not just one individual.

Does feeling part of a team, recognizing that your decision isn't the only thing that's going to make a film work or fail, in some ways mitigate the awesome feeling of being alone at the top?

It does. But the most important thing is working in an atmosphere that makes you happy to get up and come to work in the morning, looking forward to seeing every-

body in the hallway as you walk in. It would be horrendous for me to think, "Here's somebody I *have* to work with. He may be terrific, but I really can't tolerate this human being." That's a terrible thought.

Do you think that Kanter and Wigan feel they can come and confront you as easily as they can talk between themselves? Do you have a sense that there are eggshells subtly strewn around your office?

They're just as quick to confront me about something as they are each other. It worked the same with the group at Fox, not just Jay and Gareth. I never got upset when somebody in advertising came in and said, "I read the script and I don't like it."

How big a group had access to you?

Hundreds of people, actually. I've always had an open-door policy.

Isn't that distracting?

Yes, but it's important to the quality of work. For instance, at Fox the production and marketing people would come in and openly discuss what they did or didn't like about an ad or a script. But we were quick to say, "We'll do the best we can." And they really worked hard whether they liked a picture or not. If people feel free to say what they don't like, they're more open—and that's important.

You couldn't possibly be a personal friend to hundreds of people. Did some get jealous?

When you work with that many people, as long as they know you care, you don't have to have dinner with them every night to prove it. If they know you're trying to do the best for them in terms of salaries and are working on their behalf, and they know they can come in anytime and have a conversation about anything, they know you care.

Is it important to you that Kanter and Wigan are friends with each other as well?

Yes, because if something were wrong between them I'd be in the middle of it, like an arbitrator. It's best to let them arbitrate their own problems. As friends they can discuss problems openly between themselves. The people I've been close to all get along very well.

One senses the film business is exceedingly risky. When you decided to do The Turning Point and Julia, numbers of people thought it was a bad idea to put out two so-called female films so close together.

Followed by a third, *An Unmarried Woman.*

With The Rose in the background . . .

And *Norma Rae.*

Was it easier to make decisions when you had friends around who respected them?

Not all of the six people or so who were directly involved were thrilled with the possibility of making *Julia* and not everybody was thrilled about *The Turning Point,* but enough people did care about making them that the decisions were easier. And then it gave me a great deal of security to know that those who didn't like them were not going to walk around saying, "The fool."

People who have worked for you—creative people, production people—have been quoted as saying one of the things that makes them want to work for you is that you leave them alone. How do you leave

them alone on the day the rushes you've seen make you say, "Oh, God."

Well, there's leaving people alone and leaving them alone; the difference is how you approach your involvement. If I see something in the rushes I really dislike, I don't immediately stomp over to the stage and say that what I saw was terrible. I catch the person at the end of the day and tell him of her, "Something's bothering me here." It's the same when Jay, Gareth, others, and I talk out a problem without getting into confrontations. You talk with the creative people in the same manner; you don't say, 'I'm right and have all the answers," because they may be right too.

Are you conscious of trying to make people feel free from pressure?

You try to make them feel free. I don't know the formula, but whatever you do, it just has to be natural. At Fox, I felt I had to keep the pressures off the other executives. There was no need for them to get involved in the complications of the corporate structure. If you're going to assume responsibility, it's your obligation to protect the people involved. You can't go to George Lucas in the middle of *Star Wars* and tell him, "Some of the members of the board of directors don't like your movie." It's not going to contribute anything to what he's trying to accomplish.

What underlay the conflict between you and Fox's higher corporate officers and some of the board members?

Some of the corporate people and some of the board understood charts and MBOs, and I couldn't convince them that people have needs other than getting a bonus or a new car every two years. People don't stop working once they've achieved something.

Mel Brooks is not going to make a better picture out of *Young Frankenstein* if you say to him, "Well, you know you'll get a bigger bonus if you make a better picture." He'll say, "I can only do as well as I can; I'll try my hardest." But I couldn't get people at Fox to see that.

Were there other constraints on the creative process at Fox?

Well, yes, the attitudes of the people. Nobody on the corporate side ever came to us and said, "You did a good job," or, "The film division is 85% of the company and we appreciate what you're doing." The year Fox broke all industry records, none of the corporate people ever said, "Hey, you did a nice job."

Do you think if people had made you feel that they gave a damn about what you were doing the friction might have been avoided?

Absolutely, or if they had understood *what* we were doing. A lot of the people on the corporate side thought, "Well, aren't those people lucky? They just look at movies all the time, go to dinner with movie stars, and take flashy trips almost every weekend for previews." What they don't see is the Mel Brooks who walks into my office, loses his temper over a problem, picks up a chair, and throws it across the room. Their attitudes were almost resentful. And when I said I was leaving, not one corporate staff person who worked for Dennis Stanfill came in and said, "I'm sorry you're leaving."

One of the things that seems to suit you is a lot of input—people in and out of your office, lots of data, rushes, financial information—forming a big confusing picture. Do you have a sense of riding with the confusion until the ambiguity becomes clear?

Well, you have to. And it really is a muddle determining what's important and what isn't, hoping to zero in on the most essential things. On an average day I have to juggle 60 or 70 telephone calls. It's like a chess game.

But it seems that the chaos is necessary; you couldn't do without it.

No, you can't. The creative process comes out of the chaos. No book can tell you how to make a good movie. All these involved people and all their ideas make a movie. A good director or producer will try to cast a movie as you might try to cast the people on an executive level. An accountant comes in with some ideas, and so does a script person. Good directors are receptive to that: they listen to everybody, taking a little of this, a little of that.

Would it be too difficult to do all that juggling without the emotional climate in which you work?

By myself, I'd be pretty miserable. Some people would think it was terrific, I'm sure. But it's just that the emotional needs I have are deep down. I need friends around.

JAY KANTER

When you, Gareth Wigan, and Alan Ladd, Jr., left Fox, you were quoted as saying that the MBO forms there had "sent a flash of fear into people." What did you mean?

Those things were absolutely awful. I know what goes into running a big business, or at lest I think I do; I realize there has to be some sense of order, responsibility, progression, and ways to evaluate people. General Motors is not a mom and pop business. It's run with great efficiency, and managers have to do certain things along the way. The movies business, the entertainment business—any creative group, I suppose—are not constructed that way. You can't exchange the head of General Motors for the head of production of Warner Brothers. It just doesn't work.

Why do you say that?

It would be wrong for me, and I've been in the industry for years, to have an argument about something that's vital in a producer's or director's mind and not acquaint myself with the facts. If he says, "Listen, you don't know how important this particular location is," and I argue with him and I haven't been to that location to see or don't understand the context, then I'm wrong. I'm just making an executive dictatorial decision that is not based on any firsthand knowledge or experience.

The MBO forms were an example of headquarters not knowing what you were about?

Yes. For instance, Fox headquarters sent them to quite a few people. They went to the legal department, the production department, the music department, me, Gareth, Laddie—all of us. It's one thing to

get accounting people to fill them out, but it's quite another to get the head of the music department—strictly a creative force who deals with musicians, conducts orchestras, and knows what the best scoring stages are—to fill one out. He'll look at a thing like this and throw his hands in the air, go home, and spend sleepless nights worrying about what he's going to say on it.

When I received one I had to be more tolerant because I was the head of a department. And yet I would procrastinate, get angry, and generally waste a great deal of time avoiding ever filling it out. For Laddie it was even more of a form of hatred than it was for me. It was frustrating being unable to stop a practice within your division that was a waste of people's time and certainly the company's money.

Do you think the interests of a large corporation, which needs controls, are antithetical then to the needs of a creative unit?

There's a serious conflict, no question. People require some form of discipline and begin to resent their managers when they don't get it, but they also require freedom to do their jobs without feeling that every time they're two days over schedule Big Brother appears.

But it all isn't necessarily a conflict. I must say that in spite of the fact I initially resented the regimentation of the MBO forms, I found it was good to sit down with the head of business affairs and say, "You know, we're having this discussion in both of our best interests, and this is where I think you can improve. And this where I think I've fallen down in helping you improve." If the discussion was a give-and-take thing, we both got something out of it.

What was the underlying conflict with Fox about paying extra bonuses to production people after Star Wars was such a success?

Quite simply, we three—Laddie, Gareth, and myself—were the recipients of an awful lot of money (it's no secret), and we felt that the people in the division should have gotten more. There was a windfall, an absolute windfall. The company was very quick to give the stockholders a special dollar dividend and the stockholders also profited because the value of their shares increased—tremendously. I'm very sympathetic to stockholders—they own the company—but the people who provided those windfall profits were the people in this division. We

just felt that their bonuses should have been more, especially since the three of us had had a special bonus.

So you actually shared yours with the people in your division. If fairness was one motivation, was keeping those good working relationships in order another?

That crossed our minds, but I don't think it was what motivated us. It was a way of saying to the company: we're willing to put our money where our mouths are. We asked the people in the company to do it first and they said no. I was very surprised that even after we made the gesture, they didn't decide differently.

Would you say then that having control over rewards is one of the crucial areas of conflict between creative groups and large corporations?

There lies the biggest problem. I told the chairman directly how I felt. It seems silly to us that Laddie could spend all the production and marketing money—which in itself was in excess of $150 million a year—and nobody would question his decisions. There was no logic to the fact that he could buy $4 million of television network time and nobody would question whether it was a good buy, but he couldn't give somebody a $100, a $200, or a $500-a-week raise.

The chairman told me how he felt, and I was sympathetic to what he said—that he was running a company, was responsible for all aspects of it, and couldn't have people in one division getting rewards so far out of proportion to other divisions. He wasn't wrong about that.

How would you resolve the conflict?

I think one of the things to consider is the individual who's in charge of dispensing the money. Either the person is responsible or he's not. Laddie made salary recommendations, made bonus recommendations, was certainly never known as a giveaway artist, and was always very financially responsible. Our division never went crazy on budgets; we always watched them. Given a reasonable period of time to judge a person's performance, the chairman should or could have come to the conclusion that the individual in charge was not going to give salaries or bonuses which were not deserved.

Was the fact that you knew the people involved personally part of what made you share your bonus money?

Yes, because we could really see a measure of their work. At a certain point in a year you know whether you have earned the bonus, and once you've got it there's no way in the world that anybody can take it away from you. For a couple of years, midway through the year, there was no way the film division was not going to get the maximum bonus permitted. And yet deep into the year the people in the division never coasted—they worked every bit as hard as they had earlier in the year. I didn't expect the corporate staff to be aware of that measure unless we told them, and we did. But you can only feel it if you have a working relationship with your staff as we did.

How would you describe the relationship that the three of you have developed?

We all have special abilities and talents in one direction or another, and we have confidence in our own abilities. Even more important, we don't want to prove a point among ourselves. Competition is a healthy thing. But I regard my competitors as being outside the company, not inside it. We've never been so big, at Fox or here at The Ladd Company, that we'd have to compete

with each other to reach certain goals. I've seen that happen in companies where survival is a game, but you have to have the right makeup to work in that sort of environment; we don't have it.

Do you consider Ladd and Wigan friends?

Yes, I consider them friends. I do. That doesn't mean we spend all of our time together; I have other friends with whom I spend an equal amount of time socially. We're not all joined together at the hip.

How personal are the relationships? Are there boundaries you don't cross?

There are people I'm very close to personally with whom I enjoy a different sort of relationship, but when the chips are down, you add up the people in the friend column and you've got to really ask, "What is a friend?" A friend really isn't defined by the hours spent together but by your feelings for that person. On that basis I would say that I do have a personal relationship with Laddie and Gareth because they're very close to me. They're people I can depend on. I would trust them with anything. If something were bothering me or I were in serious trouble, I feel that I could go to Laddie or Gareth and say, "Help!" And they could do the same.

Would that affect your work?

Well, it wouldn't reflect on my work; why should it? I don't think Laddie and Gareth feel any differently.

Do you feel you can blow off steam in front of each other if it's necessary?

We're not very demonstrative in that way, and only on rare occasions do we really ever blow up at all, but Laddie's done it, I've done it, Gareth's done it. It's had nothing to do with each other but is always directed at something else. There are times when I'm absolutely so angry that I scream over the telephone. If Laddie and Gareth walked in with a birthday cake it wouldn't calm me down; I'd go right on screaming and yelling. It's not something that is common with me, but I certainly wouldn't be embarrassed doing it in front of them nor they in front of me.

At Fox, Ladd was president, you were senior vice president, and Wigan was vice president. Did the titles make a difference in your relationships?

In many things I think our duties—well, Gareth's and mine—were and are interchangeable. Laddie's responsibilities were much greater than ours. But none of us ever thought it was an important part of our lives to be a vice president. I suppose the first time I became a vice president of anything was very important. It was important to my mother.

Have you ever felt frustrated when you walked out of one of these group meetings where you made a "go" or "no go" decision because it didn't reflect what you wanted?

Of course, there's a feeling of frustration.

Can you resolve that with Ladd? Does it affect your friendship or your work?

No, it really doesn't, because you know that somebody has to be, in the final analysis, responsible. All sorts of disagreements occur in making a movie—what you're going to make, who the writer is, who's going to direct it, who's playing in it. Having all been in this business a long time and knowing the number of opportunities there are for dis-

agreement, we seem to get along and skirt over those problems fairly well. When you do walk out gritting your teeth, swearing that the others are all wrong, at the same time you have to turn around and say, "Look, considering the number of times we go through this process, I'm fairly lucky." We all love our children, but there are those odd times when you're ready to fling them or yourself out the window. You can't base your feelings about the children on those infrequent times they drive you crazy.

Do you feel there is an emotional outcome of working in an environment like this that's important to the work you do?

Yes. I feel that there's an emotional satisfaction. I just enjoy coming to work. I'm very emotionally involved; it's not just a job. We all get paid very well but it's more than that. I get up in the morning and I look forward to seeing the people and exchanging ideas. It's as much the actual way we all work together that is important to me, beyond the product.

Is protecting the group process an end in itself?

We do try to respect each other's feelings, whatever they are, because what we're after is beneficial to the company. There have been things that I felt strongly about over the past few years while this relationship has existed, without Laddie having to make a career of taking me away to Palm Springs for two weeks to help me understand. We don't have the time to do that, and we wouldn't have the kind of relationship that we do if we treated each other like children. We know each other's limits.

Do the sensitivity and tolerance you have, which make it possible to work closely together, affect the creative outcome?

They have a great effect on the people we deal with and the people we try to attract to work with us. A big part of this business, in addition to money, is relationships with other people. If people feel comfortable in a particular work atmosphere, the chances of their coming to you first with a film idea are far greater than if it's just a question of how much money you're willing to pay. I'm not dismissing the value of the money, but in this business it's not leverage.

What do you mean when you say "comfortable"?

People know that with us they can come and have a discussion, that we'll be supportive, that in fact we may even have some good ideas. I think most people who have worked with us do feel that we have something to offer beyond financing. If writers, directors, and actors feel comfortable in a relationship, feel they're not being dictated to, feel they're being treated with respect as human beings, then they're willing to convey that same respect back.

We take an interest not only in seeing the picture through to the finish, but we also care about the way it's sold. People know that once a film is turned over to the distribution company, we don't lose interest in it. We try to put our money in the screen, not in six limousines waiting all night long in case somebody wants a ham sandwich.

GARETH WIGAN

When Alan Ladd, Jr., resigned as president of Fox's film division, he was quoted as saying that wherever he went, you and Jay Kanter would go as well. What do you think makes your relationship so special?

I doubt there are many people in the world who enjoy doing what they're doing more than we do, and I think a lot of that enjoyment is because of our mutual trust. I'm sure, or I hope, that when Laddie said the three of us would go together, he made the decision to move with the two of us out of pure self-interest, that he believed he would enjoy his life more and do what he wanted to do better because we were there rather than because he felt he had to take care of us.

Do you consider Ladd and Kanter friends?

Absolutely. Very much so. How do you define "friend"?

Well, I don't know. I was going to ask you.

One of the ways I would define a friend is someone you can rely on absolutely in bad times as well as good, and by that definition, they are unqualified friends.

You would not feel inhibited about going to either one of them if you were in trouble or needed to talk about something personal?

Would not, did not, and will not. Not in the least. Let me give you a rather roundabout response. One of the characteristics we all share, I think, though it materializes in very different ways, is that all three of us are reticent, un-Hollywoodish people. We are not extroverts at all. I don't honestly know what Laddie and Jay may talk about privately between themselves, but I know what I talk about with them and they talk about with me; we do not, on the whole, overburden each other with our personal problems.

When we reach a certain age, everyone has two or three people to turn to in a crisis who'll sit up all night and listen, and no, I don't think that either Jay or Laddie would be one of those two people for me. Or for any of the three of us. But, for instance, I separated from my wife at the beginning of last year, and since last summer it's been one of the bad times; they're certainly aware of that. I've spoken with Laddie two or three times about it, but not in the same way that one burdens one's other kind of friends.

So in the important ways, yes, I think we are friends. But mostly what we have, I think, is the kind of relationship that straddles civilian and professional life, in a way you can't altogether define, which is in my experience exceedingly rare.

Does this affect the way you work together?

That needs a prologue as well. This is a personality-based business. You're as good as you are. Very few objective qualifications are relevant. You may have a law degree; you may have accountancy or business management qualifications. They're all meaningless, frankly, unless you have the innate ability to relate to and judge people, as well as the innate courage and talent to interpret your own instincts about material. Add to that experience, opinions, and personal obligations, and you have a movie executive. To have a career as a studio executive requires a great deal of ego projection, and it traditionally leads to an immensely competitive spirit and an enormous amount of politics or politicking. We have succeeded in having between us at Fox and here at The Ladd Company—it would be ridiculous to say zero but—as near zero politics as it's practical to achieve. You can't ever totally overcome it, obviously, but for all intents and purposes, no politics—and thus security.

Can you give an example?

Say you're making a film like *Julia—Julia* was Jay's project, and traditionally he would

probably have meetings with the writer and the producer and not necessarily tell even his colleagues what was going on. He would seek help only when he wanted it. He would be deeply offended if anybody visited the film while it was being made or spoke to the director, Fred Zinnemann, or to anybody else who was involved in making it. And if anybody—and I'm talking about his immediate colleagues—criticized it at any point, he would instantly defend it.

It doesn't work that way for the three of you?

I can remember only once in four years at Fox when we ever had to ask, "Well, am I doing this or are you?" and then only because it happened to be a film produced by somebody with whom I had worked on three films and directed by somebody with whom Jay had worked for years. When I'm away or not available, people in a project I've been closest to will speak to Jay or Laddie; one of them will make whatever decision seems sensible at the time, and there's no problem about it.

So you feel that professionally and personally the relationships are fairly reciprocal. Can you take as much initiative with Ladd as he can with you around the projects that he's working on?

Yes. It's not because we've all worked in England—though that is a coincidence—but our company constitution, like the British Constitution, is unwritten. There is a perfectly clear understanding of where Alan Ladd's prerogatives and responsibilities as president start; I can give examples but I don't think I could define them. *I* just know where the line is drawn and so does Jay and so does he.

Can you give an example of where the line is drawn?

Oh, I consider it really as a continuity of thought, for simplicity's sake. For instance, we would not make a deal with any artist of any substance or a writer or anybody like that without his first being aware of it and approving it, if possible.

But those seem like fairly straightforward decision-making responsibilities; what about the encouragement of ideas when you're sitting together in a meeting discussing film scripts? Are you aware of deferring to him and his ideas because he's president?

The way a meeting occurs, because it isn't "run," is that it is understood Laddie's voice has and should have a greater emphasis and weight than anybody else's. But then he operates in a very individual way. He's one of the great listeners of my experience. He hears everything and forgets nothing that he's heard. When it may appear his thoughts are elsewhere, he still hears everything that everybody has to say. If we're sitting in his office, as we do every Monday morning, talking about things that we've read and there's some divergence of opinion, his tendency is to listen for some time to what everybody's saying and to cull a collective opinion allied with his own. So while his feelings or recommendations don't necessarily represent a consensus, they are colored by what he feels to be a consensus.

How do you feel having your performance appraised by a friend?

I don't enjoy it, who does? But I don't resent criticism from anybody whom I respect, and there are very few people I've known in my life whom I respect as much as Laddie. There've been a couple of times when I'd disagree or I'd think, "well, I wouldn't do that." But I know a couple of occasions when he has made more than generalized criticism, and both times his judgment was correct.

Part of the art is the way he does criticize?

Well, part of the art is that he's prepared to do it at all and not just brush things under the carpet, or that any of us are prepared to do it. The art—whether it's the art of our being together or just the art of being in business—is being able to say no to people and still retain their respect. On many occasions, Laddie has consulted at length with Jay and myself on whether we thought that so-and-so could do this job, or about situations that might blow up between X and Y and whether they weren't relating to each other as well as before. I think that he values and needs our opinions and judgments, and needs to express his own feelings and be totally confident that what he says won't go any further.

How does he nurture this peer sense in light of his position?

A cynic could say that he chooses people to work with him who are prepared to accept his position, but that's not true. He put together the team at Fox, *that's* true. He probably left a couple of people doing what they were doing and shifted around a couple of other people, but he brought in everybody else—Jay, myself, Sandy Lieberson, Paula Weinstein, Lucy Fisher, the whole creative side. Obviously, like any leader, he chose his immediate subgroup. But leaving that aside, he was very quickly recognized as the best and it didn't and doesn't have to do with his age. His judgments on the whole are sounder and his ability to listen and judge before speaking is better developed than anybody else's. He has lived and breathed and thought and studied film in a way that people are only just beginning to do. George Lucas [*Star Wars*] and Steven Spielberg [*Jaws*] do it, but Laddie did it without ever intending to be a film director, writer, or actor. He does have an encyclopedic knowledge *and* the judgmental wisdom that grows out of that knowledge and out of thinking about film all the time.

Doesn't that set him apart?

No. We work together as a team. We have to accept the bruising of our egos and sometimes we have to compromise, we have to support each other, we have to work—in political terms—in a cabinet fashion. If I love a film but nobody else does, it's no good saying to the outside person who brought in the script, "I loved it but everybody else said no." You have to say to the person, "I like it but the overall feeling was that we really couldn't do it."

How is this sense of loyalty fostered?

Laddie fosters it and also, of course, the group fosters it; if you have the good fortune to experience this way of working, as soon as any member of the group appears to betray the tribal interplay, the rest of the tribe will complain.

So it really is a small culture with its own mores and values.

It's a small culture, but it's curious that it's also pervasive. I think one of the enormous errors that Fox made in considering letting Ladd go, and in what was done at Fox after his departure, was the purblind inability to recognize the depth to which his inspiration had permeated the company. I think Fox management thought that if the three of us went, we would go and that would be it. But apart from Jay and myself, there was another inner circle of maybe 12 more people, then other circles beyond that. The sense of confidence in and tremendous affection for him had gone very deep.

What made it go so deep?

It comes, of course, from success; there's nothing like success. It comes from the fact that our greatest aim is to make terribly good and terribly successful films. You see, they don't often go together. We had the good fortune to make a lot of very good films. Some of them were very successful and some of them fairly successful, and so people have pride in the product—the people on the road who are out there selling it.

But more than that, it is Laddie's personal involvement, something that people recognize as his character. He's not an easy man to get to know; he is characterized by a complete lack of bullshit. There isn't a better word for it. He has immense concern, something that all of us have, for sharing.

How does he communicate that? How do you? You must have to communicate it to the people who report to you.

I've always made a practice of talking about people working *with* me and not *for* me. That prepositional change is very important. If it's a reasonable portrayal of an attitude, it carries through into your work. As for Laddie, he's a man who has a lot of pride, as he should, and very little arrogance. Jay has too, and I hope that I have. You see, Laddie is completely different from anybody who has ever done that sort of job before. He's rotten at self-promotion, but his self-depreciation and total refusal to speak in public under any circumstances other than one-to-one or at a table over dinner and things like that set him apart from the normal run of people in charge of a studio. And as soon as people in Dallas or Toronto find that he's not behaving as expected, nor does he tolerate it when other people at any level try to behave in the traditional way, then they think, "Hey, this is something different."

What won't he tolerate?

Anyone saying, "This is mine." To give you an example, the decision to make *The Turning Point* was very difficult. I was totally committed to the film—objectively because I did believe it could be successful, and emotionally because I had had the advantage of seeing Mikhail Baryshnikov dance; I love ballet. And I did believe that Baryshnikov was enough of a superstar to break the barrier

of prejudice against this highly esoteric subject. But we had great misgivings because we were making all of these other films with women.

Now since it became successful people have said to me that it was my film. No, it wasn't. I was involved in it, yes, all the way through. I was much more involved than anybody else—too involved at times. And both Laddie and Jay at different times and in different ways expressed quite proper and sensible concerns about the film. But whatever I did, I could not have done without their questions and, of course, their support. And I hope that works both ways.

The relationships made it possible for you to oversee the film you did?

For the film to be made.

And no one every said to you, "You've got to go handle this; this is your baby"?

It was the group working; the more confidence Laddie feels in one of us, of course, the less he has to get involved. The more confidence we feel in Laddie's support, even if we're sometimes wrong, the more we're united as far as the enemy is concerned. I don't believe that has to be questioned anymore; it's there.

How long did it take to develop this trust?

It happened very quickly, and I don't quite know why. But within a very short time after I joined Fox it was apparent to me and, curiously, to other people in the company that there were an awful lot of things which didn't have to be said or didn't have to happen—a sense there was something strange or unusual in this tripartite relationship.

Do you think that as a group you have ever made a bad business decision because of your friendships?

I think bad business decisions have been made because we are collectively sometimes reluctant to make a tough decision. But not very often. Not more often than most people. But I can think of movies that we've made which we shouldn't have, decisions that have been postponed and postponed because we were reluctant to face up to our responsibility. In the end the thing is done, but it would have been much better to do it sooner.

Is that one of the dangers—groupthink? Because you know each other so well and have worked together so long, might you collectively not see something?

I don't think that's a problem, because we see things in different ways. You see, while I suppose it's interesting to stress the sameness and the unlikelihood of three people coming together who seem to share so many feelings and attitudes and so much trust, it's also important to stress the substantial differences.

What would you say the differences are?

Well, there's a disparity of eight or ten years in age between the oldest and the youngest of the three of us. I'm 47, Laddie's 42, and Jay is 50—something like that. One is a Jew, one's an Englishman, and one's an American, I think Protestant. Not that any of us are religious, but there are those differences.

Laddie has only one passion outside the movie business—football. I'm very ignorant about football. I love music. The kind of music I love is not something in which either of them is particularly interested. I am voluble to the point of being diuretic, I think, and loud. Laddie, as you know, unless you have particularly keen hearing, is difficult to hear—if you can get him to speak.

You said you were all reticent.

In behavior, but in my case, not in speech. I think that I am the most volatile in mood. I do play poker quite well, but apart from that I've had to reconcile myself to the fact that I could never hide an emotion. I walk in thinking I'm hiding it and people say, "What's the matter?" And Laddie—well, there are people who would say he shows his emotions about as vividly as the face of a mountain. I think that when you get to know him, he does, yes, but very little.

You seem to have no inhibitions about people showing emotions and incorporating them into what they do. Is that part of what makes it comfortable here?

What makes it comfortable for me is that the others allow me to show *my* emotions, yes. And I feel much happier to be able to do that. It's a little self-indulgent at times but helps get things out of my system. And I try to make up for that in other ways. I am the scribe of the group, drafting the things that we then rewrite if we need to. I'm not particularly good at it, but it's something that I'm quite happy to do. Neither Jay nor Laddie feels particularly happy doing it. I also don't mind standing on my hind legs and talking to people, while Laddie totally refuses to; Jay will if he's asked but doesn't particularly like to. Jay says he's the one who goes to funerals and functions—and he seems to, but he also does a lot more. There are different things that we do for each other, the kinds of chores of life that are harder for one person to do than another.

Do you think you can explore options more freely in this atmosphere than you might elsewhere and thus make better decisions?

Traditionally, it's terribly dangerous to be wrong in this business. It's bad for your ego and your reputation. It's important that all the mistakes should be somebody else's. So it's very luxurious to be able to be wrong and to make a decision based on merit instead of political reasons. It's very important to be able to change your mind without someone saying, "Yesterday you said something else."

Have you found your way of managing people has changed since you've been involved in this collaboration?

I expect so. I hope that I have contributed to how the enterprise is run, but happily I've found myself working with a man who feels the same way as I do about how things should be run. Certainly, were I running it, there'd be some little things that I would do differently, but only because that would be better for me. There's not one person out of the 15 closest to Laddie at Fox who at one time or another didn't say to him, "When we have meetings couldn't we have them in the room that we have set aside for meetings, instead of four on a couch, two on a stool, in your office? It would be so much more efficient," or "Couldn't we start it and know that it's only going to run an hour and a half instead of sometimes three-quarters of an hour, sometimes four hours?" And his answer was always no, because he works much better that way. When he was away or on vacation and we had a meeting, it was held in a much more orderly or seemingly organized way. But for him to function best and for us to function with him, it has to be done in a certain way.

It needs a chaotic atmosphere?

The ants in an anthill and bees in a hive look totally chaotic, but they're not. The meetings are in fact structured. The structure doesn't always work, but then no structure ever does. But as to how we treat people, I would say that on the whole Laddie is largely apolitical and was not, as far as I know, particularly involved in student politics. I was, and a lot of the feelings that I have about the way people with whom you work should be treated stem from that sort of common effort. I don't know where his stem from but they seem to be the same. He has a very real personal concern for all the people who work with him or for him. And he takes his responsibilities and his personal relationships very, very seriously. You've got a bunch of egos that have to be fostered and encouraged; these are the weapons that the film business uses and that have to be kept sharp.

Like your own ego?

Like my own. The real reason the whole thing broke down at Fox was because the management failed to understand the importance of human relationships, because of all the betrayals, not of us, but of other people in the division.

One pictures a father with his family having the meetings in his office and everybody sitting around and feeling very comfortable. Does this whole process provide something emotionally satisfying to you?

It's difficult to define what it supplies or provides. But yes, it provides something immensely satisfying. It provides an ability to get up early in the morning and go to bed late at night. It provides the fact that people say, "You're looking good." It provides the good things that you do. It fortifies you in the bad times. It makes everything worthwhile. I can say I've had the best four years of my life without any doubt or hesitation whatsoever. And it doesn't have to do with being paid more than I've been paid in my life, or anything like that. I don't know what proportion of the population actually enjoys its work as opposed to having a job. Those of us who love what we do should be profoundly grateful.

You said that with a real sense of affection.

Oh, yes. I don't think we have to be shy. It's possible to speak of loving somebody in that sense of comradeship, joined experience in success and failure; to be able to trust them in the same way that, to be melodramatic, members of a patrol out in the jungles learn to trust and depend on each other. But what's better about our relationship is that it's infinitely broader. Basically, you need to trust your buddies when you're patrolling the jungle so you won't get shot; there's only one goal, which is to get from point A to point B without dying. We have a multitude of other things to consider, and comradeship works at all kinds of levels.

Do you think that any one of you could do your job as well alone?

I have an absolute conviction that I couldn't, and with a sense of relief, I believe the others couldn't either. I hope not. I'd be mortified if I found that they could. I set a very, very much larger store on working with them than either of them probably realizes. They probably don't know how much I depend on it.

As an indication of the importance of the trust and support that come from working in the family-like atmosphere which Ladd created in the Twentieth Century-Fox film division, since these interviews were conducted seven other Fox executives—some of them mentioned in these interviews—have joined Ladd, Kanter, and Wigan. Two other executives, not from Fox, have also joined The Ladd Company team—E.G.C.C.

George Lucas—Skywalking

DALE POLLACK

The flow takes Lucas to an anonymous business district in nearby San Rafael, site of the nerve center of Lucasfilm. The casual passerby has no inkling that five white stucco buildings, marked with orange trim and pseudo-Mediterranean tile roofs, and inconspicuously lettered A, B, C, D, and E, are a magician's lair. They include the Kerner Company Optical Research Lab, better known as Industrial Light and Magic, and, in an adjoining building is the computer division. Cheerful greenery surrounds the buildings. Inside, the walls feature original production sketches, paintings, and posters from Lucasfilm productions. There are also displays of bizarre offerings from *Star Wars* fans, the people who make this all possible.

These buildings, Skywalker Ranch, and Parkhouse comprise "Lucasland," a term that makes Lucas bristle, although his friends and employees often use it. Lucasland is a self-contained community, a new version of the nineteenth-century company town. Last Thanksgiving, the paternal owner gave away turkeys to his employees, 431 ten-pound birds in all. In 1979, the number of employees and family members attending the annual July Fourth picnic at the ranch was less than fifty; by 1980, it had grown to three hundred, and then to nine hundred in 1981.

On July 4, 1982, more than one thousand people showed up for an all-day-and-night celebration featuring barbecued hot dogs and hamburgers, beer and wine, organized softball, volleyball, and croquet games, plus bocci ball and horseshoes. There was swimming at the lake (lifeguards present), followed by a dance featuring a rockabilly band. Horse-drawn surries and haywagons shuttled Lucaslandians to and from the parking lots, and a brass band played in the meadow. Walt Disney couldn't have done it better.

Disney's dreams came true because his brother Roy ran the business and paid the bills. Lucas has no sibling to turn to, although Marcia, his wife, acts as his counselor and confidante. George sets the direction for Lucasfilm and makes everyone believe that he knows what he's doing. Richard Edlund likens it to working on a special effects sequence with Lucas: "You may not understand the sequence yet, but you know that *he* does. By talking with you, he's building his understanding and yours at the same time."

Lucas reluctantly accepts his role as chairman of the board of Lucasfilm Ltd. He started paying himself a salary only at the end of 1981. Lucasfilm has average annual revenues of more than $26 million, a number that can multiply quickly when a hit movie is released. Lucas keeps his company private so that he doesn't have to tell anyone how much he makes (except the government). But being a successful executive is not his idea of fun.

"Running the company to me is like mowing the lawn," Lucas says, coming full circle from age eight to thirty-eight. "It has to be done. I semi-enjoy it, once in a while." As a child, Lucas found a way out of his dilemma; he saved his money and bought a power mower. He'd love to make Lucasfilm a self-propelled machine—but for now, he must push it.

Pushing it means showing up at President Bob Greber's office for his twice-weekly meetings. He speaks and meets with Greber and his executives at other times, but this ritual might be called "George Needs to Know." Present are Greber, vice president and chief operating officer Roger Faxon, finance vice president Chris Kalabokes, vice president and general counsel Kay Dryden. They have a direct line to Lucas. They are his extensions, doing what he can't do. Lucas is pulled in so many different directions that he has little time to spend with his employees. "They're just going to have to do it on their own," he says. "Everybody can't have me."

For four hours each week, Lucasfilm has Lucas. The meeting is informal; George leans back on the couch, his arms outstretched. Greber, serious but relaxed, sits on his desk—in his mid-forties, he is the oldest person in the company. Faxon, a former congressional budget analyst, has his glasses perched on his nose and a yellow legal pad on his lap. Dryden also has a legal pad, on which she takes copious notes. There is no formal agenda, but Greber keeps things moving. Items are discussed briefly with occasional humorous asides; the atmosphere is relaxed and open.

The renovation of a Lucasfilm-owned office building is brought up, and George looks around the room. "What do you recommend?" he asks. When everyone agrees on a decision, he nods his head: "That's my

mind on it, too." Imperceptibly, Lucas is in charge—he rattles off questions about earthquake liability and insurance like a seasoned corporate analyst. When he's made his decision, he invariably says, "My feeling is . . ." Told that someone needs to fly to Japan on business, Lucas jokes: "This is how deals are made—all to get a free airline ticket." Then the smile disappears. "Get the specifics of exactly why this trip is necessary," he instructs Greber.

Those close to Lucas agree that he has gradually become a happier, more relaxed person; he is less shy, if still not outgoing. In Greber's office he is open and communicative, expressing his thoughts without hesitation or reserve. Lucas still shuns the limelight—a request that he autograph one hundred raiders story records elicits a look of wide-eyed disbelief. "What?" he exclaims, amazed that Faxon would dare make the request. Ascertaining that it was not for charity, he dismisses the idea with a wave of his hand. These are the times, Greber says later, that Lucas would rather be somewhere else. "He would prefer never to speak to people like me if he could get away with it," Greber states.

Lucas possesses the instincts of the natural businessman, a trait rare in filmmakers. He has the ability to make decisions and to anticipate their consequences. "Most people pass the buck," says Michael Levett, head of Lucasfilm merchandising—he is not a person who floats through life. He lays a foundation for his thoughts and then methodically builds on it. "His business acumen astounds me," Greber attests.

Lucas smiles when he hears these compliments—he almost flunked math in eighth grade. He may not understand tax shelters or oil depreciations, but as he says, "We can manage very well with things I *can* understand. If it makes sense to me, then it's okay." Lucas's business philosophy is dollar-in, dollar-out, the legacy of George, Sr.

"Survival of the fittest," Lucas is fond of saying. "I'm glad I have this simple-minded, small-town, conservative business attitude. I'm just like a small shop-keeper." Minding a $26 million candy store, he might add.

Lucas has mixed feelings about the rest of his patrimony. It wasn't fun having to buy clothes out of an allowance, or having the cost of undone chores deducted each week. "It straightened me out, so I've sort of done all right in my life," he says of his practical upbringing. "But sometimes I wonder if it was really worth it—if I've turned out that much better as a result." Lucas is tired of the hard work, perseverance, and patience that have made him a success.

Surprisingly, his father has the same doubts. "I'm kind of a perfectionist, I guess," says George, Sr., echoing his son. "To some extent I neglected my family. For years, I was at work at seven A.M., six days a week. I wouldn't quit until I had done something to *my* satisfaction, and I never wanted to lose. I was a loner—I didn't want to take anyone else on, because if I got into trouble, I'd bring them down with me." Lucas worries about the same things, an inheritance he'd rather do without.

It's 6:00 P.M. when George goes next door to the offices of Industrial Light & Magic. The company's identity is revealed by an elaborate circular logo above the receptionist's desk: a magician in full tuxedo and tails, black top and white gloves, a red rose in his lapel, a wand in one hand, surrounded by a machine gear and the curved letters ILM. Security is tight. There are two receptionists in the foyer and foreboding signs warning visitors to check in. The precautions are necessary: ILM is where Lucas's imagination becomes real. Spaceships dangle from the ceiling, rock music blares in a room lined with hundreds of model airplane and tank kits. A poster on the wall shows Sinbad flying on a celluloid carpet. In four sealed vaults lie the crown treasures:

models and miniatures of the *Millennium Falcon,* the Death Star, the Snow Walkers, even Luke, Han, and Leia. "This is where the future is made," says ILM manager Tom Smith.

Lucas comes to ILM every evening when a film is in or nearing production. Walt Disney strolled down Dopey Drive and Goofy Lane to visit with his animators; Lucas spreads his pollen from department to department at ILM. The illustrators, monster makers, and costume designers would like to see him more often but, as Lucas says, "There aren't enough hours in the day for me to do everyone I have to do."

Joe Johnston and George Jensen are working diligently at drafting boards as George enters the storyboard room and takes off his leather jacket. He picks up a red marking pen and both illustrators groan. The walls are lined with thumbtacked drawings of each shot in the climactic battle sequence in *Return of the Jedi;* Lucas immediately sees that one shot is missing. He unpins the illustrations and moves them around, projecting the moving in his head. The storyboards not only give him a sense of how a scene fits together but enable him to reject specific shots before they are filmed.

When the red marker comes out, there's no doubt whose point of view will prevail. Lucas has the last say on everything. He is brutal about what he doesn't like: large red marks obliterate several carefully rendered drawings. Lucas grunts, "Let's eighty-six this one." The goal is a smooth flow of images. "I want it all to be *action!* No waiting time!" If Lucas criticizes, he also exhorts. "This is it, come on guy, we've got to get serious about this. The time is now!" The pep talk always works—Lucas drums up as much enthusiasm as a revival preacher. "Great," he says with satisfaction as he surveys a wall blotchy with red Xs.

As Lucas picks up his jacket and heads

for the door, Johnston jokingly calls after him, "If you need us around midnight, we'll still be here." Lucas laughs, but the comment disturbs him. He is halfway down the stairs when he turns and goes back, sticking his head into the room. "Will you really be here that late?" he asks—his concern for their welfare seems genuine.

As Lucas proceeds through ILM, his invariable greeting is "How's everything goin'?" said in a toneless murmur. "The fact that I don't say hello and smile and be friendly doesn't mean I don't care," Lucas says in his own defense. "If anything, I care too much." But he seems uneasy around his employees, and they are unsure of how to approach him. Distance, not intimidation, defines the relationship, and both sides maintain it. Lucas's inability to accept his position is evident when he enters a recently completed dubbing stage and a carpenter approaches him for an autograph. Lucas is taken aback, but reluctantly complies. "I didn't ask to be famous," he says later, standing in the parking lot. He looks at his feet and mutters, "But I guess that's all part of it."

George Lucas has coped with whatever "it" is, changing little in dress, attitude, or philosophy. But when he walks through an office, an imperceptible wave goes through the room, and a small entourage amorphously accumulates around him, as if he were too special to be related to on a normal level. "I know a lot of people who are afraid to talk to him. They just don't know what to say," Joe Johnston states with a shrug. Lucas can be intimidating to those who don't know him. Jane Bay once hired a receptionist and Lucas didn't speak to her for three months, not even to ask her name.

His demeanor has improved since then. "I think he's just more comfy on the planet now," says Bill Neil, who has known Lucas since *The Rain People* in 1968. George thanks people for their contribution and oc-casionally chats with them on his rounds. He is sparing in his compliments—marketing chief Sidney Ganis remembers receiving only two in three years. "I think George would like to freeze a lot of people and bring them out only occasionally," observes a bitter Anthony Daniels. Lucas is sensitive to people's emotions—anyone who could create a Wookiee and R2–D2 can't be all bad. "George isn't a person who physically expresses his affection for people, but he definitely feels it," insists Jane Bay.

Sometimes Lucas's uncommunicativeness confuses his associates. When the computer building was under construction, Lucas questioned the placement of a door. The next day the door was moved to the other side of the room. Lucas was bewildered. "I didn't ask for this door to be over here," he said. The next day the door was moved back to its original location. Ed Catmull, head of the computer division, says, "People take him very literally."

* * *

I don't make pictures just to make money. I make money to make more pictures.

Walt Disney

After *Empire*, Lucas had to decide what to do with all the money he hadn't lost. In May 1978, George and Marcia formed a company that purchased the one hundred-year-old Bulltail Ranch in Nicasio, just north of San Anselmo. Set on 1,882 acres of rugged brown hills and deep valleys, Bulltail was once a thriving cattle and dairy ranch. Within two years, Parkway Properties bought thirteen parcels adjacent to Bulltail, including Big Rock Ranch, which climbed the nearby hills. The total spread came to 2,949 acres and cost Lucas $3 million. (The price was cheap because of county requirements that the land be kept agricultural, which scared off condominium developers.)

Skywalker Ranch promised to fulfill many of Lucas's long-standing goals: It would give him a headquarters unlike that of any other movie company. It would be a motion picture think tank, where movies would be conceptualized, rather than physically made. It would be neither a film studio nor a film campus, but something in between—exactly what, Lucas still doesn't know. Even the huge profits of *Star Wars* and *Empire* weren't sufficient to build and operate the ranch. But using merchandising as its base, Lucasfilm could expand into nonfilm investments that would guarantee Skywalker's completion whatever Lucas's future success in the movie business. Lucas liked the idea of confounding Hollywood again—his films would subsidize the ranch, not its owner.

Chris Kalabokes, the financial analyst who had reluctantly approved *Star Wars* at Fox, joined the company when he heard Lucas describe Skywalker. "That was a vision I could trust," he recalls. Other associates thought the decision was alarmingly irrational. Where would the money come from? Was George serious?

Lucas listened to his inner voice again. "I don't know why I'm building the ranch," he admits. "It's coming up with an idea and being committed to it without any logical point of view, I know. But it's just a feeling I have."

To realize his dream, Lucas knew that somebody had to take charge of his company, and he didn't want the job. "I needed a businessman," Lucas says. Charles Weber, the slim, soft-spoken corporate executive who had specialized in high-finance real estate ventures, was his choice. Weber's professional confidence impressed Lucas and soothed his worries about money matters. He gave Weber a simple directive—Charlie could run Lucasfilm, and if he made money, he could run it as he saw fit. If he didn't make money, he was out of a job. "Leave me

out of it," he told Weber, who was skeptical that Lucas could remove himself from his own company.

Lucasfilm found a home in the shadow of Universal Studios, an old brick-faced egg and dairy warehouse next to the Hollywood Freeway. When the purchase was finalized, Lucas confided to Richard Tong, "One of these days, Universal is going to really want this piece of property and I'm really going to make them pay for it."

Lucas was reluctant to set up corporate headquarters so close to Hollywood. It meant flying regularly between San Francisco and Burbank, a trip he loathed. He wanted to base Lucasfilm in Marin. But Weber, permanently settled in L.A., persuaded him that it was best to stay near Fox, which still controlled the only income-producing activity for the company, the merchandising. An ambitious remodeling program was begun on the old warehouse, renamed the Egg Company; the cost quickly went from $200,000 to $2 million.

George felt his by-now familiar premonitions of doom, as the Los Angeles staff expanded from five employees to fifteen, then fifty, then almost one hundred. "I wasn't happy with it ever," Lucas now says. But he rarely expressed his displeasure to Weber other than to remind him that Lucasfilm should be kept small and intimate. Weber patiently explained that if the company was going to pay for the ranch, he needed to expand.

Lucas wanted the Egg Company to be an ideal environment for creative and business people. The original skylight was buttressed with giant oak rafters; beneath it, an indoor courtyard was filled with tables, director's chairs, and hanging plants. George laid out the large, roomy offices, and Marcia designed the stunning interiors: dark green walls with burnished trim, antique desks and tables, and a polished oak balcony overlooking the courtyard. "I remember working at Sandler Films, sitting in a dark cubicle," Marcia says. "I want every employee to have a decent place to work.

George Lucas may have brought Hollywood to its knees, but he has also kept it alive. *Star Wars, Empire,* and *Raiders* have removed more than $150 million in profits from the coffers of two major studios that have had to content themselves with distribution fees. Tom Pollock says, "George has siphoned money out of the system that cannot be used again to make movies, other than his own." Lucas is the biggest profit participant in the history of the film business. Hollywood has benefited from his successes, however. Many movies rode the profitable coattails of Lucas's string of blockbusters. Without Lucas, the movie business might have fallen on even harder times. The success of *Raiders* allowed Paramount to make twelve less successful films.

"George Lucas is *not* what the rest of the business is about," says Ned Tannen. "Nobody has ever done what he has done. Nobody. George Lucas is over there, and the rest of the business is over here." Lucas is the man who got away, who beat the system by building his own system. "The studio system is dead," Lucas insists. "It died fifteen years ago when the corporations took over and the studio heads suddenly became agents and lawyers and accountants. The power is with the people now. The workers have the means of production."

Can that be George Lucas, the conservative businessman from Modesto, spouting socialist Hollywood rhetoric? Of course not. Lucas is talking about the *creative* power of the independent writer, director, and producer, a goal to which he has dedicated his career. With power comes the envy of those who do not possess it. Lucas and Hollywood have taunted each other for more than a decade; he finds Hollywood crooked and sleazy, while the film industry resents his success and arrogance. "They don't care about movies," George says. "The advantage I've also had over the studios is that I do care. . . ."

Lucas can't wholeheartedly embrace business practices that he considers unfair and unscrupulous. Those who violate the basic tenets of morality (honesty, fairness, generosity) are eventually undone, Lucas believes. He is so honest that during the ICM arbitration over *Empire,* his staff was instructed to tell ICM's lawyers *everything,* even if it was harmful to his case.

Lucas wants the kind of ethical company that does not exist in Hollywood. His father's employees stayed with L. M. Morris for as long as twenty years, and George wants to develop that same loyalty in Lucasfilm. He tries to set a moral example. When you have someone over a barrel, don't push your advantage. When you negotiate a deal, be tough and demanding, but never unreasonable or unfair. When you have a success, share the profits. "It's just a matter of doing what's right," Lucas says.

* * *

Han Solo: I never would have guessed that underneath the person I knew was a responsible leader and businessman. But you wear it well.

Lando Calrissian: Yeah, I'm *responsible* these days. It's the price of success. And you know what, Han? You were right all along. It's overrated.

From The Empire Strikes Back

Lucas's worst fears about what could happen to Lucasfilm came true after *Empire* was released in 1980. The *Star Wars* profits had been invested and the dividends were not only paying for the company's overhead, but also freeing George from having to make movies and providing the financial base for Skywalker Ranch. Charles Weber had turned Lucasfilm into a thriving, successful miniconglomerate—*too* successful, as far as its chairman was concerned.

When Lucas extricated himself from the financial mess of *Empire,* his small, familial company of twelve people had become a well-heeled corporation with an annual overhead of $5 million, and 280 employees spread across California. His plans to consolidate the company in Marin seemed to have been forgotten. Most of Lucasfilm was already in Northern California, but the headquarters remained in Los Angeles, a community George despised.

Lucas always came back from Los Angeles feeling angry and frustrated. The Egg Company had originally had ten offices to house executives, secretaries, and receptionists. Now the building was enlarged, middle-management executives were driving Mercedes-Benzes and Porsches leased by Lucasfilm (annual cost, $300,000), and the Los Angeles staff was requesting its own cook. "It got totally out of hand," Lucas complains. "We were one step away from the delivery boy having a company Porsche. We were up here living in poverty row and they had a palatial estate."

Lucas saw the corrupting influences of Hollywood at work: His executives joined civic organizations, went to cocktail parties, and became what George had always vowed never to become—part of the industry. "I always felt a little uncomfortable being in the Hollywood community as a representative of Lucasfilm," says Weber. "I was constantly being told by George that nobody should be in Hollywood." Lucasfilm was a Marin County operation as far as Lucas was concerned. He had to get his people out of L.A.

Chronically unable to confront difficult problems, Lucas searched for a way out. He had never taken Lucasfilm seriously, allowing executives to tell him what they thought he wanted to hear. Remembers Weber, "From the day he hired me, I was a foreign entity. He was the filmmaker, and we were the business people." Lucas's daily contact with his Los Angeles office consisted of a forty-five-minute phone conversation with Weber; he usually contributed a "Yeah" or "No" to the list of questions and issues Weber had prepared. What Lucas never said was "Stop it right now. This company is getting out of hand," which is what he was thinking.

As always, it was a question of control. "While I'd been saying, 'Charlie, this is your company,' when it came down to it I realized it was my money and I cared a lot more about how it was spent than I had in the beginning," Lucas admits. The matter came to a head when Weber wanted to borrow $50 million to turn Lucasfilm's passive investments into majority ownership in a variety of companies, from DeLorean automobiles to communications satellites.

Weber also wanted Lucas to bring other movie and TV producers into Lucasfilm, lending them his name and expertise. "Charlie is a businessman, and he doesn't realize how hard it is to come up with a creative thing, not to mention *consistently* creative things," Lucas says. Like Walt Disney, Lucas didn't want his name on anything he couldn't personally supervise. When Weber suggested that the ranch represented too much of a cash drain, Lucas had enough. "The ranch is the only thing that counts," he told Weber. "That's what everybody is working for. And if that is getting lost in the shuffle, then something's terribly wrong here."

George suffered sleepless nights, chronic headaches, and bouts of dizziness throughout the fall of 1980. "I'm not very brave about these situations," he said. "I'm somewhat insecure and slightly a coward." When he came back from Los Angeles just before Thanksgiving, he was stricken with stomach pains. Medical tests showed he had an incipient ulcer, which disappeared when medicated. Lucas internalized himself right into the hospital.

There was no one to turn to other than Marcia. It was a painful process for both of them as Lucas grappled with his dilemma. The conclusion was unavoidable: He was going to have to let half of the Los Angeles staff go, move everybody else up north, and pare Lucasfilm to a manageable size. Weber was called up to San Francisco and Lucas, sweating profusely, his voice hoarse and hollow, told him of the decision. Weber, usually impassive in business situations, was shocked. He had hoped to renegotiate an already generous salary package, and now he was told that Lucasfilm was being snatched from him.

George wanted Weber to stay with the company—he still admired Charlie and he felt guilty as hell. Weber agreed to moderate his demands and drove to the airport. Half an hour later, he was summoned back to Parkhouse. Lucas had decided that Lucasfilm couldn't be his and Weber's company at the same time. Accountant Richard Tong called George just after Weber left and recalls, "He sounded like he'd been through the wringer. Talk about ill, he sounded like he was dying." Lucas's sole comment on the firing of Weber is, "The one thing I regret is I didn't do it earlier."

When the Los Angeles staff returned to the Egg Company following the Christmas holidays, they were given the bad news. Only thirty-four of the eighty employees were asked to make the move north. There were bruised egos and bitter recriminations, mostly directed at Lucas. George felt terrible about disrupting people's lives, and went to great lengths to ease his conscience. Laid-off employees were given six months to find new jobs and generous cash settlements. Lucas even hired a vocational counselor to help them.

In a strange way, the experience was cathartic for Lucas. Marcia thought George

learned one of life's valuable lessons: "When a situation is not working out, you confront that situation and you fix it. This was an uncomfortable situation for George, and he didn't confront it. In his reluctance to confront it, it just got worse and worse." By regaining control of Lucasfilm, George was again the center of his universe.

On May 28, 1981, Lucasfilm Ltd. officially relocated its corporate headquarters from Los Angeles to Marin County, completing what a press release called "the long-planned consolidation of the company." Mistakes had been made, money had been lost, dues had been paid. Changes of direction are expensive, but Lucas knew where he wanted to go.

Bob Greber, who had been chief financial officer, was made executive vice president and chief operating officer. Lucas initially kept Weber's title of president and chief executive officer (he has since given it to Greber) as well as retaining his own position as chairman. Greber's background was similar to Weber's—he had managed $60 million worth of Merrill Lynch's investments. But Greber accepted a condition that was unacceptable to Weber: "Basically, I implement those things George wants done."

Greber had some conditions of his own. Lucas had to openly and directly express his feelings about Lucasfilm. Greber told him, "You've got to tell me whether you like something or not. You just can't sit there and take it." Greber prepared a report that explained just how much money Lucasfilm had, how much it was spending, and how much was left over. Lucas was pleased: "Before, I'd gotten a seventy-five-page report that didn't say anything." He wanted to know the bottom line: cash-in, cash-out. Greber told him and won Lucas's trust.

Greber is accommodating, but he isn't a yes-man. Lucasfilm is not a company where orders are issued and the troops snap to attention. At times the atmosphere seems unnaturally idyllic: bright, motivated people all roughly the same age, with many of the same interests. The top executives are men, with the exception of Kay Dryden and Merchandising vice president Maggie Young, but many of the middle-management jobs (publishing, merchandising, fan club) are held by women. These employees share Lucas's parsimonious philosophy: "They're looking to save every dime they can," says Charles Weber.

Lucas's belief in corporate ethics, group decisions, and a family atmosphere filters down from the top. He has instilled a sense of pride in his employees through his own example. "The best boss and fellow workers a person can have," fan club president Maureen Garrett says in earnest. "I can't put it any other way." Secretaries and stage technicians are made to feel as if *they* are the artists. Because they share George's dream, they want to help him make it come true. Lucasfilm attracts the best people because of this reputation. What other filmmaker shares the wealth of his films with *all* his employees? "One act of kindness can carry you through a year of hell on a production," says librarian Debbie Fine. "The loyalty that man engenders is incredible."

As Lucas increasingly becomes a corporate overseer, his personal contact with his employees diminishes. At the 1981 Christmas party he had no idea who most of the one thousand guests were. His friends worry that he has been consumed by the corporation, which is fast becoming a new sea of faceless workers. Lawrence Kasdan senses an "IBM military" feel to Lucasfilm's corporate offices, nicknamed The Tower, after the evil-looking black administration building at Universal Studios. If a filmmaker screens a movie at Lucasfilm, he gets a computerized bill charging him for the projection room and any telephone calls he made, just like at Universal.

As the company grows, so does the internal bickering and division between the "haves" and the "have-nots." The production staff feels bullied and slighted; once again, they see executives driving around in company-leased Mercedes. And although ILM is completely unionized, as are the construction crews at Skywalker and Sprocket Systems, Charles Weber is among those who foresee problems: "People are going to think since they work for George Lucas, why is there any limitation to what they can make?" Lucas bristles at such criticism—Lucasfilm's annual overhead is $9 million, most of it in salaries. He calls the average wage scale at his company "awesome," the result of periodic surveys that ascertain the going rate in Hollywood. But three years between movies is a long time, and Lucasfilm has had to diversify to pay for all this. The company has invested $10 million in oil and natural gas wells, and owns $5 million worth of real estate in Marin County alone. Other properties include office buildings in San Francisco and the Egg Company in Los Angeles, now leased to filmmakers like Randal Kleiser. There are plans for a new commercial development in the Bay area that will combine a marina with a shopping center, a first-class restaurant, and condominiums. Greber expects Lucasfilm's passive investments to grow and speaks of profit centers and the prospect of creating TV programs. "If we can take care of that dream that George and Marcia have, it would be wonderful—as long as it's sensible," Greber says. That kind of talk was one reason Charles Weber lost his job.

Outside of passive investments and the movies themselves, Lucasfilm's only consistent source of profit is merchandising. There are literally hundreds of licenses for toys, decorator telephones, talking clocks, bicycles, lunchboxes, letter openers, children's and adults' underwear, pinball machines, video games, bumper stickers, candy, and ice cream and the bowls to eat it from. Lucasfilm also supervises the publication of novalizations, children's books, souvenir books, and comic books based on the *Star Wars* and Indiana Jones films. The record group oversees sound-track albums, story records, and jazz and disco spinoff albums. The in-house art department designs some of the merchandise and creates stationery and company logos. No ad is done without Lucasfilm's approval, no license granted before careful scrutiny of the manufacturer and distributor. Lucas's philosophy of responsibility and control has become corporate policy.

From May 1977, when *Star Wars* was released, through May 1983, merchandising of Lucasfilm products approached $2 billion in retail sales, *before* the release of *Return of the Jedi*. The company gets a royalty of between 1 and 7 percent on most items, although on products like T-shirts, Lucasfilm's share is closer to 50 percent. Lucas always recognized the potential in merchandising, but even he never imagined that a *Star Wars* label could mean a 20 percent increase in sales.

Lucas's personal beliefs suffuse the merchandising. Exploitative items are not sold, whether vitamins (he doesn't want to encourage kids to pop pills) or Princess Leia cosmetics (makeup can be harmful to children's skin). South Africa is boycotted in every respect but film sales, which are under Fox's control, because Lucas disagrees with the country's apartheid racial policies. He reviews every prototype toy (if Kenner Toys sold nothing but *Star Wars* merchandise, it would be the fifth largest toy company in the world) and maintains a veto power on all food tie-ins. Sugar cereals are verboten, but Hershey bars, Cokes, and milkshakes are okay. That was the stuff Lucas lived on as a kid—it's part of the American way of life.

* * *

There will be no one to stop us this time.

Darth Vader in *Star Wars*

When the term "software" came to mean everything from movies and TV programs to floppy computer disks and video games, Lucas hated it. But he soon realized that he could become one of its premier suppliers. A new era was dawning and, ever the pragmatist, Lucas planned to take advantage of it. . . .

Lucas also wanted to develop a complete computerized postproduction system: editing, sound editing, sound mixing, and film printing. It let him rationalize developing computer games, computer animation, and computer simulation (recreating images) at the same time. An outside firm constructed a computer-simulated spaceship battle, and the results looked as good as anything ILM had photographed. The process was costly and not yet economically feasible, but it *could* be done.

Starting a computer company from scratch is expensive and time-consuming. Lucas has already spent $8 million and still hasn't completed his postproduction system, which will revolutionize the mechanics of making movies. The drudge work will be done by the computer, leaving the filmmaker to think about how the movie fits together. Lucas wants to be on the cutting edge of film technology. People expect the creator of *Star Wars* to be ten steps ahead of the next guy.

Ed Catmull, the young director of the company graphics department at the New York Institute of Technology, became Lucasfilm's resident electronic genius. Catmull resembles the traditional technofreak: long hair, thick glasses, and a Ph.D. in computer science. Lucas told him to spend a year studying how to marry film to computers and how much it would cost. "Trust me," Lucas said. "We'll have our computer division."

In one of Lucasfilm's nondescript buildings, Lucas's promise is coming true. Bicycles line the building's hallway; the rooms are cooled by special air conditioners that maintain the optimum temperature for computers. At the end of one hall is a room filled with twenty-five minicomputers, equipped with $1,100 circuit boards that do the work $250,000 computers used to perform. In an adjoining laboratory red, green, and blue laser beams zip around a $100,000 laser table, a prototype system built at Lucasfilm with the help of outside consultants. In the graphics room, computers generate "calculated synthetic images": a landscape of tall mountains topped by fluffy clouds is invitingly realistic; close examination reveals it consists of millions of tiny computer dots. No one wears white lab coats—the usual outfit is jeans, sneakers, and work shirts. These people *are* creating the future.

Index

Y

Z